Addicted to Love

AN AUTOBIOGRAPHY

JAN LEEMING

ROBSON BOOKS

Also by the same author:

Working in Television
Simply Looking Good

First published in Great Britain in 2003 by Robson Books, The Chrysalis Building, Bramley Road, London W10 6SP

A member of **Chrysalis** Books plc

The author has made every reasonable effort to contact all copyright holders. Any errors that have occurred are inadvertent and anyone who for any reason has not been contacted is invited to write to the publishers so that a full acknowledgement may be made in subsequent editions of this work.

British Library Cataloguing in Publication Data
A catalogue record for this title is available from the British Library.

ISBN 1 86105 671 0

All photographs from the author's personal collection except for the following: p3 (below, right) Mirror Pix; p4 (above, right) HTV, (centre) *Reading Evening Post*; p6 Mirror Pix; p7 (above) Gareth D Smith, (centre) copyright © BBC and (below) HTV; p8 (above, right) Jonathan Youens, (centre, right) Sheffield Newspapers and (below) Doug McKenzie; p9 copyright © BBC; p11 (above, left) Associated News Media, (above, right) Northern and Shell Media Publications and (below, right) Mirror Pix; p12 (above) News International, (centre) Associated News Media and (below) News International.

Typeset by SX Composing DTP, Rayleigh, Essex
Printed and bound by Creative Print & Design (Wales), Ebbw Vale

CONTENTS

	Preface	v
	Acknowledgements	vii
1	Childhood and Marriage	1
2	New Zealand and Owen	27
3	Australia, Hayo and Michael	47
4	Home Again	56
5	The West Country and John	73
6	Bristol and Jeremy	82
7	HTV and Pebble Mill at One	99
8	BBC Radio 2	119
9	Patrick and Jonathan	132
10	Eric	155
11	Leaving the BBC	177
12	The Luckiest Woman on Earth?	206
13	The Darkest Days	230
14	Kent and Chris	246
	And So ...	277

To my son Jonathan – the only 'constant' man in my life.

To my family and friends who have loved and supported me through the good and the bad days.

To Owen Leeming, my staunch friend and the person who totally changed the course of my life.

Carpe dieme.

PREFACE

I have condemned the press for intruding into my private life and that of others, so why am I now prepared to let the world at large into my life and my heart?

To be approached by a major publisher fifteen years after my departure from mainstream television was a flattering request. My son has always wanted me to write the story of my life. It has also been suggested that my book might help other women who've experienced similar trials and tribulations, to realise that you can 'pick yourself up, dust yourself down and start all over again'; being well known is no barrier to pain and hurt. I believe that, just as you give love, it flows back to you. If, after a painful relationship, one retreats into a shell, you miss out on all the best things in life – love and affection. And last but not least, so many people have sat in judgment upon me without knowing the facts, they might as well be acquainted with them and then see how they feel. So that is why I spent the winter of 2002–3 joined to my computer with an umbilical cord. I should add that I have changed a few names to save embarrassment for some people.

I have been financially independent from the age of seventeen and a half. Not one of the men I married had any money, so that was not my motivation. My divorces haven't brought me substantial settlements, only heartache. I haven't needed a man financially, but I do need to love and be loved. In this book, I have used a quote from Audrey Hepburn's character in *Roman Holiday*. She said, 'I was born with an enormous need for affection and a terrible need to give it.' Well, that is how I feel. I have loved not wisely but too much.

I have been blessed with wonderfully supportive family and friends. I have a son who is also my friend. Despite his youth, he has given vital support in the last few years. I am proud of him and love him very much.

I have my health and a renewed excitement in and expectation of life. I now have freedom and a chance to move on to pastures new. Looking back I don't really think I would have changed any of it. If I hadn't made the mistakes I made, there would have been others. There's no gain without pain. And in the great scheme of things, I see the balance in my life as being more weighted on the side of the good than the bad.

Jan Leeming

ACKNOWLEDGEMENTS

I would like to thank Jeremy Robson for his belief that I had a story worth telling and the ability to write it and to his kind and helpful assistant, Melanie Letts. In my working life, special thanks go to Ron Evans and the late Tom Salmon, who had faith in me and spurred me on to higher achievements, and to Alan Protheroe, who appointed me to the newsreading team at the BBC.

Thanks also to Jane Donovan and Rob Dimery, who edited the book with sensitivity and were very sparing with the scissors. I take my hat off to Art Director Richard Mason, who sifted through dozens and dozens of photographs and came up with an entertaining and meaningful selection. A big thank you must go to Yvonne Ridley, who mentioned me to Jeremy Robson and the rest is history, as they say.

It is difficult to single out individuals for thanks because so many have helped over the years. They know who they are. However, I would like to express deep gratitude to Sue McFarlane, Jean Mays, Sarah Marshall and Chloe Smillie, who have always been there for me in the darkest hours. I must thank John Turner, who patiently read this book and corrected my punctuation. It was a big job. I may be able to speak the English language, but grammar was never my strong point. My solicitor, Sue Black, saw me through two divorces and was kind and supportive way beyond her professional status.

Apart from loving them, I give thanks to the following:

My father, for my education and a strict upbringing.
My mother, for her unquestioning love and generosity.
My sister, because she is my sister and friend.
My son – the best production of my life and the source of my greatest joy.

Owen – my mentor, inspiration and friend.

Patrick, for helping me produce Jonathan.

Eric – who gave so much love, adventure, passion and romance.

All my friends for their love and unstinting loyalty.

And I would like to thank the viewers for their kind letters, good wishes and support throughout my career in television.

CHAPTER ONE

CHILDHOOD AND MARRIAGE

My entry into the world was inauspicious. My mother almost gave birth in the lavatory. If that was my first view of the world, it might account for my outlook on life and some of the disasters since! I was born in 1942 in the middle of the Second World War, and have hazy memories of doodlebugs, or V-1s – the flying bombs used by the Germans to blitz London. They made a whining sound and while you heard them you were safe – when the whine stopped, they dropped and exploded. There was an air-raid shelter in the garden and I remember being taken there in the middle of the night during the bombing raids – to which we were highly susceptible, as we lived in Woolwich, south-east London. Woolwich boasted the Woolwich Arsenal, where armaments were made. It was an important town on the River Thames; I remember the river used to stink of rotten eggs in hot weather.

My maternal grandmother rented 109 John Wilson Street – a large house on four floors. Because the house was on a hill, one bottom room was below pavement level at the front and the kitchen at the back was at garden level. The kitchen-cum-sitting room was the only room for which I can remember the decoration. The wallpaper was a pattern of autumn leaves, very dark and oppressive, and on the mantelpiece stood two Dutch

1

china figures – a boy and a girl carrying baskets in which we'd put spills for lighting the coal fire.

There were two more floors with two large rooms on each and then an attic with two rooms large enough to take beds and accommodate servants – except we didn't have any; far from it. The house may have been large, but it was old and had no modern conveniences. The lavatory was outside and in winter you had to break the ice on the pan first thing in the morning. Despite this, it did have mains drainage. Toilet paper was an unheard-of luxury – squares of newspaper suspended from a string was our double velvet. There was a cold water tap in the kitchen and we heated water in a kettle on a gas stove. Large amounts of hot water had to be boiled in a huge copper in the scullery across the yard. It was here that Mummy did the washing, scrubbing it down on a corrugated-iron washboard and squeezing most of the water out by putting the clothes through a mangle. A large tin bath was filled up on Fridays for the weekly ablutions. It was in the scullery in the warmer months and in winter carried to the kitchen and placed in front of the fire. For daily cleaning we had top-to-toe washing in a bowl in the kitchen. Either that or we'd go to the communal baths where you queued for your immersion. You could usually feel the scouring powder under your behind from the previous cleaning and, if you stayed too long, a rap on the door would make you scurry to dry and put on your clothes.

We weren't poor, it's just that bathrooms and conveniences inside the house were not commonplace as they are today. So much of what we now take for granted was looked upon as sheer luxury in the forties. We didn't have fridges, telephones, washing machines or vacuum cleaners, and televisions and cars were the exception rather than the rule. In fact, for Queen Elizabeth's coronation in 1953 my father and I travelled all the way up to Chester to stay with friends who had a television and we watched that wonderfully colourful occasion on a small twelve-inch black-and-white screen!

My father was born in 1915 at Coonoor in south-west India into a relatively comfortable family. His forbears had left

England for India towards the end of the eighteenth century. The Atkinses made their life in India and, as far as we know, none had come back until my father at the time of Partition. My paternal grandfather was Church of England and his wife was Catholic, so they employed the rather odd habit of giving alternative religions to alternative children – Daddy was C of E and his brother Gerald was a Catholic. Another son, Oscar, died in infancy and then there were three sisters, Marjorie, Norah and Dorothy who died in her twenties from tuberculosis.

My mother came from a very ordinary family background, although her mother was a Pettet and the family can be traced back to the sixteenth century. With a French name, they may have been Huguenots escaping religious persecution. The original Pettets were Yeoman farmers who lived in Kent, and the original Pettet home – Coldred Court, a beautiful Elizabethan farmhouse near Dover – is still extant. Generations of Pettets lived in Deal, and because it is on the sea and was a naval base many of the men in the family were mariners and seafarers. When the family fortunes waned, many Pettets made their living by smuggling and hovelling.

Grandmother was one of the first Pettets to leave Deal. Having been widowed and left with three sons and a daughter to raise, she married again and my mother and her brother were the offspring. Mummy left school at fourteen and went to work in a drawing office. She was very beautiful. As they had virtually nothing in common, I once asked my father why he married her and was told simply that, 'She was the most beautiful girl around.' My father too was extremely handsome, with matinée idol good looks. They married at the town hall in Woolwich and lived in rented accommodation in Bromley. Mrs Wilson was their landlady – a large, kindly woman, whom I remember always smelling of bleach. In the forties none but the rich had holidays. However, Mrs Wilson had a beach bungalow at Jaywick on the east coast and used to take me down there for long weekend breaks. I had many happy hours at the seaside and one overriding memory. That was the man we called 'Dan-Dan, the lavatory man' who used to come around in the evening emptying the old Elsan toilets with the accompanying perfume. One year there was dreadful flooding in Jaywick and Clacton and our family never heard from Mrs Wilson again, so we assumed she'd died in the floods.

Memories of my childhood are fragmented but some remain quite vivid. My parents had moved in with Granny at 109 John Wilson Street. I remember many of the characters who lived in our road. Next door was a Mrs Chapman who, though her hair was incredibly fine to the point of being almost non-existent, was never seen without metal curlers. Our houses were ugly terraced brick, but one house was different because it had a beautiful bow window and the owner was equally striking – a very well-dressed woman called Nancy Catt. People in the street gossiped about her – don't they always – as they said she had many gentleman friends.

At the end of our road, next to the Star pub, was a family with a child called a 'blue baby' – a very fragile child with auburn hair and freckles who used to sit in the tiny front garden watching the world go by. She had a hole in her heart. Today it would be operated on, but in the forties nothing could be done for her and she died very young. We used to wave to each other as I walked to the bus stop on my way to school in the morning. If the weather was fine and she was outside in the evening, I'd stop and talk to her. Opposite us lived Mary Panel, a very homely woman who looked after me when Mummy and Daddy went out.

Then there was the tailor, Johnny Heath, whom my mother swears purloined a map and a glove belonging to Granny at the time of her funeral. Who knows whether this was true? The story went that there was money to be had by this map, but it needed money to get at it. I always thought this was the product of mother's fertile imagination, that she had dreamed up a bricked-up smuggler's tunnel somewhere in Deal with a hoard of precious stones. Fifty years later, when I encountered a Pettet who'd done extensive research on the family, I discovered there was some truth in the rumour – it all centred around land rights and many documents that needed to be collated in order to make a claim. By now any rights the Pettets had would have well and truly lapsed.

Next door to us was an old bachelor, Mr Blade, who lived with his even more ancient mother. When she died, I was taken next door to pay my respects and I remember an open coffin with her lying in it. I was very young and the memory remains as something quite frightening. There was also a chap who came round the streets with a cart shouting 'Rag and Bones' and collecting items you didn't want, for which he gave a few old pennies. Folk used to run out with buckets and spades in the hope that his horse would oblige – 'Good for the roses,' they said.

Despite Daddy being C of E, he received his education at the hands of the Catholic Brotherhood of St Patrick at St Joseph's College, Coonoor. Because he had a very good education, and despite not having a great deal of money, Daddy decided to send me to a small private Catholic school in Charlton, south-east London. The convent was run by nuns called Oblates of the Assumption. The church and the house in which the nuns lived are still standing, but the school has been replaced by a modern one. I remember the layout of the school and the chapel in particular. The Catholics used to wind up the non-Catholics with stories of ghosts and strange happenings and we used to long to go into the chapel to find out for ourselves.

It was at Charlton that I launched myself on to the unsuspecting public as an actress. In front of a very select and captive audience of mums and dads I played the title role in *King Canute*, complete with cardboard crown and bath-towel royal robe over gymslip. We played to a packed house for all of one afternoon and the brilliant review we got in the school periodical spurred me on to greater things. My next starring role was as the Wicked Queen in *Snow White and the Seven Dwarfs*. Mind you, my career practically came to an untimely end when the floodlight box toppled off the stage on to the floor, being restrained only by the back of my foot, which almost parted company from my leg. I had severed the tendons in my ankle and was off school for many weeks and unable to audition for the next epic at Assumption Productions.

I don't remember hearing my parents argue and was blissfully unaware of any tension between them, but when I was seven, an event occurred that was to have a very great bearing on the rest of my life and that of my sister. I'd caught the bus home from school and was nearing our house when I saw a removal van outside. My mother was leaving and taking my baby sister Gillian with her. My father had charge of me and we were to remain at 109. The house was quite large and at some stage in the intervening years, my mother's brother, wife and their daughter, who had Down's syndrome, had come to live in the top two floors of the house. They needed somewhere to live and could also lend a hand in looking after me. It wasn't easy for anyone. Daddy had to work and care for me, which meant it was impossible to invite friends home to play because there was no one to organise tea and cakes. Mummy went to live in rented accommodation with my sister. Gillian had to be looked after during the day while my mother worked and some of the places they lived in were dire. I remember being taken to visit and finding my little sister sitting with the door of the gas oven open so that she could keep warm. These circumstances must have had a deep emotional effect on both of us. In the forties, fifties and sixties, divorce was the exception rather than the norm – people stayed together and braved things out. Such was the disgrace that if you were a divorcee you were not allowed admittance to the Queen's Enclosure at Ascot. Now most of the immediate Royal Family are themselves divorced, so that ruling has had to go by the board.

My father was, as I have already said, incredibly good looking. In fact I think he resembled the film star Richard Todd. He was a disciplinarian, strict but fair. I adored him and we were very close. We shared a twin-bedded room and at weekends I used to love slipping into Daddy's bed for a cuddle and a story. Then when I was about eleven, he told me that I wasn't to continue the habit. I'd no idea why as I was totally ignorant of the facts of life.

I loved those cuddles and still find cuddling up to the man I love just about the best part of a relationship. Much as I enjoy a sexual relationship, it's the cuddles I couldn't do without. When I'm in the arms of my loved one, I sleep like a baby.

With the domestic help of my aunt and uncle upstairs at 109 John Wilson Street, we muddled through. I remember once cooking a meal of bacon and eggs for him far too early and by the time he got home the food had congealed, and was virtually inedible, but he braved his way through it so as not to upset me. I suppose the seeds of an unusual relationship were sown then – I tried to look after my father and he tried to be both mother and father to me. He took me to see my mother and sister as often as he could, but regular visits were not easy, as we had no transport. So from the age of seven to eleven I grew up without really knowing my mother or my sister.

I'm not a natural academic and study was always a hard slog and meant learning by rote. I suppose you'd call me a plodder. I'd begun to pick up the flat vowel sounds of a south-east Londoner and father, who speaks beautifully, decided to send me to Speech and Drama lessons. Although I also took ballet lessons, I'd never have had the dedication to become a dancer, but my Speech and Drama, plus my later secretarial skills, have earned me a living for a working lifetime.

The eleven-plus loomed and I passed with flying colours – so well, indeed, that I was awarded a scholarship at a girls' public school – Christ's Hospital. This was where inverse snobbery came into play. Because my father had paid a few pounds a term to have me educated privately at a convent, and we lived in a London County Council borough, the LCC would not allow me to take up the scholarship. Sounds familiar, doesn't it? *Plus ça change, plus c'est la même chose.* I was offered a place at the Catholic Convent of St Joseph's at Abbey Wood in South London. The nuns running the convent were the Daughters of Jesus, an order that originated in Brittany, France.

My father was in the army and the time was approaching when he had to do a tour of overseas duty. Consequently, he decided to make me a boarder at St Jo's. I'll never forget the total desolation I felt when he took me to school. It was a short walk from the bus stop to the convent, but I wanted it to go on forever. We went through the gates and up some stairs to the front door. A kindly nun led us to a small room, where we had to say our farewells. I cried my heart out. Although home life was far from perfect, it was a home and I really wasn't boarding material. I loathe regimentation and even now I hate being awakened from my slumbers by any kind of alarm. All those years ago, our boarding mistress, a short and attractive nun (Mother St Roman) would stride through the dormitory like the prophet of doom swathed in black, ringing a great big hand bell, and giving no quarter. Despite being a non-Catholic, and despite the promises to my father to the contrary, I too was awakened at an ungodly hour every second day to attend Mass. It wasn't the service I minded, but the early rising. We went to Mass before breakfast and the smell of the incense on an empty stomach has many times brought me close to fainting.

Our dormitory had cubicles down the middle for the 'big' girls and high hospital-type beds down the side for we little ones. I used to long to be a big girl just to have the privacy of a cubicle. Looking back on my boarding days, they weren't too bad and they do afford me the odd wry smile. When I saw the musical *Oliver!* I was highly amused at the children holding out their dishes for more. As an adult I rarely eat a cooked breakfast and then only very late in the morning, or if I'm travelling on a train. What is it about the magic of eating when you are bulleting through the countryside at over a hundred miles an hour ... even if the food is indifferent? At school, when we'd been awoken at 6 a.m. to attend Mass, all of us were ravenous. I remember how, on the days when we were lucky enough to have bacon, we used to jostle and push to get the congealing bacon fat handed out at the end of the meal. Makes me shudder to think of it now. Olivio and Benecol were decades into the future!

Sunday was an incredible day for boarders. We hardly got up off our knees! There was early morning Mass followed by breakfast. No sooner was that over than we got ourselves ready for the walk to the local church. We must have looked smart in our special Sunday berets. They resembled the shape of a halo trimmed with gold braid. We trooped off in a crocodile two-by-two. After the service it was back to the convent for lunch, play, homework, afternoon service, tea and then another trip to chapel for benediction. I was greatly influenced by the theatricality of the religious services, received great kindness from most of the nuns, and thought very strongly about converting. This desire diminished somewhat when I became a day-girl and the overwhelming religiosity wasn't surrounding me 24 hours a day.

I was so unhappy as a boarder that my father asked my mother to come back to the family home in Woolwich and look after me. Unfortunately, when she did we had an uneasy relationship. We'd been apart for over four years and were almost strangers to each other. Also, because they'd gone through much deprivation together, my mother favoured my sister and whatever she did wrong I got blamed for. Mind you, I deserved it sometimes, as on the occasion when I took Gillian to the Odeon cinema with me to see *Romeo and Juliet* starring Laurence Harvey and Susan Shentall. I thought Laurence Harvey was stunning and for him, I made my sister sit through the film twice. My mother was beside herself with worry when we got home. I received a sound slap and was barred from the cinema for a month. We had no television or other form of mechanical entertainment, so being deprived of cinema-going and Saturday morning pictures was a dire punishment.

My sister was six years younger than me and we were not to achieve a sisterly closeness until we were both much older, partly because we'd been separated during our bonding years and also due to my early marriage and consequent departure for New Zealand and Australia. My work has taken me to live all over the country so we have always been separated by distance and we have very few interests in common. We don't look much alike but we have the same smile, laugh and share certain mannerisms. As a little girl she was also a little minx who loved spying on me and telling tales. I am a mongrel so far as religion is concerned. Baptised Church of England, attended a Catholic Convent and went to a Methodist church on Sundays because it was just around the corner. It was here in the choir that I fell for a very tall boy called Robin. I can't remember his surname, but I do know he was old enough to have started work at an electronics company called Siemans. After many months of talking together following the evening service and then going our separate ways, he eventually asked to walk me home. Robin was six foot tall and I was under five foot. There were two steps leading up to our front door, so for ease of conversation I stood on the top step. It was there I received my first kiss, to the accompaniment of a rattling letter box. My sister had heard us talking and used the letter box as a spy hole. The spring on the flap was quite strong and it came down on her fingers. Poetic justice, some might say.

At school, I didn't excel at anything except Speech and Drama. I was hopeless at games: I was hit in the left eye by a tennis ball, which weakened my vision in that eye; at hockey I was so bad I was placed in goal and even then managed to end the lesson covered in bruises; and in rounders I got hit round the head – it takes quite some doing for that to happen.

However, I did have a competitive streak in the acting department. I regularly entered drama festivals; I usually came in the first three, and always had a cold. Colds are my reaction to nerves and all the critique forms from those days noted that '... she appeared to be suffering from a slight cold.' I'm no linguist, but on one occasion a student had gone sick just before a French verse-speaking competition. I was asked to stand in and, though I'd little idea what the words meant, learnt them by heart and had a convincing enough French accent to get through to the finals. It was really quite cheeky of me to enter and though I didn't win, it was fun trying. I was particularly fond of our English mistress. We were fortunate enough to have her for the five years up to 'O' level. Mother Mary David, who later left the order and with whom I'm still in contact, possessed endless patience and was an excellent teacher. She would organise verse-speaking contests in our form during term time. I don't know whether it was a desire to show off, or to win her approval, but for one of these form contests I tried to memorise the whole of *The*

Rime of The Ancient Mariner. I came dreadfully unstuck and never attempted that kind of bravado again.

In my school days, The Old Vic Theatre at Waterloo was dedicated to Shakespearean productions. Mother Mary David would organise trips for us to see Shakespeare performed in all his glory by some notable actors. I've still got all my little yellow programmes costing 4d (2p today) and memories of wonderful performances by young men and women, in the traditional spear-carrying roles, many of whom have gone on to great prominence in theatre and film. In 1960 the Old Vic presented a production of *Romeo and Juliet* with Judi Dench and John Stride in the title roles but with actors such as Tom Courtenay and Barbara Leigh Hunt playing minute parts. I remember Paul Rodgers playing a magnificent Macbeth and on another never-to-be-forgotten occasion Richard Burton playing Othello to John Neville's Iago. Although I was a great fan of Burton, my absolute heartthrob was John Neville. I queued at the stage door for as long as Mother Mary David would let us, and nearly swooned on seeing the wonderful Mr Neville in a navy-and-white spotted dressing gown. I didn't get his autograph on that occasion, but wrote to him and received a personally signed photograph, which still has pride of place in my autograph book. Although I've never met John Neville, I have met and interviewed many of the stars I admired as a child.

I don't regard myself as a scholar but authority deigned otherwise and I found myself in the 'Latin' stream at school. In those days there were two streams doing precisely the same syllabus, except for one notable exception. At the tender age of eleven the demarcation line was into the class that did cookery and everything else or the one that aspired to Latin and everything else. I really was dreadful at Latin and despite our wonderful Latin mistress, Miss Cronin, who selflessly gave up her lunch hours to take myself and another few 'dummies' for extra Latin, I failed my mock miserably and didn't even make it through to the exam proper. I ended up in hospital with suspected appendicitis, which turned out to be a massive attack of nerves. Miss Cronin always perched on a desk when she was teaching and I still feel bad about the verse one of the girls made up and we chanted about her:

> 'Cronibus satibus on the deskolorum
> Deskibus collapsibus
> Cronibus on the floorum.'

I longed to be doing cookery with Mother Mary Patrick, who made the most wonderful fudge I've ever tasted and whose domain was an outbuilding away from the school – a place called Ker-Anna surrounded by rhododendron bushes lovingly tended by Joe, the Irish gardener. The only men with whom we had contact at school were the priests who came to take services and dear gentle Joe. We girls loved him. I don't know if he was married, or if he had a family. I suspect he was totally devoted to the nuns and dedicated his life to being the man about the house for them. He was a gentle giant of a man. I can still see him gardening at Ker-Anna in his grey bibbed trousers, never without a cap on his head, and remember his wonderfully soft Irish voice that would have melted a heart of stone.

From 1953 to 1957, when my mother came back to the house in Woolwich to look after me, I was a day girl at St Jo's. I was a conscientious and hard worker and regretted I wasn't having as much fun as a lot of the other girls appeared to. Also, most of the girls lived very close to the school and I was a twenty-minute bus ride away, so it was difficult to integrate. We had to rely on public transport, as few parents had cars – school runs, parties and 'sleep-overs' were decades into the future. Also, as my mother worked, I wasn't in a position to ask friends home to tea. Boys started to enter the equation with most of the girls, but no one looked at me. Having been a reasonably attractive child, I was turning into an incredibly plain teenager. I remember a good-looking boy called Ken who used to wait at a bus stop near the school. I'd be on the top deck, looking with longing and willing him to look up. He never even looked in my direction and was obviously totally unaware of my existence.

While my father was away on service in Singapore, I'd often spend the summer holidays with his close friends down in Sussex. Bert Manly was in the army, like Father, and his wife, Jen, was a housekeeper for the Lascelles family at Woolbeding House in Sussex. The Manlys were warm and welcoming people and made me feel part of their family, so although I lived the life of a townie, I relished the freedom of the countryside and loved my holidays with them. Life was easy and our pleasures were simple; rafting on the river, long walks, gathering berries, scrumping apples. Nobody worried about letting us out to roam the countryside and we had so much innocent fun. On one occasion the Manlys' offspring David and Daphne and I went to the cinema in Midhurst. It was a long and late show and we caught the last bus home. It was about a mile's walk from the bus stop down the lane to Woolbeding House – totally dark and no street lighting. We were going past the churchyard, scaring ourselves silly with talk of ghosts, when we heard a weird noise. All three of us ran for our lives. It was only in the cold light of day, we realised that far from some ghoulish spectre, it was probably a cow in a neighbouring field. Being with the Manlys was my first taste of puppy love. Their son, a highly intelligent young man, was four years older than I. Four years doesn't sound much, but when a girl is fourteen and a boy eighteen, the difference might as well be twenty years. I used to go fishing with David and the highlight of my existence was the approbation that greeted the worms I dug up for his fishing rod. I was terribly hurt when, some years later, I was a bridesmaid at his sister's wedding and David announced his engagement to a German girl he'd met in Berlin while doing his national service. I remember fleeing from the room to the Ladies and crying hysterically.

As an adult, I only saw David twice, when he invited me to lunch to ask for professional advice about television – first for his daughter and then for a business colleague. He died recently at a hospice. His sister Daphne told me of his illness and when I asked whether she thought he would like to see me, she replied in the affirmative. I saw him twice in the last few weeks of his life and while I was massaging his cold hands, among his last words to me were … 'I should have married you.' Life would have been very different for both of us. He was a true academic and I think the life of a wife of a teacher at a public school might have suited me. I would have had at least four children, been bountiful to his charges at the school and been all the things I ended up not being.

Father came back from Singapore in 1957 and I was in for a total shock. He came back with a wife, Avis; I didn't even know that he and my mother were divorced. I presume they must have thought I was better off not knowing, I should have gone out to Singapore for a holiday during father's three-year tour of duty, and I'm sure he would have prepared the ground for telling me the news. It was the right of all the children of the military to make one visit in the three-year posting, but it was the time of the Suez Crisis and my trip was cancelled. Perhaps things might have been different if I'd met Avis on their home ground. It was a difficult time for the three of us. There I was, having spent so much of my adolescence as the apple of my father's eye and being a total Daddy's girl, and suddenly there was this rival for his affections. Many years later, I was to learn first-hand, and from the other side, the trauma of step-relationships. At the time I resented my stepmother and didn't understand the difficulties of being a step-parent. I think I was angry with my father, who had chosen another woman, and had divided allegiances. I was probably a thoroughly objectionable teenager. My stepmother had had a career in the WRAC (Women's Royal Army Corps), was not used to domesticity and had married my father in Singapore where everyone had servants. She came back to a ready-made family, not much idea about running a house, and a troublesome relationship with a teenage stepdaughter It was to be several decades before we understood each other and became genuine friends. Although my mother and I had not been close in the intervening years, she was my mother and when I heard her criticised, I took her side. She, in turn, did her fair share of criticism of the 'new wife' and I was like a piggy in the middle, as is the case in the majority of step-relationships.

I had taken seven 'O' levels at fifteen and passed them. I wanted to do 'A' levels and go to drama school or university, but my family were not overburdened with money. In those days only three per cent of pupils went to university and grants were almost non-existent. An added financial complication arose when I discovered the sideboard groaning with orange juice – my stepmother was pregnant. I was sixteen and the last thing in the world I wanted was a baby in the family. Regardless, I set myself the task of knitting an outfit for my sister, Mandy. I didn't realise how quickly babies grow and by the time I'd completed the outfit, it was too small for her!

Daddy and I still argue to this day over how I came to do secretarial training. He maintains he didn't know I wanted to act or go to university, and I believe he pushed me into technical college. Be that as it may, I couldn't have had a better training for the work I was to do later in life. Because I was only fifteen and too young to go on to another educational establishment, I had to fill in a year in the sixth form. My father and stepmother were living near Croydon and I entered Wallington County Grammar School for Girls. It was probably an excellent establishment but I missed the caring attitude of the nuns and felt myself to be just a statistic on a large register. However, in that year I gained another two 'O' levels in German and Economics while I was marking time waiting to go to secretarial college. My choice of career was relatively limited, as many of the jobs that exist today simply weren't around when I was at school. On one hand, the young today have enormous choice and a wonderful array of exciting futures but are faced with great competition for jobs. There was very little unemployment in my teens and if you wanted a job you could invariably get one.

I did my year at Ewell County Technical College and left with a certificate from the Royal Society of Arts to say that I was proficient in the Principles of Accounts, Commerce, Shorthand and Typewriting. How on earth I ever passed Accounts and Commerce is anybody's guess. My system of accounts is that when the books don't balance, I borrow money from savings to even things up again … sort of robbing Peter to pay Paul.

Having been thwarted in my desire to go to drama school, I decided the next best thing was to get as close as possible to an affiliated industry. So I applied to join the BBC, took a test, passed and was offered a job in the Programme Correspondence Section (PCS) – which dealt with listeners' queries and complaints. I was to earn the princely sum of £6.10s (£6.50p) per week – £2.10s went on my keep at home, another £1.10s on train fares and the remainder served to pay for lunches, clothes and entertainment. You wouldn't get too far in a London taxi for £6 today.

I was very proud of being part of the vast organisation affectionately known as 'Auntie' by most who worked for her. I quickly joined the Studio Amateur Dramatic Group and the Sailing Club, worked hard and was enjoying life and relative new-found freedom. As I was still living at home, my father demanded that I had to be home by 10.30 p.m.

The BBC was once a superb employer – looking after you virtually from cradle to grave – and it enjoyed an excellent reputation for in-service training schemes and attachments. The joke was that the BBC was the training ground for ITV. So many folk cut their professional teeth there, trained at the Beeb's expense and then moved on. One of their training establishments was in Marylebone Road, almost opposite Baker Street tube station. The building has gone now, replaced by yet another soulless concrete edifice. I had to attend an induction course there and remember the rickety old lift, which bounced up and down several times before it came to a halt on the designated floor. It was a slow process using that lift, so one day, when I was in danger of being late for a lecture, I decided my own two feet were quicker and went haring up the stairs, only to butt headfirst into an extremely tall gentleman. As I raised my eyes to apologise, I went weak at the knees. I was gazing at that wonderful black singer, the late Paul Robeson. I blurted an apology and can still see his lovely smile and hear his beautiful voice as he excused me. That was my first *contact*, one might say, with the famous. I still thrill to this day when I hear his dark black velvet voice singing the title song from *Sanders of the River.*

My boss in PCS was a Mrs Kitcat – she had a feline face, which suited her name, was built like a stick insect and smoked like a chimney. I loathe smoking and as a child one punishment for being naughty was to be sent for my parents' cigarettes, which I used to collect in a paper bag – I so hated the smell of them and wouldn't touch them for all the tea in China. Mrs K's smoking, plus the fact that I had ambition, meant I didn't stay long in PCS. Jobs within the BBC are posted on noticeboards and there was one going as Junior Secretary to the Science Unit. I applied for and got the position and went to work in offices just to the left of the clock in Broadcasting House (BH) I mention the clock because whenever I walk into BH I remember where it all started for me. I don't know why or how I got that particular job, because at school I failed my science subjects miserably and it was a wonder that I kept my head above water.

The Science Unit comprised a senior producer, a wonderful quietly spoken Aberdonian, Dr Archie Clow; a junior producer, mad on the scouting movement, Dr David Edge; Caroline Post, a senior secretary who had a love/hate relationship with a Lambretta scooter; and a junior secretary – me. Our regular output was a scientific quiz called *Who Knows?* and two other regular programmes, *Science Survey* and *Science Review*. We also did extremely erudite one-off programmes, so technical and high-flown, I barely understood what I was typing as I pounded away at the keys. I do remember one programme was about DNA – an absolute breakthrough in the fifties, and a total mystery to me. As speakers, we had top men from the scientific world, one of whom, Professor Peter Medawar, was destined to become a Nobel Prize winner.

After Caroline left the Unit, I stepped into her shoes – though not on her grade (a typical ploy of the BBC) and had to accompany Dr Clow to gatherings such as the Annual Meeting of the British Association for the Advancement of Science. Initially I was petrified. How was little Janet Atkins, hopeless at science and a miserable failure at chemistry, going to hold her own with these learned people? I soon learned that though they were experts in their subjects, they were kindly and not averse to a chat about the world of entertainment with a young secretary. And I felt very honoured when Archie Clow took me for dinner at a super restaurant in Oxford, the Elizabeth, during one of the Annual Meetings. It made such an impression on me I even remember what I had to eat – trout with almonds served on a rectangular plate.

I worked hard during the day and had an extremely full social life. I joined the local theatre group – The Harlequins – it was the best amateur society in my area and was conveniently near my home in Wallington, Surrey. Their standards were high, their shows exciting. We staged the World Amateur Première of *Expresso Bongo* – in which I played the cockney sister of the singing hero. I think Cliff Richard played the part of the hero in the West End show. We also staged *The Madwoman of Chaillot* in which I played Irma. Much of my spare time was spent with The Harlequins or at a local youth club attached to St Mary's Church, Beddington. St Mary's Youth Club (SMYC) also maintained a high standard of amateur dramatics and I remembering receiving my very first corsage of flowers (heavily wired and heavenly perfumed hyacinths) on stage at the end of *The Happiest Days of Your Life*, in which I played the vicar's wife – I was only about twenty years too young for the part!

I enjoyed working at the BBC and was fascinated by the 'characters' in Talks Department, BH. The poet Louis MacNeice was a producer, as was a white Russian, Anna Kallin, who was rumoured to have had a long-standing affair with the expressionist painter Oskar Kokoschka. Anna was so elegant with her grey hair swept back in a French pleat and on her little finger she wore an exquisite baroque black pearl set in diamonds, which is where I'm sure my love of pearls originated. Our family didn't have any jewels, so I doubly admired them on this attractive woman. Then there was Owen Leeming – a radio producer destined to alter my life dramatically and remain a friend for life. We often talked in the corridor and I suppose, looking back, we were attracted to one another. But Owen was involved with someone else and, though the affair had almost run its course, he would not have entertained the idea of cheating on his girlfriend.

Coming from a broken home and being looked after by my father between the ages of seven and eleven, I was very naive. I imagine it would be difficult for any father to discuss sex with a daughter, but fifty years ago it would have been impossible. My mother was from a generation where you didn't discuss the subject – it just happened. School wasn't much use either, being a Catholic convent. Sex was a taboo subject and the closest we came to being relieved of our ignorance was in biology lessons, when we were taught about the birds and the bees. Somehow I couldn't see the connection. Consequently, when I first went to work at the BBC at seventeen and a half, I knew nothing of life and was highly flattered that the toast of the BBC's Studio Amateur Dramatic Group, a man fifteen years older than I and much sought after by the ladies, should have found me attractive. I had no brothers and didn't really know how to cope with men, but I found the attention of this urbane and charming man highly gratifying. John had played the field and why he was attracted to an innocent young thing like me is a mystery. How I wish he hadn't happened, but he did and our relationship was the cornerstone of the rest of my life. I was sexually naive. He wasn't. If only Owen Leeming had been a free agent at the time, I don't think the liaison with John Staple would have developed.

John and I had a stormy relationship – many quarrels and making up – and then he asked me to marry him. Our engagement night was spent at the Apollo, Victoria, where we saw *West Side Story* starring the American George Chakiris. The show was like nothing ever staged before – electrifying, dynamic and different. I suppose even then I realised that I wanted more from life than a secretarial job and domesticity. Because of the strained relationship between my stepmother and myself – with my father in the middle – I wasn't happy at home and wanted to flee the nest, so I suppose I was ripe for the picking. I was heading for disaster and I think I knew it. My engagement ring came off with monotonous frequency and on one occasion John opened the bonnet of his Mini and put the ring on the fanbelt, threatening to destroy it unless I put it back on my finger. In the sixties people didn't live together; if we had, I know we'd never have married. Thinking about the film *The Graduate,* I should have run screaming from the church.

John was an obvious womaniser and by the time of our marriage, I was no longer in love with him and we rowed constantly. At this period of my life, I wasn't close enough to my mother to confide in her and I certainly couldn't discuss my relationship with my stepmother. People were aware of our differences and our rows and no one could understand why I agreed to marry him.

★   ★   ★

I'm sure people will find it hard to believe in this permissive day and age but John and I did not have a full-blown relationship before our marriage. We did indulge in what was archaically called 'heavy petting'. I was young and fertile and John should have known better. In my ignorance, I believed that you could only fall pregnant through penetrative sexual intercourse. How wrong I was. To my horror, just before my nineteenth birthday, I missed a period and then another.

Some weeks later, on a referral from a GP, I found myself sitting with John in front of a psychiatrist who held my future in his hands. 'You are not emotionally unstable and there is no medical or psychological reason why you should not have this *baby.*' We walked out of his office with me totally stunned. I'd expected John to look after me and here I was, an immature and emotionally needy young woman, being told that I would have to become a mother whether I wished to or not. At the time there was no right to abortion. A cold, clinical psychiatrist gave one the choice between unwanted motherhood or a back-street job. Coming from a broken home, being naive and with absolutely no maternal instincts, I felt as though I'd been sentenced to life and had the key thrown away. What were we going to do? Even at the age of 34, John also had no desire to become responsible for a new life. I knew that if I gave birth I would not be able to hand over the child for adoption. We would have made dreadful parents. As far as we could see there was only one alternative, and we took it.

Although I've tried to blot it out of my mind, I can't. It was a seedy, demeaning process and the sense of guilt is with me even now. John found a doctor who had been struck off the medical register and operated from an address in Kingston upon Thames. We were advised to book a room for the night somewhere in the vicinity for my recuperation and, I suppose, proximity to the 'doctor' if something went wrong. John picked me up after work and we drove in silence to Kingston, where we checked into a B&B. Our room was stifling in its smallness, with hardly room to move around the bed. I was scared stiff and had to be anaesthetised with whisky, a drink I loathe to this day. We made our way to a large house in a nearby leafy street with a wrought-iron gate and long path leading to the imposing front door. It was, to all intents and purposes, a normal family home. Sadly, it was a house of dark secrets, shame and guilt. How many other girls before me, and for many years after, went through the same demeaning process? The whole operation was seedy. The room was dimly lit and a kettle whistled in the corner, boiling the water for sterilising the instruments. And there was Him. Naturally, I never knew his name but I do remember that he took advantage of my inebriated state to touch me in an intimate way. I felt tarnished and dirty. The atmosphere was surreal. I cannot express the guilt strongly enough, it just came over me in waves and did so for many years. After the 'operation', John and I returned to our rented room and a night filled with tears of remorse.

In my opinion, the Catholic religion uses guilt like building bricks that accumulate around you, creating an edifice from which you cannot escape. I felt so badly about my 'sin', I knew I had to pay for it. In my cock-eyed logic, I thought if I agreed to marry John I could somehow cleanse myself. I knew I didn't

love him, had mistaken age for maturity, and was looking for a
father figure. I was desperately unhappy, in total turmoil and
didn't know to whom to turn for advice. But I had to expiate
my sin. Four days before our wedding, my nerves gave way and
I knew I simply had to get out of the situation. On the way
home from work I changed direction, got off the tube at
Charing Cross, and caught another to take me to where John
lived in East London. I repeat, there was no, or very little, living
together in the late 1950s. As I walked along the pavement from
the tube station, I tried to gather my courage. Knocking on the
front door, I was hardly over the threshold before blurting out
'I'm very sorry, but I can't go through with this marriage
because I don't love you.' I thought it would be a simple case
of John accepting that the relationship was over and we'd get
out of the wedding arrangements as quickly as possible.
Instead, he talked to me persuasively and assured me, 'It's only
pre-wedding nerves. Besides, all the arrangements have been
made and we've received presents; you can't let everyone
down. You'll be all right.' But I wasn't. Daddy must have
sensed my unhappiness, because even in the car going to the
church he assured me that it wasn't too late to change my mind.
Poor Daddy had saved to give me the best wedding he could
afford with a reception at the Aerodrome Hotel just off the
Purley Way. I was all trussed up in a nylon wedding dress from
Faimans of Oxford Street and my hair (which had gone too
chestnut at the hairdresser's) was primped into a beehive set off
by a coronet. I cried throughout most of the ceremony. People
are used to brides crying with loving emotion, but I was crying
with sheer terror. Never mind, thought I, it's bound to be all
right later. But it wasn't.

The wedding breakfast passed in a haze – you know the
feeling you get when you are detached from reality and
watching yourself from the outside. All the friends and relations
were laughing and having a lovely time; but not the bride. All
too soon it was time to change into my going-away outfit – a
lovely golden-coloured suit set off by a green pillbox hat. In
traditional fashion, the guests gathered to wish us well as we

climbed into John's Mini, suitably daubed in the usual wedding greetings and dragging an old boot tied to the exhaust. Although our honeymoon was to be spent in a B&B in Cornwall, John had pushed the boat out and booked us a wedding night at Skindles, a rather posh hotel in Maidenhead. Far from being a wonderfully loving and romantic experience, I spent most of the time in tears, and frigidity was setting in fast. I can't remember anything about the honeymoon except that it rained most of the time, which was suitably appropriate for the commencement of this disastrous relationship.

John was not a bad person but he was a charmer, a womaniser, prone to being dramatic, and a normal hetero-sexual male. To be married to a snivelling, unhappy, frigid girl-woman must have been an impossible situation for him. It's little wonder that he turned his attention back to an ex-girlfriend, older and more experienced than I, and happy to 'oblige' him. We staggered on in our increasingly unhappy relationship for seven months until one night I went for a bath and locked the bathroom door. He was incensed and a row ensued until in his rage he threw himself against the door and broke the lock. He hit me around the head and I know what people mean when they say they saw stars, because I did. Although a highly dramatic man, John wasn't an habitual wife-beater. I knew I didn't love him, was making both of us desperately unhappy, and was frightened that the situation might arise where I would become pregnant. He immediately apologised, but that was the point at which I knew I had to end the farce. Next morning, after he had gone to work, I put my toiletries in a small bag and left with just the clothes I stood up in. The irony of the situation was that I'd paid our rent out of my weekly salary and hadn't got enough for the train fare to my mother's home in Windsor, so I went to his parents in London instead. They were very kind and understanding and not at all judgmental. I remember John's father commenting that he hadn't expected the relationship to last, as John was very much a bachelor and was used to playing the field. I went back to the flat a few days later to collect some clothes but John had changed the locks. He did deliver a parcel of clothing to Broadcasting House for me, but I never saw most of my personal belongings again, or the wedding presents given by my family and friends.

How had I reached this point in my life? I'm sure that much of my behaviour had arisen out of the dysfunctional family life I'd lived through from a very early age and my need to be loved. My sister also went on to make two disastrous marriages and had relationships with totally inappropriate men.

★   ★   ★

Owen Leeming told me he had watched a person he described as 'bubbly, laughing and full of life' turn into a morose, depressed creature. By the time my marriage was over, so too was Owen's relationship and we often talked in the corridor of BH with me spilling out my problems to him. So when I left John, it was Owen who helped me find rooms to rent in Eton Road, Chalk Farm. The accommodation was in a large house owned and run by a retired matron. You could not only see yourself in the floors, you could have eaten off them the place was so pristine. As we lodgers came through the front door her stentorian tones would ring out, reminding us to change into our slippers. It was an all-female establishment and men were not allowed into the sanctum under any circumstances.

In the late fifties we still experienced pea souper fogs. One evening, when I returned to my rooms, a figure loomed out of the fog at the front gate. It was John, demanding to speak with me. I was frightened of him but he simply wouldn't go away. Somehow I managed to smuggle him into the house, past the dragon, and went to the shared kitchen to make us a drink. I'm sure he was only being histrionically dramatic but when I returned to the room, he was sitting in a chair pulling a pair of my stockings through and through his hands. For one fleeting moment, I thought he was going to strangle me. John liked being dramatic and I'm sure this is what he hoped I'd think. I don't remember the substance of our conversation, but I got the strength from somewhere to resist his demand for my return – I knew it would be disastrous.

Meanwhile, Owen was an absolute rock – understanding, helpful, intelligent and mature. He was just what I needed at that period in my life. There was still a strong moral climate in our country in the fifties and he too lived in an establishment with a landlady who frowned on any assignations. Owen lived at the corner of Cadogan Square and I remember the first meal we had together after he'd managed to smuggle me into the flat. He cooked me steak with garlic – a taste with which I was unfamiliar – followed by tinned guavas and cream eaten out of Poole pottery cups because he didn't have any pudding bowls. I'd never experienced guavas before and to this day they remind me of Owen and our first night together.

Was I in love or was I in need? Perhaps it is difficult to separate the two. Owen brought me emotional security and was also to bring about an enormous change in my life. The change was one that greatly affected my future. The nerve-wracking experience of being smuggled into Owen's accommodation, although great fun, became a strain and we decided to move in together. Our flat was in the basement of a house in Oakfield Road. It was owned by the Marquis of Queensberry, who had just opened his Reject China Shop in Chelsea. We looked out onto a small paved courtyard where His Lordship's dogs relieved themselves. Well, I suppose they had to go somewhere and it was better than fouling the streets! It was most definitely not glamorous accommodation.

By this time John, quite rightly, had decided to divorce me and I couldn't be bothered to go through the process of a counter petition because of his adultery. Owen and I had to experience the slightly quaint and amusing business of being visited by a private detective. A little man in a bowler hat came by prior appointment. He didn't have to witness anything other than the fact we shared a double bed. You did not have to be caught 'in flagrante delicto'. The chap doffed his bowler at the front door, exposing a shiny bald pate. It was all so silly we got a fit of the giggles. We showed him the bed and offered him a cup of tea, but he refused on the grounds of impropriety. It really was farcical. Why is it assumed that a couple only have sex in bed? And would the grounds for divorce have been acceptable had we had twin beds? The mind boggles.

So far as my marriage to John Staple was concerned, that was that. Moreover, I thought that he had blocked my path to promotion and better things at work. I had applied for and obtained an attachment to BBC Television as a production assistant. When John heard about it he conveyed to me that life would be difficult for me if I took up the position. I don't know if he could – or would – have done anything but I had no desire to experience any more unpleasantness, so I stayed working in Sound Radio at the BBC, going to Speech and Drama lessons and taking Guildhall exams in my spare time.

CHAPTER TWO

NEW ZEALAND AND OWEN

Owen was an intellectual, academic, kind and loving man. What he saw in me, I'll never know. As a talks producer, and then on secondment to television as a drama producer, he mixed with and met actors, writers, poets and people from a world of which I longed to be a part. At Television Centre, Owen was charged with producing *The Grass is Singing* by Doris Lessing. The play starred a very good-looking actor called Walter Brown, who seems to have disappeared from the acting scene. Through Owen I met people from his exciting and stimulating world. We saw the musical *Oliver!* and went backstage because Owen knew the actor John Bluthal, who played the part of Fagin. At one dinner gathering I met the poet Ted Hughes, although he didn't have the acclaim then that he now posthumously enjoys. I was frightened witless and hardly opened my mouth. It was all heady stuff, although I remained largely on the periphery of discussions, not having the intellectual background to feel that I could make any worthwhile contributions. But I sat, listened and absorbed the information like a sponge.

Owen had an MA in French and studied music to BMus. level at Canterbury College in New Zealand. While working as a radio announcer, he won a bursary to continue his studies in musical composition at the Conservatoire in Paris. He fell in love with Paris and had a great love of France and the French; today he is a naturalised French citizen. Recently I e-mailed him to check on a few facts of our life together and asked why he'd not continued his musical studies. His reply was, 'I decided that I wasn't up to European standards and decided to return to New Zealand but not before seeing something of Europe, ending up in England. I landed a post as a BBC Talks Producer and fatefully crossed paths with a cute and fairy-like Talks Secretary in Broadcasting House.'

Owen loved planning trips and wanted to introduce me to the delights of France, so we took his little frog-eyed Sprite down to Lydd in Kent and loaded it on to a plane to Le Touquet. From there we drove south. I'll never forget my first experience of French hospitality. It was only a Relais Routier at which we stayed. Mine host apologised for the frugality of his table, but explained that we had arrived quite late. The *frugal meal* comprised an hors d'oeuvre of so many different delicacies, it was a meal in itself. We feasted on artichoke hearts, oysters, marinated mushrooms, haricots verts and so much else that the main course was superfluous.

On our travels we encountered an old man by the roadside, sporting the traditional French beret and distilling Marc – the rough brandy made from what's left of the grape skins after the wine has been pressed. The locals brought their residue to him and he processed it. Under EU rules, this practice is not acceptable and has virtually disappeared, though a few die-hard old Frenchmen ignore the rules and continue plying their trade. We were making our way slowly to Paris, where we were to stay for a couple of days. There is a song – 'April in Paris' – which talks of chestnuts in blossom and romance under the stars. It was spring, the chestnuts were in blossom and romance hung heavily in the air. I even found romance in what I call the threepenny bit green and gold cups from which many Parisians drink their *café crème* halfway through the morning. We raced around Paris trying to buy some, but they were only on sale to the catering trade. We made do instead with a rather naff couple of cups sporting the words *moi* and *toi* with *nous deux* in gold on the coffee pot. I have so much for which to thank Owen, not least my enduring love affair with France. On our return journey, we were overjoyed when the plane took off and the sun came first through through the windows on one side of the plane and then through the other side – there was fog at Lydd, the plane couldn't land and we had to spend another night in what was now 'our' beloved France.

Owen had always intended returning to his native New Zealand, taking the production experience he'd gained at the BBC back to the fledgling New Zealand Broadcasting Commission. Now he was going to take me with him. My divorce hadn't come through, but that didn't matter. If it had, maybe Owen and I would have married. Although he no longer practised his religion, Owen's parents were staunch Catholics. We didn't want to hurt them and I didn't want to go to New Zealand bearing my married name. So for the princely sum of 12s10d (about 65p) I changed my name by deed poll to Leeming and Owen told his parents that when we arrived in New Zealand my name would be his. It was the truth and they made the assumption that we'd married quietly before leaving England.

In the sixties, a plane journey to the other side of the world was a lengthy affair and you didn't do it in one or two legs like you do nowadays – apart from anything else, the planes simply didn't have the capacity to fly enormous distances without refuelling. We flew KLM and at every meal we were given delicious handouts of Dutch chocolate. These were to act as currency when we had a stop at Delhi. We disembarked at the airport to be driven to an hotel to freshen up and rest before the next stage of the journey. I shall never forget the beggars and poverty there. I saw a way of life about which I was totally ignorant. At the hotel we were waited on by an old Indian who looked careworn, tired out, and as though he should have been at home with his feet up being pampered by his grandchildren. We had absolutely no Indian money on us with which to tip him, so I left behind all my accumulated chocolate bars and hoped he would appreciate them and understand.

Our next stop was Bangkok, where we were to stay for a few days. My introduction to theatre had been a production of *The King and I* at the Theatre Royal Drury Lane. When I was eleven, Lady Loewen, the wife of my father's army boss, took me to a matinée performance with tea and cake in the interval. I had fallen under the spell of the theatre at that performance. Suddenly here I was, the sets had come alive; the temples, the tinkling of the temple bells in the wind, the vibrant colours, the smells, the noise. Bangkok had a magic despite the traffic and the pollution. We stayed in a small guest house – clean and comfortable with no frills, and that included no air conditioning. It was the lack of the latter that led to me being confined to bed for several days. I hadn't been drinking enough liquid and went down with a case of heat exhaustion. I thought I was going to die.

Norah Boylan, my Speech and Drama mistress in England, had given us an introduction to a friend, a ballet dancer, who in turn introduced us to Jimmy Thompson. Jimmy was an American who stayed in Thailand after the war. He single-handedly got the Thai silk industry on to a commercial footing. He was a fascinating man who ran a good, successful business but kept the creation of his wonderful silks very much a cottage industry. He took us on a tour of his 'silk village', which was close to the Chao Phraya river so the huts were on stilts. The employees and their families lived in the huts and worked on the premises where all the spinning, dyeing and weaving of the cloth took place. I remember huge baskets filled with the most glorious coloured silk threads wound on to bobbins. Jimmy would help the workers decide on colours for the individual pieces they were to weave. He gave me a length in muted shades of green. I wish I'd kept it as a simple stole, but had it made into a dress, which eventually wore out. Jimmy invited us to dinner at his home – a combination of several old Thai houses blended together to form the most extraordinary dwelling. Jimmy was a great lover of Thailand and his fortune had allowed him to amass a wonderful collection of antique artefacts beautifully displayed throughout his home. He cared so much about his adopted home he'd willed everything to the state as a permanent memorial to his love for that country. I remember he sent his car for us. I'd never been chauffeur driven before and though it was an experience, I was absolutely frozen in its air-conditioned splendour. Many years later, while reading a magazine at the hairdressers, I saw an article about Jimmy Thompson's mysterious disappearance. He had just walked into the jungle and was never seen again. As far as I know the mystery was never solved and his body was never found. Rumours were rife; was he involved in politics; had he displeased someone? We'll never know, but I do treasure my meeting with him.

We took a trip down the Chao Phraya river, which runs through Bangkok – what an experience that was. The Thais live on and by the river, they drink and bathe in it; the river is the centre and mainstay of their lives. Along the waterfront houses we saw coffins where the relations were still paying homage years after a death and the deceased hadn't been interred. We visited the lovely beach resort of Pattaya, lined only with a few beach bungalows and bougainvillea. When I see pictures of the resort in today's brochures, I thank God I saw it and a few other places in the world before they were spoilt by wall-to-wall skyscraper hotels bowing to the tourist industry.

Today we are familiar with the four corners of the globe. Without leaving our homes we are taken on magic carpet rides around the world via holiday programmes and intrepid reporters. But in the early sixties these wonders were a well-kept secret. I was astounded at the beauty of the temples in Bangkok. They rose in magnificent splendour from the otherwise drab surroundings. Their roofs were bright orange fringed with green and everywhere you heard the tinkling of the temple bells. My overriding memory was of the Temple of the Emerald Buddha. The Buddha himself was almost insignificant as he sat on top of a 'pile' of gifts. There was a stack about six foot high with chairs, grandfather clocks, boxes, vases, gifts of every description left in the hope of intercession with the Lord. It looked like a junk shop on a bad day.

There were incongruities everywhere in Bangkok. On a busy
street, we stopped at a shack of corrugated iron strung between
two buildings and open to the elements. Having admired some
of the pretty things on sale, we started bargaining for a gold-
coloured metal belt. We couldn't understand why the price was
so high until we realised the belt was pure gold and, though we
didn't have that kind of money, the cost was surprisingly low.
Who would have expected a street vendor to be trading pure
gold in a street with open sewers? That's the East for you. We
also went to the cinema and had to stand for about ten minutes
at the end whilst the national anthem was played. Every time
we thought it had finished, they struck up another verse and
everyone stood stock-still and respectful.

We had hoped to visit the temple of Angkor Wat, but there
was a border war with Burma and no foreigners were allowed
into the area. Instead we visited the ruins of one of the many
ancient capitals of Thailand – Ayudhya – and encountered
something I found difficult to accept: the rickshaw coolies. I am
not comfortable with a man taking the place of a beast. Our
rickshaw 'boy' was a man of indeterminate age, and emaciated.
Going up a slight incline, he appeared to be struggling, so I
hopped off the rickshaw and walked with him. I didn't realise
how much I must have hurt his pride.

From Bangkok we took another plane to Australia. We
touched down at Darwin to let off some passengers and to
enable a very large Australian, with hairy legs, shorts, and knee-
length white socks, to debug the plane with a can of spray – this
was supposed to blitz any foreign bodies we might have picked
up en route. Next stop was Sydney and a change of planes. I
was doing some shopping when the terminal announcer
drawled in broadest Aussie that the next plane to Mugee and
Dubbo was about to depart. What improbable names they
were. I was just buying a toy koala bear and promptly
christened it Mugee. He lives with me still.

From Sydney we flew to Melbourne and a stay with
Owen's old university friend David Moody and his wife
Pippa. I thought they were the height of sophistication – and

their lifestyle was so much more grand than anything I'd experienced in England. I was very impressed with what little I saw of Australia.

I suppose we were both a trifle apprehensive as we left Australia for Christchurch, New Zealand, and the meeting with Owen's family. Mother, father, brothers, sister were all over us at the airport; totally open, warm and friendly people who welcomed me with open arms. I think they imagined Owen to be a confirmed bachelor so this addition to the family was doubly welcome, which made me feel even worse about our deception.

We stayed with the family for days of partying and, for Owen, renewing acquaintances. It was then that the first pangs of 'homesickness' hit me. I wasn't pining for England but I was apprehensive about this huge step of having come halfway across the world to a country and a people who, though they spoke the same language, had an entirely different culture. I walked down the main street of Christchurch, looked in the window of a millinery shop, and cried. It wasn't that I wore hats a great deal, it was just that everything seemed so old fashioned and about twenty years behind the times. Although those I met were very kind, I found the New Zealanders insular.

I didn't have long to wallow because Owen, ever the adventurer, arranged a trip taking in most of New Zealand's South Island. The Maori name for New Zealand translates as 'The Land of the Long White Cloud', and the country has an example of every kind of land mass in the world. Mountains, glaciers, lakes, thermal regions, deserts, plains and fjords make it a stunningly beautiful place. We stayed at the hermitage on Mount Cook and made a trip to the Fox Glacier, where we had an eerie and potentially dangerous experience. A guide took a party of us on to and around an area of the glacier. I remember huge waves of frozen water; looking down cracks and seeing lakes of brightest blue; hearing cracking noises all around us. The experience was awesome. When we got back to our hotel, Owen realised he'd put down his glasses while he took a photograph. I remembered him taking them off and felt sure I could find them. We were totally stupid in going back without a guide but we did and we found the glasses. The noise of the ice cracking all around us was frightening. Just think, we might have ended up coming out at the end of the glacier round about now – forty years later!

Owen was to take up a position as a producer with the New Zealand Broadcasting Commission (NZBC) at Wellington in the North Island, so we bade goodbye to the family and took the boat from Christchurch to Wellington. Wellington is very impressive when approached from the sea, with the harbour surrounded by high hills. It is an extremely windy city, to the point that sometimes it blows so strongly you are unable to turn a corner from one street to another. Initially we rented a small house at Lower Hutt, just north of Wellington. Owen had been to university with many of the people who were now working in the field of broadcasting, so for him it was familiar territory.

One evening we had his boss and wife, a glamorous model, to dinner. At that stage of my life I wasn't a particularly good cook and had done no entertaining. I was desperately overambitious. Remembering a lovely dinner in London where the Italian mama of our opera-singing host cooked a whole fish in foil, I decided to do the same. I'd no idea how long it needed cooking, or that you prodded it with a fork to test whether it was done. I served it and suffered the embarrassment of finding it still raw in the middle. As far as I was concerned the evening went rapidly downhill. I'd also been far too ambitious with the dessert and attempted a chocolate soufflé. Soufflé is not a dish for the beginner. The meal was pretty awful and I was absent from the table most of the evening. Now I only serve recipes I've tried out first and I simplify my meals into cold starter, warm middle, and cold dessert. That way I get to talk to the guests.

Owen was at work all day and I couldn't drive, so Lower Hutt was a bit of a no-no for me. We soon moved into Wellington proper: 56 Salamanca Road, Kelburn was situated close to the top of the funicular railway. We had a ghastly landlady who knocked on our door one day and told me the reason I had so many colds was that my underwear was scanty! Scanty it was, but that was not the cause of my ill health. I'd had asthma as a child until my tonsils were taken out at the age of seven. The asthma went but I've been heavily prone to colds and throat infections all my life.

I wanted and needed to work, so Owen encouraged me to phone the head of the NZBC. Miraculously, I was given an appointment. I can just imagine trying to do that in England. You'd never get through the smokescreen of secretaries and PAs. I must have been a good talker because all I had to my credit were reams of certificates for poetry speaking and drama, a fair amount of amateur theatrical experience and a great deal of enthusiasm. I was given a try-out doing presentation for television on Sunday evenings. I think my fee was £5. Such riches had to be supplemented by clerical work during the week, but it was *experience* and that's something money can't buy. The equipment was very Heath Robinson and I remember having to flick a switch on the desk when given a signal in order to fade in my microphone.

At the time, I was also doing some modelling. I had applied to the Lucy Clayton modelling school when in London, but in England a model had to be 5′7″. The New Zealanders were traditionally a shorter race and 5′5″ for a model was acceptable; I could also do photographic and hand modelling. I did some hat modelling too and after a particularly difficult session the photographer offered me a drink. I accepted and drank several martini cocktails, not realising just how potent they were. For a while, I wondered why he didn't use me again ... but then I did knock over his highly expensive camera as I exited!

Owen was working at the NZBC for a living but was producing drama at the Victoria University Drama Club for fun. One of his productions was Aristophanes' *Lysistrata*. Although the play is a great and ageless comedy it is primarily concerned with the issue of war and peace and not, as it seems on the surface, with sex. It says, with logic and power, that the personal lives of men and women are of a higher value than the impersonal demands of the state. The plot centres around the women of Athens and Sparta who get so fed up with their men going to war they eventually withhold all conjugal rights until the men stop fighting. I auditioned for and got the part of a sexy little piece called Myrrine. The play is a riot of double meanings and was great fun to do. Priapic men and scantily clad women racing over the stage must have rocked dreamy old Wellington to its foundations.

The English Department at the university put on a production of Arnold Wesker's *Roots* and I played the part of Jenny Beales. The producer decided that Jenny had to be overweight so I was padded for the role. Although the two productions at the university were not strictly professional productions, they were of an extremely high standard. One could draw a comparison with the standard of the English OUDS (Oxford University Drama Society) and Footlights, the Cambridge equivalent. I learned a great deal.

My 21st birthday arrived while we were in Wellington. As we'd only lived there a few months, we didn't know enough people to throw a party. Owen wrote me a beautiful poem, which was later published in an anthology, bought me a fox fur stole and took me out to dinner at the best restaurant our finances would bear.

Owen was my guru and had brought so very much into my life. He was forever opening doors to new, interesting, and intellectual experiences, forever encouraging me to push back the boundaries I imposed on myself by my own self-doubt and insecurity, but something in the relationship wasn't quite right. Then it happened ... I was chatted up by my hairdresser (not an unusual scenario for women). Bob Witting was a charming man of Dutch origin who'd been through awful experiences as a child with his mother in a concentration camp. He wore dark glasses all the time, not as an affectation but because his eyes had suffered due to the poor diet in the camp. The glasses gave him a mysterious allure. We embarked on a passionate affair, somewhat lacking in conversation! Owen knew about it but, with his usual maturity and wisdom, let me get on with it. I'm sure he thought it would just be a fling and then I'd come to my senses and return to him.

It was at this stage that my normal mousy hair became very dramatic. Bob entered a hairdressing competition and dyed my hair blue-black with cyclamen overtones. I liked the result and, though I shed the cyclamen rinse, stayed with the blue-black for twenty years until wisdom dictated that a lighter colour would be more befitting my ageing skin tones. I got myself into a total mess with the two men. I knew a long relationship with Bob was out of the question; you really do have to be able to converse with your partner. On my side, there was great love but a lack of passion for Owen, I didn't know what to do, Neither man was right for me and I knew I was making all of us unhappy. So, I decided on a tactic I often employ when in difficulty, and that is flight. I think I must have taken the old adage to heart that 'he who fights and runs away, lives to fight another day'. I only had £35 in savings, so returning to England was out of the question. My money would allow me to go as far as Australia and it seemed like a good idea at the time, so I booked a passage. When I left Wellington, there was Bob at one end of the boat saying goodbye and Owen at the other. I've never been in that situation since, and don't ever want to repeat it.

The crossing only took a couple of days and I remember nothing about it except my total excitement and anticipation as we manoeuvred into Sydney Harbour. In 1963, the tallest construction in Sydney was the Harbour Bridge and it looked magnificent. Today it is almost insignificant, dwarfed by multitudinous skyscrapers and pushed out of pride of place by the Sydney Opera House. I shall never forget docking at Wooloomooloo and a port official saying, 'Can I help you with your bags, Miss Hepburn?' I like to think he meant Audrey and not Katharine, but I was incredibly flattered. At times in my life, people have been kind enough to say I bear a resemblance to Audrey Hepburn and, as she is one of my heroines, the compliment is doubly acceptable.

Bob had stuffed £10 into my purse, so I wasn't destitute. I was soon working as a temporary secretary, so at least I now had a small income with which to put down the deposit on rented accommodation, which I found in a leafy suburb of

Sydney. It was a house in Edgecliffe, not far from the harbour. In Sydney, until you get to the outer suburbs, nearly everywhere is close to the water. I shared with three other girls about whom I don't remember much except that as Christmas approached, we made a totally daft decision to have a traditional Christmas lunch and invite guests. There was the turkey and trimmings, flaming Christmas pudding and mince pies. The temperature soared to over 100°F. We were almost passing out with the heat and dripping with sweat as we prepared the meal. We soldiered on and served up a hot meal that nobody wanted. We would far rather have been at the beach so, with stomachs groaning, we gathered our bathers (the Aussie word for a swimming costume) and raced off to the sea. We didn't use sun-screens then and many of the Aussies used to coat themselves in a mixture of oil and vinegar and literally 'fry'. I take a tan quite well but I've never burned so badly as that Christmas of 1963. The next few days were spent alternating between calamine lotion, cold tea, feeling very sorry for myself and staying out of the sun.

Even though I'd done no professional acting, armed with my sparse television experience I decided to look for an agent. I really don't think you could do it now without letters after your name, but a respected Sydney agent, Gloria Payton, took me on her books. It was at this stage that I became Jan. Aussies like short names and Janet was automatically shortened. I like it and found it flowed better with Leeming. Owen's pet name for me was Jani, pronounced with a slight French intonation, but Australians just couldn't get their tongues around it. More often than not it ended up as Jenny. So Jan Leeming I became.

Gloria put me forward for an audition as a continuity announcer with the Australian Broadcasting Commission (ABC). Originally they were looking for one announcer only for Sunday evenings but they reached an impasse trying to choose between the final three and decided to use us all. I seem to recollect we were paid £10 for the evening's work and as this was only going to be for one Sunday in three, I had to continue my temp-seccing. The power of television is awesome. After only a couple of Sunday appearances, I'd find people in the offices where I worked looking quizzical and then the questions would start until finally they sussed where they had seen me.

Gloria continued to send me to auditions and finally I got a break in professional theatre. John Trevor was an English actor of the old school who had found his forte in adaptations of Shakespeare edited down into versions suitable for touring with the minimum of characters; seven, to be exact. The Young Elizabeth Players were founded in 1958 and funded by the Arts Council. The Players' role was to take Shakespeare to the Bush, performing in village halls, cinemas, theatres, in fact anywhere the local arts councils could gather a quorum of enough people to make a performance worthwhile. Because everything was done on a shoestring, the local arts council members invariably put us up in their homes. We travelled in a van with our rostra, costumes, props and suitcases.

The experience was a baptism of fire for me. I had never even been camping in my native England, being your archetypal stay-at-home-don't-like-to-get-wet-and-please-don't-ask-me-to-rough-it person. I was now about to embark on a seven-month tour of New South Wales covering 17,000 miles and roughing it, travelling in a van with eight folk who represented almost every category of sexual preference known in the sixties. Was I particularly ignorant or were most of us blissfully unaware of 'differences'? Here I was with a gloriously handsome, reputedly bisexual leader; a rampant 'sex maniac' from Scotland who leered 'Git your gear off' to every passably good-looking female; two gay guys; a chap who appeared to be totally non-sexual; and, the biggest shock of all for me, the other woman in the group, Laura, joined by her female 'flatmate' one weekend on tour. The flatmate came down to breakfast with a neck full of love bites! Our driver/manager was a gentle heterosexual man who'd come on tour to get over a broken marriage and often burst into tears. Then there was me. I think I'm 'normal' but then what's 'normal' any more?

We were to take out two plays: *The Merchant of Venice*, in which I played Portia, and *Macbeth*, in which I was a witch. It was very hard work performing, often driving hundreds of miles to the next venue and then loading and unloading the gear. After a very hard day, we had to be sociable with and entertain the hosts who were giving us beds for the night. We weren't always lucky with billeting, especially in the larger towns, and on those occasions we'd stay at motels or inns or anywhere inexpensive. I remember a couple of our billets quite vividly. One was in a town called Tumut and the local vet put up both of us girls; he was good-looking and had two equally handsome red setters. The vet and I got on well and some months later, when I was back in Sydney, he came to see me and take me out to dinner. He was a very quiet man with little conversation so unfortunately the relationship petered out, otherwise I might have ended up being a vet's wife in the outback!

On another occasion we were all staying at a modest hostelry in the back of beyond. The New South Wales folk have an expression, 'Back of Bourke', which means way out in the boondocks. That's where we were. In the sixties, women were not allowed into bars anywhere. Laura had a stinking cold and I needed to get her some medicinal brandy. At the bar door I stopped and waved frantically to catch the eye of a male company member. To my surprise, I was invited in. They were all sitting in a dim corner talking to a person so black I could only make out his eyes and teeth. It was the first time I had encountered an Aborigine. The guys introduced us and in typical English fashion I put out my hand, expecting a rough calloused hand to grip mine. It was like touching velvet. After I'd taken my companion her brandy, I was allowed back into the group and spent a fascinating evening listening to our Aboriginal friend and mysterious tales of the outback.

We were performing in a town called Walgett a few miles from Lightning Ridge, centre of the Black Opal Mining Fields. We prevailed upon Wally, our driver, to take us there. Nobody had prepared us for the landscape that met our eyes as we came over the brow of a hill. I will never forget it. The terrain looked like the surface of the moon, with gigantic white mole hills dotted all over the area. Today it is probably ultra-sophisticated, but in the sixties people bought a concessionary plot of ground in the opal area and started digging. They dug down and shovelled out the 'potch' (the matrix in which you find opals), chucking it out rather like a mole does. To say the place was primitive was an understatement. There were a few shacks with corrugated-iron roofs and a bigger shack that was the bar. It did a roaring trade. The prospectors were men on their own and after a hard and invariably fruitless day's digging, all they wanted to do was get drunk.

Because we were so far from civilisation, Laura and I were invited into the bar, where I talked to an old prospector sporting a hat with dangling corks (the only time I ever saw this phenomenon). The corks are not an eccentric adornment but a very useful method of keeping away the flies. We talked about opals and this character opened a match box and took out a perfect, solid opal about one and a half inches long and an inch wide. It was a stunning stone and he placed it in my palm. I was terrified I'd drop it. When I asked how often he found a stone like that he replied in his broad Aussie drawl ' ... Oaawa, just often enough to keep me here.' I reckon a stone like that at today's prices would be worth about £10,000. He also showed me an almost perfect round 'fire' opal, so-called because they really do look like coal fires with red flames licking around inside. He wanted £30 for it but, even between us, the company couldn't russle up that amount of cash and a cheque is useless on an opal field. I have thought often of that beautiful stone, which today would probably have two noughts added on to the end. He gave me a bit of potch that did contain some opal, but he could tell just by looking at the lump that it wasn't worth working. However, I took it to the opal cutter on the field and he coaxed out of it a thin opal, including its impurities; I later had it set in a ring of silver.

Everyone associates Australia with beaches, heat and eternal sunshine. Let me tell you, I have only once been colder than I was in the Motel Titania at a place called Oberon in the Blue Mountains west of Sydney, and the other place was Siberia. We were all so cold, we slept in our clothes in addition to having our coats on top of the bed covers. There were many venues on that tour where our breath hung in clouds of condensation around us and the audience were rugged up in as much clothing as they could wear. It is a country of extremes. There are desert areas where they don't see rain for years and any 'roads' disappear under a cover of 'bull dust', which is a fine coating of drifting sand that makes driving incredibly difficult. It was while we were crossing one of these strips without seeing anything other than the odd cactus that we unanimously decided we needed a comfort stop. It was dusk and we'd see nothing for hours, so Wally stopped the van and it was girls one side and boys the other. Yes, you've guessed it: out of nowhere came a four-wheel drive with its headlights blazing. We must have presented a pretty sight.

I don't know whether it was the strain of the tour, but the day before we were due to return to Sydney for a few days' Easter break, I had an attack of amnesia. We were performing *The Merchant of Venice* when suddenly I dried up completely, didn't know where I was or what I was doing and had to be prompted and cajoled through the remainder of the play. It was a frightening experience. I got back to my rented accommodation and slept endlessly. A few days before the tour was to resume I had a panic attack. Would I be able to remember my lines? And what would I do if they didn't come back to me? The first couple of performances were difficult. I left notes for myself pinned all over anything that would take a pin and a piece of paper, but I did get through and after a while the fear left me. I've never had an amnesia attack again but I get so nervous before a performance – television, stage, after-dinner speaking – that I get a lump in my throat that I sometimes fear I will not be able to clear before it's my turn to speak.

We were billeted with lovely people, some of whom I remained in contact with for many years. That tour left me with many sweet memories of the great open hearts, the naturalness, of Aussies; the wide open space; greeting pet sheep at kitchen doors; being offered huge steaks for breakfast, which I declined; going mushrooming with a huge bucket rather than a tiny bowl because everything is big in Australia; little children, with feet barely touching the floor and with absolutely no knowledge of Shakespeare, coerced into attending performances to make up the arts council quota; endless hours before performances spent in coffee bars eating cake.

During the tour, I was also getting back to Sydney on a Sunday to do my one-night stint of continuity announcing with the ABC. All the to-ing and fro-ing was taking it out of me. But as our seven-month tour was nearing its end, Laura said to me, 'If you can get through a Young Lizzie gig, you've got the staying power to get through anything this business [theatre] throws at you.'

Saying goodbye to my companions was a tearful experience. We'd been together through thick and thin, exhausting heat, mind-numbing cold, hard work, great companionship, and now it was over. This is the price you pay for a life in theatre, or even television for that matter. You work together on a play, a series of programmes, form close relationships in the short term, and then disperse. It is difficult to form lasting friendships because of the nature of the business, but while they are there, they are meaningful. It has become easier to accept as I've grown older but I used to pine a great deal over the friendships that just petered out because of distance and work commitments.

Returning to Sydney, Gloria told me I had an interview with a much-respected ABC drama producer for a part in Farquhar's *The Recruiting Officer*. Donning my smartest outfit, I caught the bus to the ABC Studios at Gore Hill and was ushered up to wait in his office. I had my back to the door as Henri Safran entered; he was a very good-looking Frenchman. Taking one look at me, he didn't mince his words: 'You 'ave put on ze weight.' End of interview. I was crestfallen as I realised I was paying the price for all those hours on tour sitting around in cafes drinking milky coffee and eating cake. I'd gone from a size ten to a tight twelve or a loose fourteen; from just under eight stones to almost ten. It is so easy to put on weight and so difficult to get it off.

Diets do not work. In the short term, they fool the body, which then readjusts itself. The weight comes off . . . the weight goes back on. The only sure way to lose weight and keep it off is to alter your approach to food and follow a healthy regime for the whole of your life. Losing weight and staying slim is not a quick fix. After dieting unsuccessfully with the usual yo-yo of weight loss and weight gain, I eventually took several years to lose my excess weight and have watched what I eat ever since. After a while, your mind controls your eating and you would no sooner indulge in 'bad' food than jump off a cliff. Don't get me wrong. I do have the occasional piece of cake, or chocolate; I love to drink wine with a meal but I get on the scales regularly and if there is a weight gain I readjust by having a very 'careful' day or two of just salads and no wine. I find the best way to keep my body healthy and happy is not to combine protein and carbohydrate in the same meal. I eat very little meat, but lots of vegetables and fruit.

A farce called *Boeing Boeing* had enjoyed great success in London and Australia. In early 1964 it had run and run in Sydney. Capitalising on this success, Phillip Productions decided to try again a year later and were casting for a similar farce. They say that every cloud has a silver lining and though I'd lost almost a stone in weight I still had a fairly voluptuous figure, one of the requirements for a part in *The Diplomatic Baggage*. It was to be directed by a Brit and to star Jack Watling, a very well-known English actor. Auditions were held. Eloise was the French mistress of the lead character and as I was petite, had a healthy tan, and black hair, I probably looked the part more than many Australian actresses. We worked hard, had fun, opened at the quaint non-air-conditioned Palace Theatre in Pitt Street, Sydney, on Wednesday, 3 March 1965 in a heatwave. We closed on Saturday, 13 March! I like to think that we got bad reviews because the heat in the theatre was unbearable and the critics in their DJs were crotchety, but we probably were just not good enough.

It was around this time I was approached by the news department of a commercial channel in Sydney. Channel Ten – 10 required a woman newsreader; I'm sure it was more as a gimmick than due to political correctness. In Australia in the sixties, a good, clear Queen's English accent was quite sought after. You would not have been able to tell the ABC announcers and newsreaders apart from those in England. I had the voice and was already known to television viewers, so I was an obvious choice. The news department was a totally male preserve and I felt honoured to be part of it, whether using me was a gimmick or not.

After I came off air one evening I was given a message asking me to phone Robin Bailey. I don't usually respond to requests to phone strangers, male or female, but I knew Robin was an actor and that he'd had an extremely long and successful run on both sides of the Atlantic a few years earlier in a production of *My Fair Lady*. He had directed and starred in the show and he was back in Sydney to do the same in a production of Iris Murdoch's *A Severed Head*. He had seen me on television, knew I was also an actress and invited me to audition for the juvenile lead. I got the part of Georgie Hands, the totally screwed-up mistress of Martin Lynch-Gibbon, a wine merchant played by Robin. I must mention that the part of the psychoanalyst was played by Michael Blakemore, a native Australian, who now enjoys a fearsome reputation as a theatre director.

We opened at the end of May to super reviews and this time not only did the show run, but we took it on tour visiting most of the major towns in New South Wales. It was a tour again but with a trifle more luxury than the previous year. I loved every minute of it. Not only was my part challenging, but the cast were all friends – none of the bitching one often finds in theatre companies – and Robin was such fun. He often waited for the scene where he'd gathered together his mistress and her new boyfriend, his wife and the psychoanalyst, place himself with his back to the audience and then do something to make us laugh. Robin could carry off most events with great aplomb including the ability to keep a straight face; we couldn't. On another occasion a door handle came away in his hand and as it was imperative he got off stage, he exited through the fire place with great elegance. No one in the audience even tittered.

The show toured until the end of the year and then it was back to Sydney and searching for work again.

My agent, Gloria, sent me to audition for a part in a comedy film starring a famous Italian actor, Walter Chiari. It was the usual kind of scenario, the star and several women all believing they were his one and only love. To my surprise I was given one of the 'girlie' parts. On the day that Mr Chiari arrived at Sydney airport, we girls were there to greet him along with a huge press contingent. I obviously displeased Walter or wasn't sexy enough. I remember wearing a fashionable straight coat in green velvet that hid any curves I might otherwise have displayed. The next day Gloria rang to say the offer of a part had been withdrawn and as no contract had been signed, I didn't get a penny.

CHAPTER THREE

AUSTRALIA, HAYO AND MICHAEL

It was the summer of 1965 and though there was no work, it was great to be able to spend my days doing something I love best: chilling out in the sun on a beach with a bag of fruit and a good book. I was sharing a large and beautiful flat in Mona Road, Darling Point, with two English girls and one Australian. Anne and Nancy were British nurses and Jan was a secretary so they were out during the day and, when working, I was out in the evening. It suited me down to the ground. Although I love people, I like my own company and to have the house to myself most of the time was ideal. I'm a house-proud person and didn't really object to clearing up after the others when they went off to work. I counted myself lucky that I wasn't on a daily treadmill. We had a view of Sydney Harbour Bridge and I often stood at the window metaphorically pinching myself. It was like a dream. I was in a country I'd come to love and lived in a large and comfortable flat with the most idyllic view. I often played Rodrigo's *Concierto de Aranjuez* while I sat gazing out of the window at the harbour, the boats and the bridge.

I loved the work I did and was thoroughly devoted to my life in theatre. But I hadn't had a serious relationship for nearly three years. There was the occasional date but nothing more and it didn't bother me. I became mystified, therefore, when cards and posies of flowers began to appear at the entrance to our flat. Many of the missives bore westernised versions of the sayings of Confucius. One of these was hung around the neck of a wooden cat. Curiouser and curiouser! I was making no headway at all in discovering who the mystery admirer was until, one evening, I started chatting to the owner of a restaurant we actors frequented in King's Cross – Sydney's equivalent of Chelsea in London. He was a well-educated and charming Greek called Vadim. During the course of conversation, he made a reference to Confucius and I realised he was my mystery admirer. We had a couple of dates but on my side there was no spark to be ignited. However, I still have a book he gave me with an inscription of which I wish I'd taken more notice throughout my life: 'In times of personal stress, it is best to pause a while and ponder on the absurdities of Life. Laughter especially at oneself is the best remedy.'

I had a good circle of friends, not all from the theatre. One of them is now famous, extremely rich, the owner of a highly successful fashion house that bears her name, and still living in Sydney. When I knew her, Carla Zampatti had just started to design clothes and cut them out on her kitchen table. I must have been one of her first customers, buying a charcoal grey shift dress decorated with a white crocheted false collar. She was married to a Dutchman and they lived on the other side of Sydney from me. They invited me to lunch one day and, as I had no transport, organised a friend of theirs to give me a lift. Any time friends organised blind dates for me they were disasters so I expected nothing. The French have a delightful expression for it: *un coup de foudre*. Its literal translation is 'a hit by lightning' – love at first sight. I suppose you could argue that you can't possibly love someone you don't know, but that irrepressible sexual magic occurs and we believe it is love. If we're lucky the love grows alongside the sex, but I firmly believe that the initial attraction between two people is sexual.

Well, there at the door stood this dark, handsome man with Latin matinée idol good looks. Hayo Niebor was actually half-Dutch/half-Swedish, had served in the Merchant Navy and had come to rest in Sydney. The lunch was a great success. I'm afraid we were very rude, had eyes only for each other, and hardly spoke to anyone else.

We hadn't been dating for very long when Hayo invited me to an unusual lunch. He picked me up at the flat and drove out to one of the small coves around the corner from the harbour. He had a small basket containing a bottle of wine and some bread. 'This is going to be a frugal picnic,' I thought. Then I noticed the rocks were covered with oysters just below the water line. Hayo had brought an oyster knife with him and proceeded to prise the delicacies from the rocks. I doubt very much that you could do it today because of pollution. Sydney oysters are different from the ones we have in England. They are smaller and sweeter and I loved them. As we were feasting on our free harvest of oysters with chilled white wine, Hayo asked me to be his wife.

I loved him and it seemed the most natural thing in the world to agree, even though we'd not known each other for long. You can be with someone for years and still not know them. You can be with someone for days and know them intimately. There was no sparkly ring slipped on my finger, but it really had been a most romantic afternoon. A few weeks later, Hayo gave me a highly decorated gold band that had belonged to his deceased mother. Many continentals give a gold band to be worn on one hand during the engagement and changed to the other after marriage. Hayo was following the continental fashion. The ring was much too big for me and sizing it was difficult because of the intricate ropework adornment but he had it done and engraved inside with J.L. – H.N. j.a.d. (jag alska dag), Swedish for 'I love you'.

It was at this time that I learned to drive, which was fortuitous as I landed a part in *Semi-Detached*, being staged at the Ensemble Theatre outside of Sydney and not the easiest of places to get to. The play was a comedy by Englishman David Turner. It is quite strange how in the sixties so many plays indigenous to England were staged with great success in Australia, where the whole culture and way of life were different. The play was to run for five weeks, opening on

27 December 1965. Hayo lent me his car, which was extremely good of him as I'd no experience other than passing the test. I don't remember much about the play, except that I had a fun-filled five-week run.

I still retained the flat in Mona Road, but spent an increasing amount of time with Hayo in his apartment in King's Cross. One Sunday morning, as we were enjoying the luxury of a lie-in, the doorbell rang. Hayo was gone a very long time until eventually I threw on a robe and went to the front door to find him speaking Dutch and deep in argument with an extremely attractive blonde woman. So, who was she? I was told she was a jealous previous girlfriend who wouldn't accept their relationship was over.

Success breeds success. I was getting very good notices and the gaps between being in and out of work were narrowing. Just after the run at the Ensemble, I had to pack a suitcase and decamp to Melbourne for a season in the prestigious Union Theatre Repertory Company (UTRC). The season was seen as the most ambitious season ever, comprising four thought-provoking plays. The first was *The Representative* by Rolf Hochhuth, a highly sensitive work exposing the passivity, or non-intervention, of Pope Pius XII in the extermination of the Jews in World War II. It was a play for the male members of the Rep; we women appeared in Act Three as inmates of Auschwitz. It was a harrowing work in every aspect. A highly acclaimed Melbourne actor, Brian James, played the Pope and an actor I'd seen in many productions in Sydney, Michael Laurence, portrayed Father Riccardo, the priest appealing to the Pope's conscience.

The next production was Tolstoy's *War and Peace* in which I was cast as Natasha, with Michael as Prince Andrei. Although it was Rep, and shows were mounted on small budgets, I remember my costumes as magnificent in their simplicity and beauty. They were designed by Kristian Fredrikson, who went on to giddy heights of achievement and is still today designing for the ballet in Australia. The sketches were beautiful but on our small salary, I couldn't afford to pay £8 for the one of my ballgown. I don't suppose it would be worth a great deal today, but as a memory for me it would have been priceless. I adored playing Natasha and unconsciously modelled my performance on that of Audrey Hepburn.

Being apart from Hayo was difficult, as we hadn't been together long enough or known each other well enough to establish the kind of relationship that can withstand absence. He was very possessive and long phone calls were not helpful. If relationships are difficult, phone calls can make them worse. You are unable to see your loved one's facial expressions and conversation is open to misinterpretation. A smile, or the fact that you are making a comment tongue in cheek, can't be seen. You might have a disagreement but are unable to touch and cuddle afterwards, by way of forgiveness. I have discovered through bitter experience that the man who suspects your fidelity is usually the one playing around and judging you by his own standards.

Hayo had just bought himself the car he'd hankered after for a long time: a Porsche. I'd been away from Sydney for nearly three months and we really needed to be together, so we made arrangements for him to come and see me in *War and Peace*. At dinner afterwards he said, 'I've fallen in love with you all over again.' As I was unaware that he'd fallen out of love, this comment took me by surprise. I wondered if the mysterious blonde was playing a part in the drama. We had a glorious weekend, cleared up all our differences and it seemed as though our romance was back on track.

Paul Riomfalvy was a director of the Sydney production company that had staged *Diplomatic Baggage* and *Severed Head*. He came to see me playing Natasha and took me out to dinner after the show. He wanted to talk about a forthcoming production of a three-handed play called *Luv* and the possibility of my playing the lead. Dinner was enjoyable, conversation plentiful and then came the invitation to round off the evening with coffee at his hotel. I am a fairly naive person in many ways, but even I could see where this one was heading. I've never been good at turning down a man with a blunt 'I don't fancy

you' or 'You're not my type'. I usually soften the blow with the
excuse that it's the wrong time of the month, or that I have a
headache. I must have hurt Paul's ego dreadfully, because I
remember saying, 'I'm sorry but I really have to go home and
do my washing.' I don't think any man would believe you
would do your smalls at midnight. I did not get the part.

The next Union Rep production held another big role for
me. I was to take the lead in a play about the Greek community
in Melbourne and the difficulties of uniting the old ways with
life in a new country. In the mid-sixties there were more than
sixty thousand Greeks resident in Victoria, so the problems of
adaptation were shared by a vast number of people. The
author of *The Young Wife*, David Martin, was a highly
successful playwright and novelist. He had written the novel
Tiger Bay, which was made into a successful film starring
Hayley Mills, John Mills and Horst Buchholz. In *Young Wife*
I had the lead role of Anna, a young Cypriot girl sent to
Australia to marry a much older man, Yannis, chosen for her
by her family. Brian James as Yannis was a kind and gentle
man and a wonderfully giving actor with whom to work. You
work very hard in Rep, learning one play and rehearsing during
the day while performing in another at night, so it is doubly
valuable to have the support of and to be on good terms with
your fellow actors. The play was full of complexities, but the
plot revolved around Anna falling in love with a younger man.
The Young Wife had all the ingredients of a modern-day *Romeo
and Juliet.*

Yet again, separation from Hayo was affecting our relationship. I was desperately upset and longing to go back to Sydney
so that we could sort out our life together, but I'd signed a
contract and had to honour it. *The Young Wife* had been
running for a couple of weeks and almost every time we spoke
on the phone, we were into disagreement. One Friday night, we
had an argument and I put the phone down on him. On the
Saturday morning, one of the girls who shared the boarding
house knocked on the door and told me Carla Zampatti, who'd
introduced us, wanted to talk to me. I hadn't seen Carla for

months and thought it was a ploy to get me to the phone so that Hayo could speak to me. I didn't take the call.

That night, while preparing for the show, the stage manager came to our shared dressing room and told me Carla Zampatti needed to speak to me urgently. I began to get a sinking feeling in the pit of my stomach. Why was she phoning the theatre just before a performance? Was Hayo sick, had he been hurt? I went through the empty theatre to the box office to take the call. Hayo wasn't sick; he was DEAD. I was told afterwards they heard my cries echoing from the box office down to the backstage area. It couldn't be true. Was it some sort of sick joke? Carla repeated the dreadful news again. It wasn't a joke. He had decided to surprise me by driving overnight from Sydney to Melbourne, a distance of 500 miles. He always drove fast, but Australian roads are wide and empty when you get away from the towns. Nobody will ever know exactly what happened, but I was told he was in collision with a truck. The car caught fire and though he was thrown clear, he died from a ruptured spleen.

I was in shock and a doctor was called. In Rep you don't usually have the luxury of understudies and in *The Young Wife* there was no one who could take the part of Anna. The doctor told the stage manager if he gave me a sedating injection, I would not be able to go on stage. It was suggested that a large and strong brandy was the only remedy. You can imagine how supportive the cast were. I went through that performance like a woman in a dream. It was only at the end of the play that I returned to reality. The curtain comes down on Anna weeping over the body of her young lover. That night I got a standing ovation from the audience. I didn't deserve it – they didn't know I was weeping real tears for a dead love.

Michael Laurence and I were good friends and that night he came back to our digs and stayed the whole night cradling me in his arms. I remember he was wearing an off-white Aran sweater and it was rough against my face. I marked it badly with my running mascara. On the bedside table were the flowers my mother had sent for the opening night. She is highly superstitious and would have been horrified to know the Australian florist had sent an arrangement of red and white flowers – a sign of death.

Carla and some other friends very kindly offered to pay my return airfare to Sydney so that I could attend the funeral. I refused. I couldn't bear the thought of seeing a box containing the mortal remains of such a vibrant, life-loving man. I just wanted to remember him alive and smiling. I have his ring and wear it to this day. I was not only having to face the trauma of his death but couldn't forgive myself for putting the phone down on him. It was Owen who came to my aid over that particular problem. We wrote regularly and in one of my letters I told him of how I couldn't assuage my guilt and the feeling of '… if only I hadn't put the phone down'. He replied by return of post, 'Nothing will stop this, but it may help to realise that everyone's conscience contains several "If I had nots" and that in nearly every case there is no direct responsibility. As far as indirect responsibility is concerned, it's better to forget about it – there's no end to it, and it's a splendid gateway to neurosis. If Hayo gets in a car and drives badly (or is the victim of a traffic circumstances), it's not the reason for which he got into the car that is to blame. The only way you could be to blame would be if, in hanging up the phone, you said to yourself "Now I know he will get into his car feeling angry and he'll drive so badly he will be killed". Which is absurd.' Owen's common sense helped, but I did feel guilty for a very long time.

Michael was also coping with his own sadness. A young man he loved had committed suicide and our shared grief drew us together. There are men and women who, when they lose a loved one, retreat into a shell and shun love. There are those who, to go on living, have to love and be loved again. I am one of the latter. It doesn't lessen one's love for the deceased, but the grief would kill if you weren't able to give love, a different love, to someone else. Michael and I did share a bed on a few occasions – not out of passion or a need for sexual fulfilment. Our need was to feel a closeness, to give and receive affection.

The season was nearing its end and I was in total turmoil. I was still grieving over Hayo. I loved Australia, but there was no work on the horizon and I really wasn't thinking straight. It was an act of kindness on the part of my mother that brought matters to a head. She sent me the money to return to England and I booked passage on an Italian ship, *The Castel Felice*, which was to leave from Melbourne and had a Sydney stop on its itinerary. I'd left many of my belonging in Hayo's flat and Carla had put them in a trunk stored in the basement so the Sydney stop was useful. Carla and I met briefly for a coffee before the boat sailed and I asked her about the mysterious blonde in Hayo's life. She admitted that he did take out other women while I was in Rep and later sent me a letter in which she wrote: 'You asked did he go with anyone else. Well Jan, as only to be expected he did I think take other girls out sometimes, but of this I am quite sure, no one ever meant anything to him because he used to ring and talk about you several times each week and no one was ever mentioned. I feel quite sure if there were anyone of importance to him, he would have told me.' She assured me that when he took that fateful journey to Melbourne, he had decided I was the one he wanted.

CHAPTER FOUR

HOME AGAIN

The Castel Felice left Melbourne on 11 July 1966 and docked in Sydney on the 13th. I had some misgivings about leaving my much-loved Australia and by the time we pulled away from the harbour with the bridge diminishing in size, I was totally choked with emotion and knew, absolutely knew, I was taking the wrong action. *The Castel Felice* wasn't an easy boat on which to be travelling, as a high percentage of the passengers were disgruntled returning Poms. They couldn't understand my fierce loyalty to all things Australian, having made the assumption that every one on the boat must loathe the country they were leaving behind.

The journey was going to take the best part of six weeks, which is a long time to spend within a confined space and with no means of escape from anyone. The Italian crew worked hard at diversions for the passengers, when they weren't chatting up the ladies. They put on bridge and chess lessons, lectures, painting and Italian classes. I joined up for the latter but I'm no linguist and it was a bit too much like hard work. One of the first officers took a shine to me but soon realised his wooing was falling on stony ground and changed allegiances, though not before he'd presented me with a large bottle of 'Mitsouko' by Guerlain. I can detect that perfume at ten yards and remember balmy nights at sea and glorious starry skies.

The Castel Felice was not the most stable of ships and we went through some pretty awful weather. We'd been at sea for over a fortnight so, as we steamed into Hong Kong on 26 July, we were extremely glad to set foot on dry land. Hong Kong was noisy, dirty, busy and utterly magical. The sights, sounds and smells assailed the senses. A group of us did the usual tourist things, such as crossing on the ferry to Kowloon, taking the cable car to the Peak and shopping, shopping, shopping till we dropped. I remember buying a heavily beaded skirt and top for about £10. (I kept it for years, until I felt beads would never be fashionable again, and gave it to a charity shop. Beads did come back and that little outfit would have cost forty times as much!) We also ate authentic Chinese food, which is so different from what one gets in a Chinese restaurant in England as to be unrecognisable.

It was a shortish hop of only three days before our next port of call. Singapore in 1966 was dirty and crime ridden. Raffles was the place to go and we went to take afternoon tea and look out over the sea. No, I haven't made a mistake. Today there's been a great deal of land reclamation and Raffles is now a fair distance from the sea. The world-famous Raffles Singapore Gin Sling was the drink to have, so we had it. That was a precursor to dining at the renowned Singapura International Hotel. There I made an absolute fool of myself. The menus were handed round the table and I started blubbing. My dinner companions were alarmed. Why was I crying? Australian rock oysters were on the menu and it brought back painful memories of Hayo, our lunch and the country I'd regretfully left behind.

It was another ten days at sea before we docked at Aden. We had a stop-over of only a few hours and my overriding memory was of myriads of little craft hemming in *The Castel Felice* as the natives bartered their wares, predominantly leather goods, camel stools and small wooden tables, winched up and down with great dexterity for us to see, admire and buy. We steamed on up the Red Sea for three days to Suez, where there was a choice. You either stayed on the boat as it went through the canal or got off and took one of President Nasser's trips. We called them that, because there was no alternative. Nasser was the boss and ran a state monopoly. You paid £7 and were transported, on a ropey old government-owned coach, through endless miles of desert. I took the trip because, for as long as I can remember, I've been fascinated by the civilisation of ancient Egypt and dearly wished to visit the pyramids and Cairo museum, particularly to see the artefacts from Tutankhamun's tomb.

The battered old coach took us to the largest of the Seven Wonders of the World, the pyramid of Cheops at Giza. If you wished, you could enter and, half crouching, make your way at an angle of forty-five degrees up a long, low tunnel to the centre of the pyramid and the burial chamber that held the sarcophagus of Khufu, a fourth-dynasty king. The sarcophagus was broken and eons ago the tomb robbers had taken everything of value. Although there was nothing there but an old bit of broken granite, I experienced the strangest feeling. There was a chilling presence that brought me out in goose bumps and precipitated a hasty retreat back down the passageway. We were lucky to have seen that particular pyramid, for a short time later it was declared unsafe and closed to visitors for many years.

Cairo was next on the agenda, dirty and noisy. The museum was poorly laid out, badly lit and fabulous artefacts from the tomb of Tutankhamun were thrown together in glass cases in too much of a jumble to be appreciated. The one poignant memory I took from there was the desiccated spray of flowers, no colour left, which his queen had placed, centuries ago, on the Boy King's tomb.

We rejoined our boat at Port Said and sailed for Naples, where we had enough time to visit the ruins of Pompeii and sample genuine Italian food before the last leg of our journey. People get very nostalgic about the White Cliffs of Dover, but I failed to see their magic. Whether it was the misery in my heart or my desire to be back in Australia, I thought they looked decidedly in need of a wash. They didn't lift my spirits one little bit. The only bright spot on the horizon was the thought of seeing my family again.

My mother and stepfather offered me a home until I got on my feet with work, which was a blessing and one less thing to worry about. I've still got my diary for 1966 and from the moment I got back to England on 24 August, it is full to busting with the names of people and agents I had to contact.

Robin Bailey and Jack Watling had given me introductions to their agents and I did all the necessary phoning around, but to no avail. I may have been a little special in Australia with my Mediterranean looks, heavy tan and black hair, but in England I was just one of an enormous band of out-of-work actresses. I couldn't even transfer my Equity card. In Australia I'd been assured that British Equity would honour my card but they didn't, so I had to set about getting one. It's a silly catch-22 situation. You couldn't get a card until you had a job and you couldn't have a job until you got a card. Somehow I managed to acquire the part of a French maid in one of a series of highly successful comedy programmes called *Hugh and I* starring Hugh Lloyd and Terry Scott. The contract had a 'Special Low Engagement' fee of £31.10s, but at least it got me my card.

I pounded the West End pavements, visiting agents and making contact with Aussie actors I'd either known or who were friends of friends. One day I was walking down Shaftesbury Avenue and a few feet in front of me I saw what looked like the back view of Hayo. The powerful shoulders, the dark hair, the walk, all created an impression that virtually propelled me down the street until I got abreast of the man. It wasn't him. I don't think I ever quite believed Hayo was dead. Because I hadn't attended the funeral, there was no closure. I had some ridiculous idea that it was all a bad dream where he'd run away from me with the unnamed blonde and his friends had covered up for him. At this point I needed to get a grip on myself and when I got home to my mother's house, I phoned the crematorium in Australia just to doubly check that my Hayo really was dead and gone.

There was no theatre work on the horizon. I needed to earn money, but I also needed my days free to go for auditions, so I decided to do what a lot of out-of-work actresses did in those days; I applied to be a Bunny Girl at the Bunny Club in Park Lane, Mayfair.

At the duly appointed hour I turned up for my interview. Whether I wasn't attractive enough or whether I was being paid a compliment, I don't know, but I was offered a position as a Bunny Mother in charge of the other hostesses. I was about to gratefully accept when a man came into the room and, in front of me, openly discussed a stabbing that had taken place in the club the night before. I was out of that office so quickly, you couldn't see me for dust. Can you imagine what the press would have made of me, as a Bunny Mother in her scanties, some fifteen years later when I became a newsreader on national television?

As I wasn't destined to be a Bunny Mother, office work beckoned again. I signed up with a temporary agency and worked all over London. I like to be committed to a job and didn't really enjoy temping but neither did I want a regular job where I couldn't have time off to go for interviews and auditions. I lived in hope. I was also coming to the decision that if something good didn't happen fairly soon on the work front, I was going to return to Australia; I missed it so much. I knew I could get work in theatre if I returned, and Michael had started writing loving letters to me.

Around this time, my agent was offered an audition for me for a part in a new series that today we'd call a 'soap'. The programme was *Crossroads*. She advised me against going to the audition, saying it would be bad for my career. Looking back, I find it really funny. It might have been bad for my so-called acting career, which was in its death throes anyway, but it would have been good for the bank balance.

I was doing a week's work for a firm called Cubitts when I met Martin Watson. He came into the office to talk to the boss and stopped by my desk for a chat. The next day, he came by again and this time we discovered our homes weren't far apart. I was in Windsor with my mother and he lived in Maidenhead. 'Why don't I give you a lift home and maybe we could stop off for a drink,' he said. I didn't enjoy strap-hanging on the tubes and trains and readily accepted the offer. He then ran his hand through his thick black hair and I saw a gold band on the third finger of his left hand. 'No way,' I thought, 'I'm not accepting a lift or having a drink with a married man.' I let a few hours elapse and went to his office to decline his offer politely.

That evening, when I left work, he was sitting outside the building in his dark blue Peugeot. He got out and repeated his offer of a lift, declaring that as we were going in the same direction, it was a bit daft not to travel together. So we did drive back together and we did stop at an inn. While we were drinking, he asked why I'd declined his offer and I told him why with total honesty. That was the first time I was given the line about a wife not understanding, that they stayed together for the children and weren't intimate any more. Despite being a short man with a slight lisp, he had Continental dark looks and was seductively attractive. I should have followed my initial intuition, but didn't. How we poor mortals fool ourselves when we want to be fooled.

Martin and I started seeing each other occasionally. I enjoyed the attention and the dinner dances we went to at Monkey Island near Maidenhead. I love dancing and he was a superb dancer. He was also a great womaniser. I reasoned that, as he was free to see me so often, his tale of disharmony at home was credible. He had also rented a flat in London, ostensibly to use as a work address, so he was a relatively free agent. I was getting into deep water and, as with most affairs, was soon too far in to extricate myself.

I thought salvation, or an answer to my dilemma would come in the shape of a job in the north of England. I'd been to an audition for a newsreading position with Granada Television in Manchester. I vividly remember walking into a room where other hopefuls were sitting. My heart sank when I looked at one stunningly beautiful woman and thought I hadn't got a chance. She was a painter called Sara Leighton, who went on to relative acclaim. To my surprise, she didn't get the job; I did. I can only think it was because I already had experience of newsreading and the others hadn't.

Granada offered me a six-month contract to work four days a week. This meant travelling up to Manchester by train on a

Monday morning and returning after the early evening news on a Thursday. I loved those Thursday evening journeys back to London. I always had dinner on the train and though the dinner was typical fare for trains, the ambience was delightful. You sat at tables for four, lit by bracketed lamps, and never knew who would be dining with you. I had many entertaining journeys over the next six months chatting with strangers I knew I'd never see again.

For the first few weeks in Manchester, Granada paid for me to stay in a pub close to the studios. I am not a lover of pubs and this one was particularly grotty. The rooms were adequate but, when you went down for breakfast in the morning, you were overwhelmed with a stench of stale beer and smoke. It was pulled down many years ago, amidst much sorrow from the Granada regulars, who regarded it as a home from home.

I was only too happy to move out of the pub and into Mrs Hoey's boarding house. It was a bus ride from the studios but clean and comfortable, and full of actors, so it suited me much better. Although I wasn't resident at the weekends, I had the same room for my four days each week. One Monday, I'd been out to dinner after work and got back late, only to find a stranger in my bed. A great big mound of sleeping man. He was an actor who'd had a trifle too much to drink and fallen into the wrong bed in the wrong room. I couldn't wake him, didn't know what room he should have been in and couldn't go around trying doors at midnight, so slept on the sofa. The poor man was mortified when he woke in the morning and realised what he'd done.

It was at Mrs Hoey's that I met Sue Michison. She worked as a production assistant at Granada and was a great straight-talking northern lass. We got on extremely well and decided that, much as we like the boarding house, we'd rather have a place of our own. We made enquiries and ended up renting a small miner's cottage in Sale owned by Pat Phoenix. Pat was one of the stars of *Coronation Street* and had obviously realised that money was safer in bricks and mortar than in stocks and shares. She owned quite a few cottages, which she rented out.

She was a fun lady and I was sad when I read of her death, relatively young, from cancer. Sue and I have remained friends now for almost forty years. We are godmothers to each other's sons. Although we don't see each other often, we can always pick up our friendship where we left off. She has helped me through many of my traumas and I have enormous affection and respect for her.

I enjoyed my work at Granada, but was so depressed by the seemingly endless rain and longed even more to return to the sunshine of Australia. I was getting more deeply involved with Martin and didn't know what to do. I'd hoped distance would have ended the affair, but it didn't. He was romantic, attentive and very persistent. I would break away from him but he would always win me around with false promises.

I was becoming more confused than ever because I'd written to Michael Laurence in Australia. His initial letters had been full of regrets that he'd not had the courage to grab our relationship in both hands and see if it would work. He was now writing urging me to come back and see if we could perhaps make more of our mutual affection. He wrote beautiful letters apologising for his uncertainty and assuring me that if I returned to Australia he'd ensure I wasn't homeless, would look after me and help me back into theatre, and allow us to see if we could have a future together. Michael is a wonderfully frank person and incredibly honest about himself. I was fully aware of his doubts about his sexuality, but we both thought it might be worth having a go at a relationship. His lovely, loving, funny, self-deprecating, newsy letters continued for three years during which time he blew hot and cold about 'us', alternately longing for me to return and assuring me that all he wanted was a normal life and babies, then holding me at arm's length by insisting that, should I return to Australia, it must be first and foremost because of the country and not him.

I was into my fifth month with Granada and no one had said a word to me by way of encouragement, approbation or indeed continuity of work. I am a natural born worrier and financial security is very high on my agenda. In one of his letters to me,

Owen Leeming commented '… you were never prepared to put sacrifice ahead of security', and he was correct. I was scared stiff of not earning a living and not being able to put a roof over my head. Like many in the acting or television world, I have suffered from deep insecurity all my life and wonder why on earth people like me are drawn to these insecure professions.

My agent was aware that the six-month contract was close to expiry and sent me to an audition for a continuity announcer post with Westward Television, based at Derry's Cross in Plymouth. I was offered the position but really wanted to progress to something more substantial, like interviewing work. The Head of Presentation, David Sunderland, gave a verbal assurance that Westward would try to give me the experience I required. Arrangements were made to visit the studios in Plymouth for some pre-publicity photos and a look around. I liked what I saw. The people were friendly, I preferred the open spaces around Plymouth to the more industrialised areas close to Manchester and I was assured it rained less!

Returning to Manchester to complete my contract and say my goodbyes, I was met with incredulity. Why was I going? Everyone was perfectly happy with my work but no one had thought to tell me and I was assured my contract would have been renewed. A valuable lesson was learned the hard way. If no one says anything, just keep your head down and go on working. Contracts departments get round to doing the necessary in the end. But there was no alternative for me because once again I'd signed a contract and had to honour it.

It was at this time I decided to buy a car. In typically female fashion, I knew only how to drive and where to put the petrol. Apart from that I was ignorant as to what one looked for in purchasing a four-wheeled beast. My stepfather, Geoff, offered to help and, after much looking around, I decided on a racy little white soft-top Austin Healey Sprite, which we found at a garage between Windsor and Staines. It was, of course, second-hand and cost a few hundred pounds. Geoff gave it the once-over and the purchase was made. I was so proud as I drove it away from the garage. The next day, 14 April, I would be going to Plymouth, to take up my post with Westward, and was really looking forward to the journey in my very own car.

In the morning, Mummy came into the bedroom to say goodbye and to wish me luck in the new job. It was a sunny day but I experienced a strange feeling as we hugged. I felt as though I would never see her again. Four hours later, on the straight road leading into Salisbury, the car zig-zagged out of control, went into the nearside bank, continued travelling for about ten yards and then came to a halt, turning over in the process. Somehow the car had come to a stop trapping my hands. I couldn't move. Hayo had died in April twelve months earlier and I remember repeatedly saying, 'Please God, don't let the car catch fire.' The coincidence was frightening.

A motorist came to my rescue and managed to lever up the car enough for me to wriggle free. I was frightened because I couldn't see. Blood was pouring into my eyes from a cut, a fractured nose and cuts above my eyes. I'd been wearing glasses and they'd caused the damage as my head hit the windscreen. The kind motorist who came from Windsor cleaned up my face as best he could and to my great relief I realised I hadn't been blinded.

An ambulance took me to Casualty at Salisbury General Hospital, where I was assigned to a female doctor. Apart from my nose, I had gravel embedded on one side of my face, a badly cut elbow and glass had severed a nerve in the little finger of my right hand. The doctor sewed me up as well as she could, but my right eye was so tightly sewn, it kept watering. It was the complicated fracture of my nose and proximity to a hospital renowned for its plastic surgery that saved my looks. After lying around on a trolley for hours (do things ever change?) I was transferred to Odstock Hospital. Odstock was a collection of Nissen huts that had housed military personal during the war. It may not have looked very grand, but the plastic surgery carried out in the shabby 'huts' was of a very high standard.

It was evening by the time all the to-ing and fro-ing had taken place and I was ensconced in a hospital bed. My nose had a compound fracture and was swelling by the minute. Someone made a decision that the senior surgeon should take a look at me. The surgeon, John Barron, had trained under Sir Archibald McIndoe, who remade the burned faces of RAF pilots in World War II. Mr Barron was located at a formal dinner and came to assess my damage, all dressed up in his dinner jacket. I'll never forget his kind face and the gentle way he touched my wounds and said, 'I think we can tidy this up a little but the nose is so swollen, I will only be able to splint it for the time being.' They took me into theatre round about 11 p.m., where Mr Barron, splinted my nose with a piece of metal (he said it was part of a tobacco tin!) and re-did all the stitches so neatly he'd have won a needlework competition. The side of my face which was covered with embedded gravel was sanded and looked like a piece of raw meat. The damaged finger was stitched and plastered. Incongruously, my painted nail had remained intact and was left sticking out of the bandage. That made me laugh a lot.

By the next day the accident was reported in the papers and the story made its way to Australia. A few days later I had a frantic letter from Michael. I had told him about Martin but we were still close friends and Michael is a very caring individual. The staff at Odstock were wonderful and Mr Barron assured me that when all the swelling went down I'd be as good as new. 'We'll see what happens with the nose. It might be all right but if not, we can consider plastic surgery.' I wasn't allowed to have a mirror for many days, which was just as well. When I did finally take a peek, my heart sank. I was worried by what I saw. My face was very swollen and badly bruised, particularly around the eyes and nose. However, relief that I was alive overrode most other emotions.

Because of the pre-publicity and the fact that I was on the front cover of *Look Westward* (the West Country ITV Guide), the viewers sent me so many get-well cards, presents, baskets of fruit and flowers, that I was overwhelmed by their kindness. However, with a metal splint on my nose and a clown-like red blob on my cheek, work was out of the question, so I went to my mother's house in Windsor to recuperate. The accident had frightened Martin and he made all sorts of promises about his honourable intentions. I looked frightful, so having him reassure me that he'd love me whatever the outcome was a great comfort.

When I had the accident, my father had engaged the AA to do a check on the car. The predominant fault contributing to the accident was one radial tyre on the front of the vehicle. Evidently, you should always have two radials and they should be at the back. Not long after my accident, a law was passed making it illegal to have radials on the front of a car unless they were coupled with two at the back. I was advised to see a solicitor, who assured me that I definitely had a case for damages, as the car should not have been sold in an unroadworthy state.

When I returned to Odstock to see Mr Barron, we were both unhappy with my nose. It had a decided bump on it. I was well enough to go back to work but Mr Barron wanted the nose to settle down even further before we embarked on a 'nose job'.

I hadn't the money to replace the car and David Sunderland wanted to make sure that this time his announcer arrived in one piece. He came up to London, took me to see *Fiddler on the Roof*, which we greatly enjoyed, and then drove me down to Plymouth. I liked Westward and there were some great people at the station. The anti-social hours didn't bother me too much as I was still involved with Martin. He didn't get down to see me all that often. I'd organise my time off, often refusing invitations to dinner and social gatherings from other members of the Westward staff, and then there would be the last-minute letdown. Frequently, I would come off air and be told there was a message that regretfully Martin couldn't make it. My time in Plymouth became a lonely time. I would go home to an empty house and my knitting. I was making Martin a huge navy Guernsey-type sweater. By the time I finished it, our affair was over.

As soon as Mr Barron felt my nose had inwardly healed enough I was booked in for the operation. I remember him doing his rounds and stopping to ask me what kind of nose I'd like. I suggested retroussé, but he advised against it. There was a copy of *Vanity Fair* on the bed and he thumbed through it, finally stopping at a particular page and saying, 'I think this nose will suit you', and that's what I got. I wish I'd kept the magazine.

The shock of the accident and two spells in hospital had a remarkable effect on my figure. I lost almost two stones in weight over the summer of 1967 and looked a little like Twiggy. I decided to complete the transformation by having my long hair cut and went for an urchin look. The transformation was dramatic to the point that on my return to the studio, several colleagues did a double take.

I wasn't happy. The interviewing work didn't materialise. My relationship with Martin was going nowhere. Michael was writing regularly, urging me to go back to Australia. And I really wanted to go. I'd always regretted leaving and greatly missed the theatre and the wonderful climate. But I was scared. I didn't have enough confidence in my own ability to grasp the bull by the horns and go for it back in Australia. Michael kept assuring me that the Philip Theatre Management would look very favourably on my returning. Once again it was the need for security that won. For the time being at least, I had a job and was earning a salary and I was frightened to give it away on the chance that I could pick up where I left off in Australia. I re-read my notices. They were good – surprisingly good.

My rented cottage was at Sparkwell, a few miles north of Plymouth. Although I loved it, it was a bad choice because of its isolation. To keep me company, Martin bought me a black miniature poodle. Her name was Sheba and she was the most loving, intelligent, wonderful little companion you could ever wish for. You'd never get away with it now, but I was allowed to take her into the continuity booth with me and she would lie at my feet for hours on end, without making a sound. The combination of living out of Plymouth, away from the action, and turning down a social life waiting for Martin to visit was taking its toll on me. I didn't really give myself a chance to integrate into the life at Westward and the West Country in general. So at the end of my contract, I left and went back up to Windsor in the hope that I could get some acting work.

I can't remember much about it but I was given a part in the Bournemouth Theatre Company's production of *Let's All Go Down the Strand*. I had to smoke on stage, which was an ordeal for me and must have been incredibly unconvincing. The best things about those few weeks were being able to go to the beach during the day and meeting Ian Ogilvy. I think his mother was in the next production and he'd come down to visit. His mother was nearing sixty, was stunningly attractive and had a ravishing figure. I found myself hoping the years would be kind and I would wear as well.

There is a saying that one man's misfortune is another's fortune. In this case it was one woman's misfortune that gave me a lucky break. An actress with the highly respected Oxford Playhouse Repertory Company had an accident and they were desperate to fill her place at short notice. An Australian actor called Lewis Fiander had seen my work at the Union Rep in Melbourne and suggested me to Frank Hauser. Frank had reopened the Oxford Playhouse in 1956 and was Director of Productions for Meadow Players, with a policy of staging important new plays and classical revivals. He trusted Lewis's judgment and with only a cursory audition I was invited to join the company and appear in two productions – *The Silent Woman* by Ben Jonson and a world première of Robert Browning's *Pippa Passes*. It might be sacrilege to say it, but I should think it was the first and last time Pippa Passed! Stephanie Beacham, who went on to dizzy heights in American soaps, was in the company and a lovely lady she was too. She didn't stay for *Pippa Passes* (can't say I blamed her) but sent me an opening-night card, of three incredibly starchy-looking Brontë sisters painted by their brother, with the words, '... Nearest I could get to you three grotty bags. [I was playing one of three grotty street women.] All luck and love, Stephie.' Other names in that production who later became famous were Simon Ward and Roy Marsden.

It was during the Oxford run that Martin suggested we rent a house together and so we went house hunting. As the time approached for us to sign the documentation for the rental, however, Martin became elusive and evasive. I began to smell gigantic rats. After work at the Playhouse one Friday evening, instead of driving straight home to my mother's house, I came off the motorway one junction early and drove to what I knew was Martin's home. My heart sank when I recognised his car outside the family home, which was in darkness. The next morning before contacting him, I rang the estate agent to enquire why there was a hold-up on the rental contract and was informed that Mr Watson had cancelled the deal.

When I finally got hold of him, I was fed a tale about his wife being unwell; he'd had to return to the family home but he'd slept in a separate room! By this time I was getting tired of, and distressed by, all the lies and deceitful acts. Acts such as receiving postcards from Scotland (posted by a friend of his) where he was supposed to be working, only to discover he was actually on holiday with his wife. I did eventually meet her and found her to be a charming woman who informed me she had a perfectly normal relationship with her husband and was unaware of the London pad. Now I look back, I really do have to laugh at the situation. Martin had been on a business trip to South Africa and had brought me back a pair of gold nugget earrings with the explanation that he'd been torn between some gold hanging baskets and the nuggets and had decided to give me the latter. When his wife and I met, she was sporting the baskets!

Once I was back on his home territory, Martin 'came on strong' again. More promises, more lies, more deceit. But he was an out-and-out womaniser and his promises meant nothing. At one stage in our relationship my mother went to an hotel where he was conducting a management course and told him she would involve the police if he didn't leave me alone. He was making me very unhappy and weight was dropping off me.

I simply had to get away and my salvation came in the form of a phone call from the Controller of BBC Plymouth. Tom Salmon was a wonderful man; a talented broadcaster with a beautifully mellifluous voice and a superb administrator, who encouraged talent when he saw it. Angela Rippon had defected from the BBC and gone to Westward, so Tom was short of a continuity announcer and was offering me the job. I explained that I really wanted to be an interviewer, so a deal was struck that if I took the position, Tom would ensure that I got experience with radio interviews. It seemed like a good deal. There was no theatre work on the horizon; I needed to work and also to put distance between myself and Martin.

So in 1969 I went back down to Plymouth. This time, I had a ready-made home. Whilst at Westward, I'd made friends with their Presentation and Promotions writer and she had rented a large house at Budshead Road. My rent would help her; the company suited both of us and she allowed me to have my lovely Sheba with me. Joan was a fantastic cook and a superb hostess and I learned a great deal from her, including the imbibing of large and lethal Manhattans, which we'd drink after a hard day's work, declaring all the while that, 'Men are bastards.'

Joan had spent a large amount of her married life in Africa, but before that her circle had been in the West Country and she'd kept in touch with many of her friends. One weekend she suggested we go down to St Austell to visit very dear friends of hers. I took an instant liking to Cecily and George Dobson. Joan had told me the couple had a very amiable son called John, but she wasn't sure whether he would be at home or not. We spent a most enjoyable afternoon and were about to leave when John returned. We only exchanged a couple of sentences, but I liked him. He was tall, blond, slim, good looking with lovely eyes. A few days later, I had an invitation to a dinner dance and decided to go for it and invite him. After all, the worst he could say was 'No'. He said 'Yes'.

I believe we were good for each other. John had been in a dreadful accident. He was a passenger in a Morgan sports car driven by a friend, which had been in collision with an English China Clay lorry in one of the numerous narrow lanes around St Austell. Fortunately he was wearing a sheepskin coat, which saved his body, but his hands were very badly burned, as was part of his face. His mother told me he gained confidence from the fact that I cared despite his hands being in such a dreadful state. He was so courageous and absolutely determined that he wouldn't lose the use of them. He endured so many operations and did retain almost total mobility.

Shortly after I went to Plymouth the second time, Martin's friend Ken rang to tell me Martin had had a heart attack. He blamed me for it but I'm sure it was the pressure of his double life and all his lying that put the stress on him. Martin started to phone me again but on one occasion when John was with me, he took the phone out of my hands and told him politely to leave me alone and get lost. Fortunately, I didn't see Martin again for many, many years. When I did bump into him, I wondered what on earth I'd ever seen in him. His flirtatiousness was totally transparent. I suppose I had matured enough to see him for what he was. But sadly, I was to go on making poor judgments about other men for a long time into the future.

CHAPTER FIVE

THE WEST COUNTRY AND JOHN

Life was highly enjoyable. Tom Salmon was as good as his word and ensured that I got out and about with a Uher (the old and heavy recording machines we reporters used to lug around with us). I shall never forget the first interview I did. It was with an old sailor who sang sea shanties and told fascinating tales of the sea. I did a sound check, turned on the machine and sat back while we chatted. I didn't understand the discipline of an interview and came back with two and a half hours of tape. I had no idea where to start when Tom told me he only wanted two and a half minutes. I was close to tears. Anyway, Tom edited the tape for me and taught me a huge lesson. With both radio and television interviews, you work on a ratio. It may be different now, but for radio if you wanted a final three-minute piece, you could afford to tape roughly twenty minutes. For television, the ratio was less, at three minutes for every one you wanted, because it was more complicated to edit. It's all quite different now; the advent of Electronic News Gathering (ENG) and digital tapes has speeded up the process beyond belief. When I graduated to television interviewing, we would rush the film back to the studios, where it would go into the 'soup' to be developed. Then, we reporters would sit with the editor as he cut and we scripted. It was a lengthy process but was also a means of learning. To this day, I have a built-in clock and can usually time a piece accurately to within a few seconds. Throughout the day, I usually know the time to within five minutes, without looking at a watch.

I'd been back in Plymouth for six months and was happy both professionally and personally. Then, in November, Tom called me into his office to tell me auditions were being held in Bristol to find a Presenter for *Tom Tom* – a sort of junior *Tomorrow's World*. He suggested I should apply even though it would mean him having to find a replacement if I got the job.

I was told that the BBC had received over two hundred applications for the position. I remember the audition quite well. You were put on the spot by having to talk knowledgeably about a scientific object that had only been cursorily explained to you. Then there was one minute describing a strange blob of black wood with a hole in it and suggestions as to what it might possibly be. This was followed by a two-minute talk on a subject of your choice, with no chance to write any notes. I went into full flow about my meeting with the opal miner in the outback of Australia. Being able to ad lib was very important in the earlier days of television because so much of it went out live and if a film went down, you just had to talk your way through until the operator was ready to roll again. I preferred 'live' television because, although it was far less polished, it was more immediate and far more fun.

The producer of *Tom Tom* was a highly intelligent Oxford graduate called Richard Wade and he chose me for the job. I was sad at leaving Plymouth and not being so close to John, but in any business you have to be prepared to move to improve. That is very true in the cut-throat world of broadcasting; you go where the work is and you work anti-social hours because that is what the job demands. And if you don't want to do it, dozens of other hopefuls will step into your place.

I moved to Bristol and found a tiny house to rent in Cliftonwood Crescent. Bristol is a hilly city and the suburb of Clifton is on one of its many hills. I was able to look out over the garden wall and see the river Severn bustling with activity.

It proved a superb vantage point for viewing when they brought the SS *Great Britain* back home.

I thought *Tom Tom* might have afforded me the opportunity to go abroad but it was very much a home-based programme for most of us. I remember one of our presenters, John Earle, going off to Tibet but I'm not sure whether that was for work or a holiday. He brought me back a Tibetan prayer wheel, which I now keep in front of a beautiful Vietnamese Buddha head.

Remember, I'm not good at scientific subjects, so working on the programme was very challenging for me. Just occasionally I was in danger of finding the subjects over my head. I had to interview Edward de Bono, the leading exponent of the art of lateral thinking. I'm a very straight-up-and-down thinker. Logic is not my strong point and interviewing Mr de Bono was like talking to someone in a language you don't completely comprehend. He was extremely patient with me.

In the world of broadcasting, you are only as good as your last job and can never afford to let the grass grow under your feet. As well as working on *Tom Tom* I also contributed the occasional pieces to both the television news programme *Spotlight South West* and to various radio programmes. When *Tom Tom* came off air for the summer break, I had to work harder than ever picking up freelance interviewing work. When a programme is off air, you don't get paid.

On Friday, 8 May 1970, I was asked to do a radio interview and the location was close to Plymouth. The story was something to do with a farm dog but when I got there the farmer refused to play ball and wouldn't submit to the interview he'd agreed to do. This meant that I didn't need to get a tape back to the studio; the weekend was coming up and I was already halfway to Cornwall. The 10th was John's birthday, so I found a phone box and rang John's mother to ask if I could stay for a couple of days. She was delighted, so was John. Although I only had the clothes I stood up in, it didn't matter. I could buy some underwear and a toothbrush, which was a small price to pay for being able to celebrate John's birthday with him.

I rang my flatmate to let her know I wouldn't be coming back that Friday night only to be told that she was about to get a train down to Cornwall to see her boyfriend, Clive Gunnell, a very well-known West Country television presenter. As we were both going to be in the West, she asked if I would give her a lift back on the Sunday. I agreed without realising that Clive lived in the depths of the Cornish Moors.

We had had some totally marvellous and unseasonal weather for two weeks. It had been exceptionally warm and not a drop of rain in the sky. Then, just before I left, the weather changed and we experienced that dank, dismal drizzle that is so indicative of the Cornish Moors. It took me two extra hours to find and collect Claire in my relatively new, second-hand Triumph GT6, and then we commenced our long journey back to Bristol. There was no motorway network in the West in the late 1960s and it was a difficult journey on not-too-brilliant roads. We were coming up the A38 close to the Weston-super-Mare turn-off when I took the corner too fast. Had I not been tired and had the roads not been 'greasy' from a dry period followed by drizzle instead of good solid rain, maybe it wouldn't have happened. I lost control on a bend and skidded, coming to a grinding and noisy halt against a telegraph pole. Claire was OK, so was Sheba, and I thought I was, until I put my right foot on to the ground and crumpled into a heap.

The area in which we'd had the accident was a known black spot and kind people rushed out of a nearby cottage very quickly. They covered me with blankets and phoned for an ambulance. I can still remember the pain every time it hit a bump; the road was a stretch of road between the A38 and Weston-super-Mare General Hospital and it was being resurfaced. The ambulance men rushed me into Casualty. I had what is known as a Potts fracture of the ankle and the legbone a few inches above the ankle had broken and come out through the flesh. It was a mess and there was no orthopaedic specialist on duty late at night, so the duty doctor decided, in the short term, to immobilise the joint. He did so by cradling my leg and ankle on a huge lump of plaster of Paris.

There was no room in Orthopaedic, so I was sent to the Geriatric ward. I was in so much pain, I wouldn't have cared where they put me. The nurse administered F8s (strong painkillers) every hour. My bed was opposite a clock, which I watched like a hawk as the minutes ticked past until another painkiller could be administered.

The next day, it was decided the leg couldn't be splinted and plastered because of the wound, so I spent several days immobilised, with the leg under a cradle supported on the plaster, I couldn't be left in that state for too long or my foot would have set at the wrong angle. Eventually the specialist had to put the leg and foot in plaster with a screw through the ankle to hold it together.

Then the fun began. The power of television is staggering. I'd only been on national television for six months and yet it felt as though the whole world knew me. At visiting time, I was recognised and strangers would come over and talk. In the first few days, enduring excruciating pain, the last thing in the world I wanted was to make conversation with strangers, but in our business you are never off duty. I don't always manage it but I do try to be polite to members of the public who, after all, are largely responsible for the success of the programmes on which we work. If they don't watch we don't have jobs. Even the nurses would sit on my bed and chat when all I wanted was to be left alone.

While I was in hospital, some friends brought me my mail, including a bill, from the local council for the telegraph pole! What insensitivity. There was also a letter from Monica Sims, Head of Children's Programmes, BBC Television, in which she told me that the autumn series was to be the last of the *Tom Tom* programmes ... 'I know this will come as a great disappointment and we have only come to this decision after much discussion and heart-searching. We feel, however, that there are now too many magazine programmes for children and would prefer to use the programme time for several different series. Meanwhile, I do wish you great success for the next series of *Tom Tom* and hope you will enjoy working on it until

November.' Richard Wade had left the programme and a new producer, Andrew Smith, had taken over. Andrew visited me in hospital as a courtesy and to assure me that my job was secure, come the autumn. They would work around me. I could stand behind a demonstration table and the plastered leg wouldn't be a problem.

So there I was with a smashed-up leg and no means of income for the summer months. How was I going to pay the rent and what was I going to do for money? My friends sorted out the rent problem by persuading me to take, as a lodger, a chap who'd had a bad car accident himself and lost the sight of one eye. As someone who'd just been in a crash, I felt sympathetic and accepted even though I'd never met him. The rent had to be paid somehow.

I couldn't work or do anything for myself, so John suggested that I went down to Cornwall for a month. He'd just rented a house in Fowey and could offer me accommodation. I had a magical month despite my plastered leg, because the weather was simply amazing. When the sun shines in England, you wouldn't want to be anywhere else and whilst John was at work, I sunbathed and loafed around.

John and I had never had so much time together. He borrowed a friend's small cabin cruiser and we had many happy hours mackerel-fishing. We often went into inaccessible coves, approachable only by sea, and John would give me fireman's lifts out of the boat, over the water, and on to the beaches. It was a lovely time and I felt this was definitely a silver lining to the cloud.

All good things come to an end and eventually I had to leave John and return to Bristol. It was time for the plaster to come off. I went to the Bristol Royal Infirmary (BRI) and sat in the queue forever. The specialist cut off the plaster and I had to laugh at my totally white leg up to the knee, in stark contrast to my very bronzed body everywhere else. My mirth was short-lived; the plaster needed to be redone. Even worse, I was not to put any weight on it. An ambulance took me home and I was dumped in the living room. I rang my mother and asked her to come down for a few days. Bless her, she has no sense of direction whatsoever. The journey from her home to Bristol should have taken two hours maximum. Four hours later, I was desperately worried that she'd had an accident. But she eventually arrived having missed the turning to Bristol and motored on over Severn Bridge into Wales. How she found her way back to me is a mystery, but she did.

As my bathroom was upstairs and I couldn't walk, I had to wriggle up and downstairs on my behind. I've never had such slim hips. The *Tom Tom* producer came around to see me one evening amidst great assurances that I need not worry about work. I would be kept off filming and do all studio work. The leg wouldn't be a problem. Mr Smith had to commute to Bristol from his home near London and on the evening he visited, he surprised me by asking if he could stay the night. I wasn't too happy about letting an almost total stranger stay in my home, but he was the producer and surely could be trusted. He slept on the sofa but in case he had other ideas I locked the bedroom door.

The next day, I had a phone call from the production office and was told that although the programme was about to start, it had been decided I wouldn't be required for a week or two. No plausible reasons were given. The timing was more than a coincidence and I smelled a rat. I had been assured by Monica Sims that my job was safe for what was left of the programme's life, despite my bad leg, and yet I was being fobbed off with reasons for not using me. I was hoping the plaster would come off that week and praying the leg and ankle would be mended so that they didn't need replastering. At the BRI the specialist gave me the 'all clear' and I was discharged.

I took a taxi straight from the hospital to the BBC building in Whiteladies Road. As I entered the *Tom Tom* office, the staff went quiet and looked sheepish and embarrassed. Nobody said anything but someone pushed across the desk to me the script for that week's programme. My name had been crossed out and replaced by one of the researchers called Michele Brown (married now to Gyles Brandreth). I was stunned, shocked,

and very, very upset. Why had they lied to me? Why couldn't
someone have had the guts to let me know what was going on?
This kind of cowardice and lack of communication was a facet
of the industry I would meet often over the next twenty years. I
didn't work on *Tom Tom* again! Some of my colleagues were
incensed at the cavalier treatment meted out and urged me to
insist that I should be paid for the series whether I was used or
not. I'd been out of action for almost two months with my leg,
and desperately needed the money so I did take on Goliath and
won my case. I got paid for the series despite not working on it.

I had another financial problem. My tenant was not paying
his rent and I couldn't possibly afford to renew the rental lease
on the house whilst my work prospects were looking so bad. My
love life was also falling apart. John was progressing in a career
that would become enormously successful, and had moved to
London. He was spreading his wings and I didn't have a part in
the script. I was extremely upset at the break-up, not only at
losing John but also the friendship of his parents, whom I'd
come to regard as family. John is a very tall, big chap and I had
spent months knitting him a sweater. That was completed at
the same time as our relationship broke up. After the sweater
scenario with both Martin and John, I vowed I'd never knit for
a man again!

For reasons of economy, I gave up the house and moved in
with a very pleasant young woman who had an apartment in
one of the many large old houses in Cotham. She and I got
along well together and I enjoyed her company. It actually felt
good to be sharing a home. And then I had a stroke of good
fortune. The damages case from my accident in 1967 finally
came to a conclusion. I was awarded £1,500 compensation and
though £750 went on solicitors' fees, I felt as rich as Croesus.
The vagaries of my profession, where you are in and out of work
with monotonous regularity, had never allowed me to save
money long term. When I was in work, I had to put money
aside for the times I would be out of work. I had always wanted
to own a home and the compensation money was a good
enough sum to use as the down payment on a flat. I was still

worried about paying a mortgage but I had another stroke of luck in the form of a phone call from Mike Towers, one of the producers at Harlech Television (HTV) in Bristol. 'We are about to launch a new programme for women which will go out twice a week, and wondered if you would be interested in coming over to the studios for an audition.'

Women Only was the programme and I was to be the main presenter/interviewer. Mike offered me £14 per programme and no dress allowance. The money wasn't brilliant, but the programme appealed to me. Besides, if the trial period was successful, I could look forward to short-term financial security. As is often the case in television and theatre, nobody wants you and then everybody wants you. I had just auditioned for a job on the BBC's *Tomorrow's World* and was filmed explaining how to erect a folding bike. As far back as the seventies people were looking for ways around congestion in London and the idea was to take your bike with you in the car boot, travel up to the city by train with the bike, and then avoiding the tubes, cycle to your destination. (The bikes never caught on!) My time on *Tom Tom* had given me many opportunities to do demonstrations so the audition didn't phase me. I know I handled it well and Andy, the producer, was delighted with my work. I was offered £45 per filmed item but, and it was a big but, the work was to be on an ad hoc basis. I needed a regular income.

Owen's appraisal of me is absolutely correct. I play safe in the workplace. Though the thought of being on a national television programme was appealing, the security of longer term regular money with HTV won the day. Also, I liked living in Bristol and was building a good social life for myself. I accepted the HTV job and started house hunting with Hartnell, Taylor, Cook, the most prominent and established estate agency in Clifton. And that is where I met Jeremy Gilchrist.

CHAPTER SIX

BRISTOL AND JEREMY

Jeremy Gilchrist was attractive and, initially, arrogant. The latter I attributed to his having attended public school. Arrogance is a trait I've often observed in public school chaps. Jeremy had been to King's College, Taunton, where he made friends with St John Hartnell, the son of the senior partner with Hartnell's. It was a natural progression for St John to join his father's firm and as Jeremy hadn't any other plans, he followed suit.

Jeremy and I didn't hit it off when we met in his office, but he assured me of his best professional attention and would keep his eyes open for a modestly priced apartment. Some days later, by accident, we met in Clifton Village, where he apologised for his brusqueness and took me for a coffee.

We are all attracted to different qualities in the opposite sex. For me, a big turn-on is a man's voice and Jeremy's was about the best I've ever encountered. He spoke beautifully, with none of the mannerisms of a public schoolboy but all the clarity of diction that I love. In terms of colour, his voice would be golden brown and sexy. He also had beautiful eyes and lovely hair. The rest of him was pretty damned perfect as well!

There was a very strong mutual attraction and a distinct drawback. Jeremy was married. His wedding had been a shotgun affair. He'd got a girl pregnant and did the honourable thing by marrying her. He must have been reasonably happy in the early stages of his marriage because the second child followed quite rapidly after the first.

Because of my Catholic upbringing, and having had a strict father, I would say I am a fundamentally moral and honest person. But as anyone who has ever been in love will testify, reason and logic desert you when Cupid shoots his arrow. No one is easier to fool than yourself, so I believed the story of the mutual unhappiness of Jeremy and his wife, because I chose to. I really didn't want to go down the Martin path again; I don't wish to bring unhappiness to anyone and I am definitely not mistress material. If I love a man, I want to be with him and share a life. I don't want to meet in the shadows and spend Christmas, New Year, birthdays and holidays on my own.

Just after we met, I had to return to hospital for a minor operation. The screw that had pinned my ankle together was working its way to the surface and needed to be removed. Jeremy took me to hospital and came back for me at the end of the day. He was bit of a hippy at heart, and I'll always remember him with his jeans and a long white cheesecloth shirt, buttoned at the top with two engraved gold dress studs. (He later had them made into earrings for me.) He was so kind and attentive and, after a dose of anaesthetic, I was more than usually vulnerable; and that's when we became lovers. Although my flatmate was understanding and accommodating, we felt embarrassed at subjecting her to our liaison, especially after we broke the bed! It was a brass bedstead and I'm positive the bolts must have been working loose over a period of time, but we did break it. One minute we were in the seventh heaven of our passion and the next we were unceremoniously tumbled on to the floor. It was time to move.

Jeremy had been looking around for a suitable place for me to buy and found a basement flat in a large house back in the Clifton area. The cost was £3,300 for two rooms plus a kitchen and bathroom. For years, I'd lived in rented property with other people's choice of fixtures and furniture, so it was really exciting to have a home of my own. It was a blessing the place was small, because I didn't have much money for furniture. Friends have called me a natural home-maker and I suppose I am because I've managed to make my homes attractive on a relative shoestring. The flat had a small room at the front on the street side leading to a much larger room and then through to the other facilities and a tiny garden. I didn't fancy having my bedroom facing the street, so the small room became the living room and the large one took the bed. And what a bed! Jeremy's boss was in the throes of a divorce and was getting rid of some furniture. Among the items to go was a beautiful Victorian four-poster bed, which had come originally from Powderham Castle in Devon. It had a glorious dark burgundy and gold canopy, bedspread and curtains. Jeremy persuaded me that it would be an investment, and like the flat, could be sold at a profit if the need arose. Apart from being an investment, it was extremely solid and would not collapse under us! Shortly after this, Jeremy moved in.

Now that we'd regularised our relationship, Jeremy wanted me to meet his parents. Their home was at Walberswick in Suffolk and, on the first meeting, we weren't offered accommodation so had to book into an hotel. I was absolutely petrified of our first meeting and remember it vividly. Jeremy's parents came, by prior arrangement, to the hotel. Jeremy went downstairs first to greet them and after a while came back up for me. I could hardly move from fear. I needn't have worried about his father. James was a larger-than-life, almost Pickwickian C of E vicar who took to me immediately. The feeling was mutual. Despite being a man of the cloth, James was totally non-judgmental. I wish I could have said the same of his wife. Norah frightened the life out of me. Matters were not helped by the extremely close relationship she had with Jenny, the mother of her grandchildren. I was definitely *persona non grata*. I like people and dislike atmospheres, so I tried hard to win her over. I never really succeeded and she was one of the few people with whom I never felt comfortable or completely relaxed.

At HTV, life was getting better and better. *Women Only* was attracting a good audience and was beginning to be syndicated – shown in other regional areas for which HTV received a fee. Unfortunately, I wasn't a beneficiary in the revenue. I'd

signed a contract and what HTV chose to do with the programmes was their business. Besides, I'd never have thought to
have had a clause giving me 'a piece of the action' if the show
were successful.

Success breeds success and I was invited to a meeting with
the Head of HTV News, Ron Evans. Ron offered me the
chance of being a reporter on the local news magazine
programme *Report West*. I was to be paid on an ad hoc basis per
interview, but this didn't bother me as I had my regular £28 per
week for the *Women Only* programmes. I readily accepted and
was sent on my first television interview. Fortunately, I wasn't
let loose entirely on my own with the crew. Tony Holmes, one
of the newsroom producers, came out with me.

On one occasion, I was to interview an air hostess about
conditions of service in the airline business. It was a sunny day
and we talked outside the Grand Hotel in Bristol city centre.
Tony called for a wrap (termination of the interview) and then
said, 'OK now we'll do the cutaways and noddies'. I was
nonplussed. I thought Noddy was a character in a children's
programme and a cutaway was a piece of material cut away on
a garment to reveal extra flesh. Tony explained that in order to
cut the film, the interviewer had to repeat his/her questions to
camera, so that if a response needed to be cut, the interviewer
could interject with the next question. If the answer needed to
be shortened, the camera would cut back to the interviewer
wisely nodding, shaking his/her head, or looking quizzical, and
then return to the interviewee's answer. I couldn't even
remember all my questions. Tony had anticipated this and
made a note of them. Just as in my first radio interview, I'd not
been concise and had asked far too many questions. But it was
a learning curve. There were no television schools, you just
learned on the job. In many ways, I feel this was a good way to
experience the business, because you had to be aware of the
needs of other members of the team. If your interview were
overlong, it was not only extra work for you but for the film
editor as well. Because we were all so interdependent there was
a great team spirit and I experienced many happy days going

out in the TV car with the camera, sound and lighting men. And in the 1970s, the jobs were all held by men. In fact, I think HTV was one of the first companies to have a female boom operator. She was a tiny dot of a girl called Patty, who had worked her way up from the HTV post room and was justifiably proud of making it into a job traditionally held by a man.

Only a few months into reporting Ron called me into his office and offered me the job of co-presenting *Report West* with Bruce Hockin. Bruce was already an established and much-loved figure and it was a great compliment to be asked to join him. Again HTV was ground-breaking in that it was one of the first companies to have a female co-presenting news. By now, it was decided to regularise my finances with the company and, instead of being paid piecemeal, I was offered a contract for a year. The contract was for five news programmes and two *Women Only* recordings per week and the salary was £3,000. The only drawback was that although I would be working on contract, I was taxed as a PAYE employee but without being on the company pension scheme. Oh well, retirement was a lifetime away so I didn't let it worry me.

Although Jeremy's salary was almost totally taken up supporting his wife and children, I earned enough to keep the two of us and was only too happy to do so. He loved his children and visited them frequently but I remember how worried I was every time he went to see them; worried that he wouldn't come back. Eventually their mother allowed them to visit us and I found them delightful. Little Polly took a shine to me and one day presented me with a great big sparkling Christmas cracker ring. 'Please have it Jan 'cos it's my bestist,' she said with her almost imperceptibly lisping voice. I felt overwhelmed by her sweet gift and still keep the ring in my jewellery box. Jonathan was more wary, but even he began to warm to me after a period.

Women Only was great fun. I met and interviewed so many interesting people. The current Marquis of Bath came on the programme in 1972 to talk about his book *The Carry Cot* – a psychological whodunnit. It was a strange book, but then Lord

Weymouth, as he was then, has always been hippy and anti-Establishment. I had met him in the summer of 1970 when doing the odd bit of reporting for the BBC in Bristol. The interview was about the wing of his stately home, which he'd decorated entirely with scenes from the Kamasutra. I found it all slightly embarrassing and there were very red faces from the crew when I asked if he was worried about the mirror astride his four-poster bed crashing down on him and any 'wifelet' who happened to be in bed at the time. Despite his strangeness, he was the soul of good manners and propriety. He's never caved in to the Establishment and you have to admire him for that.

Nanette Newman, whom I had always admired both for her acting talent and for her beauty, came on the programme with a little book, *God Bless Love*. To benefit The Invalid Children's Aid Association, Nanette had compiled children's sayings about their concept of love. The whole book is a giggle a minute, from, 'I think you can fall in love if you have your picture taken in front of the church' (Eric, aged five), through 'I saw a book once with all drawings in it about falling in love and I think you have to have eggs' (Vera, aged five) and 'Love is hard to do to people you don't perticuly like (Deborah, aged ten), to howlers such as, 'King Henry the eight fell in love lots of times and in the end they had to chop his head off because he was geting fat' (Sidney, aged seven). When you admire someone and have the fortune to meet them, you always pray they will live up to your expectations. Nanette surpassed them. She is a truly beautiful woman in every sense of the word.

Jackie Collins was not only stunning in looks, but charming as well. She was on the programme to promote her fourth novel, *Lovehead*, a story of revenge for the murder of a good woman who'd offered hope to prostitutes and in so doing damaged the income of the pimps and hoodlums who controlled them. It was not a book to my liking, but it was well written and, despite my own feelings, I must have made a good fist of the interview because she autographed it for me, 'To Jan, With many thanks for a really interesting interview – Best regards, Jackie'.

The painter David Shepherd came on *Women Only* to promote his autobiography *The Man Who Loves Giants*. The 'giants' were the loves of his life – elephants and engines – and he's at ease painting both. He brought his beautiful wife Avril with him without whom, on his own admission, he'd be totally lost. I have interviewed and met the two of them on many occasions since that meeting in 1975, when he thanked me for 'a super interview'.

Raymond, or to give him his professional name 'Mr Teazy Weazy', was the forerunner of Sassoon, Toni and Guy, Paul Mitchell and Trevor Sorbie, to name a few. He was the first hairdresser to make an art of the whole business and even though he'd had cancer of the jaw and had had a large part of his face removed, he was still a great showman and a charming man. He 'teazed' some hair for us but he also spoke knowledgeably about Victorian mourning jewellery. He had a large collection all made from or containing hair from the beloved deceased. Many years ago, my father gave me a watch chain made out of his mother's hair. I didn't find it at all morbid, just a tangible memento of someone I'd never known.

By far and away the most colourful character to come through the studio doors and on to the *Women Only* set was Noel Barber. I remember him to this day in his cavalry twill trousers, navy blazer and red-and-white gingham shirt. Noel had been foreign correspondent for the *Daily Mail*, was the first Briton to reach the South Pole after Scott, had been stabbed five times covering the wars in Morocco and shot in the head during the Hungarian uprising and had walked across the Himalayas to report the Dalai Lama's escape to India. What a man – he was 'larger than life', with eyes that twinkled with the sheer joy of living. He'd written 22 books by the time I met and interviewed him. *Lords of the Golden Horn* was an historical reconstruction of the fall of the Ottoman Empire. I have always enjoyed history, and when it's taken away from the dry realms of academia and a story woven around the facts it is all the more interesting.

Noel enjoyed the interview and being on the programme. A few days later I received a present sent from Fortnum and Mason. I'd never had anything from Fortnum's in my life. The parcel contained a wooden box filled with chocolate-covered Morello cherries in brandy. A long-distance friendship began, with the odd letter and a couple of lunches in London. Until his death, he always sent me a copy of his latest book. My favourite is his first novel, written in 1981. *Tanamera* takes place in Singapore pre-World War II and is the story of two great dynasties – one British, the other Chinese – the society that segregated them and the passion that bound them and, of course, the star-crossed lovers from the two societies. I loved the book so much I had it leather-bound and gold-edged and bought a paperback for rereading, which is now brown with age and falling apart. Also, I named my house in Buckinghamshire *Pela* after a character in the book. Pelagius was a monk who believed there was no such thing as original sin and that the individual takes steps towards salvation by his or her own efforts. The forbidden lovers in *Tanamera* named their daughter Pela. The novel was made into a mini television series that I felt didn't do the story justice.

I never met Noel's wife Titina, whom he obviously adored, but received a beautiful reply to my letter of condolence when he died in 1988. Life without him must have been bleak.

Many other characters were passing through the *Women Only* programme: a very young Robin Cousins, the ice-skating star; the singer Dorothy Squires (ex-wife of Roger Moore); the lovely dress designer Gina Fratini, renowned for her fairy-tale gowns and for designing the wedding dress of Princess Anne. Any touring artists visiting the Colston Hall or the Bristol Hippodrome would invariably find themselves as guests on *Women Only* or *Report West*. Through the programmes I also met singers such as Neil Sedaka and Johnny Nash. It wasn't all famous folk, though. There were lovely people who did great good for others and came on the programmes to talk about their work. One of these was a woman of indomitable spirit, Marion Welchman. One of her children, whom she knew to be highly intelligent, was deemed below average. Marion knew otherwise and became a spirited fighter for the recognition of dyslexia. It was a cause for which she fought till the end of her life. I did a little to help her cause and she always gave me undue credit for it.

Although I was extremely fulfilled at work, life at home was somewhat strained. I had reached the age of 29 without ever really experiencing any desire to have children. I loved Jeremy and when a woman loves a man, she very often desires to give birth to his babies. I wanted his children and resented the fact that we couldn't do anything about it. Jeremy wasn't yet divorced and in 1971, a very dim view would have been taken of me having a baby 'out of wedlock', to use a gloriously old-fashioned phrase. I would have run a big risk of losing my job. Also, as I was the main breadwinner, I was worried sick as to how we would survive financially.

In August I had to go back to Odstock Hospital for plastic surgery on my ulcerated leg. Although it had healed, the skin was extremely thin and would have been prone to further ulceration in later life, so Mr Barron agreed to carry out the procedure. I had to have skin taken from one part of my body and placed on my leg. Mr Barron showed his usual concern for the vanities of women and took the skin from high up my thigh and well under the bikini line. On 13 August, whilst still in hospital, I received a telegram from Jeremy: 'Decree Absolute granted today stop will you marry me, Jeremy'.

Our flat in Frederick Place was tiny, and if we were ever going to be able to start a family, we needed somewhere larger. Jeremy heard of a large property for sale in a rather run-down road near the university. It was a ten-roomed, five-storey Georgian terrace house going for £6,700. The price was modest because it came with a sitting tenant who occupied the two top floors. The basement rooms were damp and needed attention, but four large rooms would be for our use, and that was enough for us for the time being. Jeremy advised me that it was in a road that would be 'up and coming' and was a good buy, so I bought it. Being Georgian, the rooms were large with high ceilings and the living room was on the first floor with French windows opening onto the tiniest of balconies. The other room on that level was a kitchen that had to double up as a dining room. Downstairs at ground level were two rooms to be used as bedrooms, so now we had a suitably large home for our four-poster bed. The damp basement rooms remained empty.

We hoped to gradually do up the house, make it into a lovely home, and see it rise in value. However, more than half the street was given over to student bedsits and the house next door to us was filled with Chinese restaurant workers who insisted on putting great heaps of left over-meat into a dustbin with no bottom. Dustbin day came and the local dogs and cats had a field day with the trail of rotting debris. Southleigh Road was going to take some time to 'come up' in the world. But it was home and we loved it. We got into a most enjoyable routine of working, socialising and keeping Sundays just for us. By now I had another poodle. Fleur was of the standard variety and apricot in colour. She had the sweetest nature and let little Sheba totally dominate her. Our Sunday routine was either to walk on the Bristol Downs or to drive, with the dogs, to Clevedon and go for long walks by the sea, returning home to the wonderful aroma of a roast – if I had remembered to put the oven on automatic.

In the early 1970s, there wasn't nearly as much 'living together' as there is today. Besides, if I love a man, I want to commit to him. Jeremy had asked me to marry him and I very much wanted to be his wife. So we started to plan our wedding. As divorcees, we had to get married in a register office but Jeremy's father had promised us a later church blessing with which we were happy.

We chose to get married on 28 July 1972. Wanting something a little different, Jeremy organised a horse and carriage to take us to the registry. The local press were out in force and headed their article 'Bride and Bridle'. I was absolutely amazed at the people lining the route taken by our carriage and the well-wishers outside the registry shouting, 'There's our Jan.' I'd been a fixture on local television for over two years, fronting seven programmes a week, and that is how the viewers referred to me – 'our Jan'. I was proud of their regard and affection.

Jeremy looked stunning in morning dress and I wore a very simple calf-length Gina Fratini organza day dress with a wide-brimmed hat. I had struck up a strong friendship with my hairdresser, Jean Mays, and she was thrilled when we asked her to be one of our witnesses. Jeremy's parents came to the wedding, as did his brother, sister and 'adopted' sister Ginny. Ginny was almost one of the Gilchrist family; she was treated like a sister and had paid me the honour of asking me to be godmother to her son. Jeremy's ex-wife Jenny very generously allowed Polly and Jonathan to attend. My mother came as well, but not my father. Sadly, since their divorce, relations between them were very strained and they never liked to be at the same function together. It was also awkward for my stepmother.

The gathering couldn't be too large, as our 'reception' was to be at home in Southleigh Road. Marion Welchman did the catering for us. All I can remember is that we had huge bowls of raspberries, as they are my favourite fruit, and a lovely wedding cake. We packed in as many guests as our rooms would accommodate. My friend from Granada days, Sue Michison (now McFarlane), made the trip from Surrey and I invited my boss and his wife from HTV. Bruce couldn't attend as someone had to hold the fort back at the studios. I know wedding photos are always happy and smiling but, looking at them now, we really did look as though we had everything going for us.

Our wedding night was spent at a lovely hotel called The Petty France just off the Bristol to Stroud road. I don't know whether it was nerves, excitement, or something that had disagreed with me but by the time we went down to dinner, I had come out in horrible red blotches and felt decidedly under the weather. It was rather a shame but it wasn't as if we'd never slept together before. We were going to have a two-week holiday in Majorca later in the summer and that was going to be our proper honeymoon.

Summers at HTV were what I called 'Muddy Field Syndrome' time. Attending fêtes and carnivals were part of our work roster. It was a chance for the public to meet us and a good advertisement for the channel. Well, it was meant to be, but I've lost count of the times I'd arrive at a venue after a long and arduous drive – West Country roads are notoriously clogged with traffic in the summer – be ordered to park in the far corner of a muddy field and then be announced as 'Miss Fleming from the BBC'.

Despite the name confusion, I always came away from those events with a good feeling. On the whole people are kind and generous and when you saw how hard they worked all year to raise money for good causes, you could do nothing but admire them. I always bought lots of home-made jam and pickles (before EU regulations virtually put a stop to the practice. I'm glad to see people are starting to ignore the stupid rules). In the summer, my home was never short of flowers presented by the fête organisers. If I thought it appropriate, I would take the dogs with me too. Most children love pets and when they were charged with looking after Sheba and Fleur, they glowed with pride.

September came and Jeremy and I took off for our delayed 'honeymoon' in Majorca. Because he had been flying back and forth to the island on business, he had many contacts and knew the northern part of the island well. We stayed at the Golf Hotel, which in the 1920s had been a watering hole for the jet set who came to the island to play golf. It sat alone amid grassland and on arrival you looked through the entrance hall straight out to the beach and the sea. The hotel had lost most of its former glory, but we loved it. A father and son owned and ran it and their personal care and attention gave the place a family atmosphere. On Sundays, the hotel always produced an enormous paella. Maybe it was because I'd never tasted paella before, or maybe it's just time making memories special, but I've never had as good a one since.

We were lent a car and drove up to Formentor, which had one of the best five-star hotels in the Mediterranean. The setting was idyllic, the hotel frighteningly expensive and we promised ourselves that one day we'd come back for a holiday. We also visited the Caves of Drach, which boasted a floodlit underground lake. As we drifted across the lake in a boat to the sound of Handel's *Water Music*, it was so romantic that we thought we were in seventh heaven.

We'd made friends with the proprietor, who invited us onto his yacht. He sailed it out to sea and then put in again at a cove inaccessible from the land. It was a magical day, diving off the boat into water so clear you could see the bottom, even though the bottom was far further than anyone could have dived without using an aid. We ate and drank and felt very privileged.

Then the holiday was over and it was back to earth with a bump. Not much of a bump, because I loved my work at HTV and knew how lucky I was to be paid to do something I enjoyed – meeting and interviewing interesting people from all walks of life. But on the home front, things were beginning to unravel. Jeremy became withdrawn and our disagreements about babies and money were more frequent. Jeremy wasn't a person with whom you could have a darned good row and clear the air. He would avoid issues and go quiet on me. I knew something was wrong and it was taking longer and longer to get back the loving feeling after a disagreement, but I was totally unprepared for what happened in February 1973. He suddenly announced that he needed space to sort himself out and was going to rent a flat near the office for six months. I didn't want him to go but felt sure matters would right themselves if he were given the time he asked for. I certainly didn't like the arrangement but wasn't unduly alarmed by the situation. Jeremy did ask me not to visit him in his rented accommodation, which I found a little strange.

My evenings were now very empty and I had to do something to fill the time whilst Jeremy was 'sorting himself out'. I'd always suffered a feeling of inferiority because I didn't possess a degree. The Open University had started up a couple of years earlier and offered a wonderful opportunity to study in your own time. I applied but didn't make the quota, which was filled with teachers improving their qualifications. Adult education night classes was the other alternative, and having always had a great love of literature, 'A' level English Lit. was the answer.

Work is a great cure for many problems, so I worked hard during the day and studied hard at night. I don't think many people knew about our situation and I was so sure it would all turn out fine in the end I wasn't unduly worried, only a little perplexed. Then, one Sunday, I was feeling particularly down and decided that, whether he like it or not, I was going to see my husband. He didn't want me to go upstairs to his flat and when I insisted, I found out why. One wall was plastered with photographs and they weren't of me. Naturally I was furious and very upset. When I asked what he was going to do about the situation, Jeremy answered honestly that he didn't know.

My sister was planning to get married in the summer and had asked Jeremy to be the best man. As matters between us were unresolved and we didn't loathe each other, it was decided that we wouldn't spoil Gilly's day. We kept to the arrangement and went up to Windsor for the wedding. Gillian looked absolutely stunning and I so hoped her marriage would be successful. The festivities went on long into the night, we'd had several glasses of champagne and it was really too late to drive back to Bristol. Mummy offered us her spare room. We hadn't been together for months and the sexual attraction was very powerful. I so desperately wanted to enjoy my husband, but my thoughts kept returning to 'the other woman. I knew I would feel used if he did decide to leave me. So we spent a very frustrating night together and it was the last in which we shared a bed.

Not long after that, the keys to his company car were put through the letter box of Hartnell, Taylor, Cook, and I received a telegram from Sweden. Jeremy had joined the girl in the photos, whom he had met on his regular business trips to Majorca.

I was shocked. I certainly hadn't expected this turn of events. The next few days were a haze of misery. I remember going to my friend Jean's hairdressing salon and being ticked off because I looked like death and hadn't put on any make-up. Jean has a glorious Bristolian brogue and remonstrated with me '... You mustn't let your public see you like this. Whatever you are feeling inside, don't let it show.' She is right. It is absolutely true, 'Laugh and the world laughs with you; cry and you cry alone.' Other than close family and friends, people do not want to share your misery and even family and friends get fed up after a time.

During this period, I also drank the drink I basically loathe. Feeling desperately maudlin and sorry for myself, I swigged out of a whisky bottle and before I knew it, had drunk half the contents. I felt so ill and woke with a massive hangover. But it was Friday, which meant two recordings of *Women Only* and the news programme *Report West*. Although Bruce could have carried the news without me, it would have been very difficult for the studio to find a substitute for my women's programme at such short notice. Every time there was a halt in the recording I would dash to the dressing room, splash my face with water and grab five minutes lying on the floor. It was a nightmare but totally self-induced. My hate affair with whisky was complete.

The next few months were very strange. I do believe Jeremy genuinely didn't know what he wanted. He phoned me and sent letters telling me how much he wanted to come back. I sent him loving letters urging him to come home and assuring him we'd work our way through the problems. I didn't know the problems were not just personal. One evening, I opened the door to a stranger who turned out to be a debt collector. Jeremy had run up debts of £1,500. That may not seem like a very large sum, but it was the same as a year's salary for him. I wasn't given details of the debts but was grateful to be assured that I wasn't responsible for them. Heaven alone knows where the money had gone because, although we lived comfortably, I ensured that we did not live beyond our means. He was also failing to meet his maintenance payments to his ex-wife. So, matters got worse and worse. Again I urged him to come home and we'd face the music together. I really thought I was winning the battle and then something trivial happened that may or may not have tipped the scales. I had a group of friends around for drinks. I'd gone to the loo when the phone rang. I would never, ever pick up a phone in someone else's home, unless asked, but one of my friends did. Maybe Jeremy thought there was another man in my life. I didn't hear from him again for many years.

Jeremy had booked another holiday in Majorca for us in the summer of 1973. Of course, he wasn't going to be taking it with me and I made the decision to keep the booking. A girlfriend agreed to come instead. Poor Celia, she must have had one of the worst holidays of her life. I found out from Jeremy's business colleagues that the Swedish woman had been in the background for some time, so why on earth he bothered marrying me is anybody's guess. I was gutted by the information and spent most of the holiday mooning around in tears and ended the fortnight catching a virus and being extremely ill.

But, life has to go on, and I was fortunate enough to be able to throw myself into work. My friends rallied around and life began to return to a kind of normality. I wrote the occasional letter to Jeremy but there was a deafening silence. When I re-read the letters he wrote in the first months after he left, they posed a total enigma. Eventually, the mental turmoil was so bad, I decided to take the letters to a psychologist for unravelling. It was a very harsh judgment, but his words were '... your husband is amoral, and should he return to you, I cannot see a happy outcome. For your own peace of mind, it would be better to seek closure and bring the relationship to an end.'

I do not agree that Jeremy was amoral, but even at the time I couldn't see him returning or envisage a happy outcome and I did need to draw a line under the affair. I was also worried that if I didn't divorce him, there might come a time when I would wish to remarry, might be unable to locate him and divorce would have been very difficult and expensive. So I divorced Jeremy for adultery. He didn't dissent but made one request that I found strange. He agreed to the adultery but wanted the other woman's name deleted from the papers. I agreed to this, but her name is there, just with a line through it. I was asked if I wished to make any future lien on money Jeremy might have or inherit. I was an independent woman with a house, a job and no desire to be a liability around anybody's neck. I wanted a clean break and got it.

CHAPTER SEVEN

HTV AND PEBBLE MILL AT ONE

I have always found solace in work. I could immerse myself in the programmes at HTV and not consider my worries until I came home alone in the evening. Thank goodness I had Fleur and Sheba wagging their stumpy tails and covering me with licks, love and affection.

Women Only was gaining in popularity and the viewing figures showed that *Report West* was way ahead of the BBC's local news programme. There was an empathy between Bruce and myself, a partnership that worked superbly. Many thought we must have been having an affair. Nothing could have been further from the truth. Bruce was firmly and happily married to his wife Caroline and utterly devoted to his children Georgiana and Giles. We socialised on high days and holidays only.

The feeling of popularity is a heady one, but it comes at a price and that price is freedom. Increasingly I was under the spotlight. The viewers liked what I wore, didn't like what I wore, criticised and applauded in speedy succession. One of the funniest events of that otherwise traumatic year was Jean suggesting that a change of image mightn't be a bad thing. I'd been wearing my hair brushed back and slightly backcombed with a flick at the sides. At that time, Jean styled hair but didn't cut it and I was handed over to a trendy new recruit called Richard. He was one of these hairdressers, and there are many, who take control of your hair and give it the style they want, not what suits you. I emerged from the salon with a mediaeval pageboy look (as one newspaper described it) with a geometric fringe cut like curtains across my forehead. The switchboard was jammed and 'for an hour no one could make a call out of the studio'. The viewers didn't like the style and told me so in no uncertain terms. The local newspaper reported that I was unrepentant and would keep the style. But I didn't, and within days was back to the old familiar one.

Clothes were becoming a big problem. The public expects you to have an extensive wardrobe and assumes it's provided at the studio's expense. Well, it wasn't and I had to find seven different outfits a week. The more feminine clothes I wore for *Women Only* were not suitable for *Report West*. There were evening functions requiring glamour clothes. Because I was a PAYE employee, I had no right to any tax allowances. I got so incensed at one point that I phoned up the tax officer dealing with HTV. The company had studios on both sides of the Severn, in Cardiff and Bristol, but the administrative centre was in Wales and so was the Tax Office. The operative who looked after me was a Mr Jones. When I finally got through to him I politely asked if he watched our channel.

'Oh, yes, Miss Leeming, you're one of my favourites and I watch most of your programmes.'

'Right,' said I, 'then you are aware of how many clothes I use and that these are not provided by the studio.'

'Oh, yes, Miss Leeming, and lovely they are too.'

'Then, Mr Jones, you know that my clothing bills are genuine.'

'Oh, yes, Miss Leeming.'

'So why am I not entitled to claim a tax allowance for them?'

'Goodness, Miss Leeming, I wouldn't let my wife spend that much on clothes.'

'So, I am not allowed to claim an allowance?'

'Oh, no, Miss Leeming.'

End of conversation. I was flabbergasted. Another HTV personality, a man, also took up the cudgels with the Inland

Revenue. He lost his case. It all revolved around the wording of our contracts. At least I've never forgotten Mr Jones!

I enjoyed living in Bristol. To me it was a city big enough to be interesting, yet small enough to be intimate. We had very good theatre, art galleries and restaurants. Evenings were often taking up attending charity functions. At weekends I sometimes visited Cecily and George Dobson, the parents of my ex-boyfriend John. He'd got married in the interim and Cecily felt that it would no longer cause embarrassment to either John or myself if the friendship between we two women was allowed to progress. Over the years she has been like a second mother to me. We share a love of antiques and would often roam around the galleries in Fowey or Truro, mostly looking and sometimes buying. She had readily taken to Jeremy and was sad for both of us when the marriage broke up. She was always there offering a shoulder to cry on. My mother is the eternal optimist and it can get very wearing when she continually assures me 'It will all be all right in the end.' Of course it will – it has to be, or you would curl up and die. But these words are no comfort when your heart is bleeding.

As a child I had asthma till the age of seven, when my tonsils were taken out. The asthma left me, but with bronchitic conditions in the family on both the paternal and maternal side, I was very prone to colds, sore throats and tonsillitis. Using my voice all the time and working in stuffy television studios was doing my voice no good at all. I was coming down with tonsillitis and laryngitis with monotonous regularity. An ear, nose and throat specialist concluded that my tonsil beds had grown again and I would require another tonsillectomy. It is not a pleasant operation, even when you are a child; as an adult it is ten times worse.

In spring 1974, I had the operation and was again greatly touched by the goodwill of the viewers. My room looked like a florist's shop and the bed was like a toy store with all the fluffy animals and goodwill gifts that had been sent. I needed a period of convalescence and as a meeting with Owen was years over-due, I wrote and asked if I could visit. We had corresponded sporadically and I knew that he had spent several years working for UNESCO setting up television stations in various parts of the world. His long-term goal had always been to make enough money for him to be able to retire to France and continue his writing. This, he was now doing. In the years since we had parted, Owen had achieved some success with both his poetry and his plays.

As my plane began its descent into Marseille Airport, I experienced a mixture of anxiety and anticipation. Although we'd kept abreast of each other's news, it was nearly ten years since we'd seen each other. I began to wonder if this holiday was a good idea. But, as I emerged through the gate, there was my dear, familiar, loving Owen with his arms held out to greet me. As he murmured 'Welcome, my Jani,' the intervening years just evaporated.

We had so much news with which to catch up, but we put the chat on hold so that I could enjoy the magnificent countryside as we drove north. It was probably my years in Australia that gave me a love of wide and somewhat stark scenery. Provence is a hot and dry area with jagged limestone escarpments and valleys filled with olive groves and almond fields. The area is carpeted with thyme and rosemary and as it was spring, the blossom was shedding like confetti onto the ground.

Owen lived north of Salon in a village called Lamanon. He had rented the tower apartment in a small château. Being a tower, the rooms were round. He had filled them with an esoteric mix of art and artefacts purchased from the countries in which he had set up TV stations. I suddenly had a panic attack – would Owen expect us to pick up where we had left off? I needn't have worried. Ever sensitive and kind, he assured me that though he'd love us to resume a physical relationship, he was content to wait and see. I really don't know why I remained so special to him after the way I'd let him down but I still have a postcard he sent me in 1971 in which he said, 'In spite of our rough times and splitting up, I must admit that in those ten years I haven't again experienced the strength of feeling which drew me to you.'

On my first evening in Lamanon, Owen's landlady invited us in for an aperitif. She was the epitome of everything one associates with a well-educated, middle-aged French woman. She dressed beautifully and entertained in style. She had an array of drinks but suggested I try her favourite and so began my liking of Ambassadeur. You can't always get it in France and I've never been able to acquire it in England. It is a fortified wine with a taste somewhere between sherry and port. It must be served chilled with a slice of orange and it is delicious.

Owen had become a very good cook and managed to conjure the most wonderful tastes out of virtually nothing. He kept a good cellar too. He had a nose for a bargain and bought well, laying down his wines and drinking them at the right time. At dinner, he wanted to know all about my work. He was very proud of what I'd achieved because he was the one who pushed me out into a world with boundaries way beyond my original expectations. He wanted to know where the Jeremy episode had gone wrong. I was at a loss to explain that what had started so well had ended so badly and really couldn't give him any reasons. We had a lovely evening but I realised, although my feelings for him were deep and sincere, there was no physical desire. I know he was disappointed but he loved me enough to enjoy me as a friend.

The next day we went into Salon, the home of Nostradamus, the sixteenth-century astrologer and physician and author of a book of much-quoted predictions. Salon is a most attractive town that has spread out from its original walls. By the clock tower is an unusual fountain surrounded by cafés. The 'mossy' fountain has been created by the action of limescale build-up on the original sculpture, which has then been subjected to the dropping of seeds by birds. The whole effect is like a large tree dripping water. Many of the fountains in the area have become mossy, but the one in Salon is the largest and most famous.

Owen gave me a wonderful holiday. Although he had a limited budget, he always managed to make experiences exciting. We were lucky enough to visit the Camargue at a time when you could take a car right across it. Today, vehicular access is forbidden. Even more fortunate, we saw the white horses, the bulls and the flamingos all in the same day. We also went to the gypsy church of Saintes Maries de la Mer – the two Marys of the sea. The saints are carried in procession once a year – one Mary is white and the other, supposedly her servant, is black. The church is fortified and stands stark against the Mediterranean. It is the centre for the annual pilgrimage of the gypsies of the Camargue. I have visited the Camargue so many times but have never been there at the time of the gypsy gathering where they carry the saints into the sea.

On our way back from the Camargue we called in at Les Baux; it is where the original bauxite was mined. On the lower slopes of the Baux range there's an old Roman town that snakes up the side of the escarpment and on top there's a mediaeval fortification From the road it's almost indiscernible until you realise the silhouette has a shape to it. It was once the stronghold of Cardinal Richelieu, who is reputed to have tipped all those who displeased him over the side and down into the valley.

Owen took the opportunity to visit some small vineyards, including the famous Châteauneuf du Pape area. Because I was an English visitor, the proprietor allowed me to buy a few bottles of White Châteauneuf, which I was told was bottled and sent only to the Hilton Hotel in London's Park Lane. There wasn't a large yield and the Hilton nabbed the lot, except my two bottles. I kept them for many years and when opened they offered the best white wine I've ever drunk.

The holiday was over and it was with much sadness that we said goodbye at the airport. The sadness was in part because we were separating and in part because we knew there was no future for us as romantic partners. We would always be the dearest of friends, but nothing more. We had moved on, but it was good that our friendship was intact. And little did I realise how significant Les Baux and the mossy fountain in Salon would be in the future.

Life was full and getting fuller. Work was burgeoning. I had another mini-series added to my workload at HTV. *Profile* was, as its title suggested, a look at the life and work of West Country characters. Meanwhile, *Women Only* was going from success to success and was even syndicated by Scottish TV.

Recording days were always a great joy; exciting people to greet, meet and chat with. I have a lovely photo of George Melly and myself in the studio. His loud suit was worse than usual and the director had requested me to ask of him the very personal question as to why he wore the clothes he did. In his gravelly voice he told me, 'Well dear, I happen to like them. They are my trademark. Mind you I'd be very careful not to sit down at the seaside in this one in case someone paid thruppence [three old pennies] and sat on me!' For the uninitiated, George's wide-stripe suits looked as though they were made out of deck-chair canvas.

I also met Wynford Vaughn Thomas, a revered broadcaster, and we had a laugh over his famous remark made at a royal review of the fleet. There was a suggestion that Wynford might just have had a wee drop before he went on air. After a rather banal comment that 'the Fleet was all lit up' he continued by saying that Her Majesty the Queen Mother was wearing 'an off the hat face' instead of the other way round. He swore to me that he hadn't had a drink or three beforehand.

In one of the *Women Only* programmes, I was scheduled to do an interview on corrective and cosmetic dentistry. After the interview, the dentist asked me why I'd not had anything done to my two front teeth. They leaned slightly backwards and had a groove across them, probably caused by a childhood illness affecting them while they were growing. As a youngster, I'd had a great deal of dentistry, during the course of which I'd had to wear a plate to enlarge my upper jaw. There had also been several painful extractions, and I was dead scared of visits to the dentist, so that's why I'd never done anything about my front teeth. Having confided my fears to my guest dentist, he persuaded me to visit his surgery in Nailsworth, just south of Stroud. I did have the teeth seen to and it made a world of difference. I had a habit, of which I was almost unaware, of covering my mouth with my hand when I smiled, because of the teeth. Now, with my beautiful new teeth, I could really flash a smile.

One of the most fascinating people to come onto *Women Only* in 1974 was Jan Morris. On the fly leaf of her book *Conundrum*, was written, 'It is now public knowledge that James Morris, the author of *Venice, Oxford, Pax Britannica, Heaven's Command,* and many other books, has undergone a sex change and is now Miss Jan Morris.' Jan had won innumerable awards for her writing, had been married and was the father of four children. She maintained a relationship with her wife in what she called a 'family bond of passionate friendship'. Her book discussed the tangled meanings of transsexualisation. It was a searingly honest account of how she came to terms with her sexuality and of the appalling operations she had to endure to put herself into what she considered her 'right body'. In the seventies no surgery was available in England and Jan had to go to a Dr B— in Casablanca. He specialised in transsexual surgery and unhappy people from all over the world flocked to his clinic. I would have liked Jan whatever sex she had been. She empathised with me and we exchanged Christmas cards and postcards for several years.

The West Country is a swinging place once you get to know what's on and where and I went to many thoroughly enjoyable events. At the Bristol Arts Centre, I'd met a very interesting couple who staged recitals at their beautiful home at Auton Dolwells near Taunton. What had started out as a thank-you performance from some grateful actor, who had been given bed and board hospitality by Bryan Catley and Tom Cassidy, had turned into a regular festival. I went to their sixth, which was a solo performance by the actor Marius Goring, who usually played tough Germanic types in films. The evening was dedicated to the 150th anniversary of the death of Lord Byron. As I was a Byron fan and also greatly admired Marius, the evening was to be a double treat. A champagne buffet supper was thrown in, and all for £3. For several years I went to super, magical events there and saw artists such as Judi Dench, Barbara Jefford, Richard Pascoe and Barbara Leigh Hunt. I've never lost my respect for the magic I find in theatre and meeting these stars was a great treat for me. I suppose it's like a lad meeting his football hero or a girl meeting some male heartthrob from a pop group or a television series.

In 1975 I had a bear named after me. Bristol Zoo enjoyed an enviable reputation for rearing 'babies' in captivity. On 19 March (the coldest day of the year) a four-month-old baby bear got her first taste of snow and was officially christened. HTV had run a competition for children to name the baby and to my delight a large number wished to call the bear after me and 'Jan' had come out as the overall winner. 'Jan' was a trifle short, so a decision was made to couple the baby's name with that of her mother Nina, and 'Janina' was the result. They will be grown now, perhaps with children of their own but I wonder if Simon Monks and Kenneth and Rebecca Milliner will remember coming to the zoo to meet Janina and me?

Women Only was now five years old; *Report West* was hugely popular, but I was getting restless. I'd seen researchers and producers come and go on *Women Only* and felt that as the longest serving member of the team, I probably cared for and knew more about the programme than those who passed through the studio on short-term contracts. My interviews were chosen by the researcher or the producer and I had no say in the overall shape of the programme. I wanted to be more involved in decision making. I made noises but no one listened. However, I did nothing pro-active about moving on because I was predominantly happy with my working life.

In 1976, not only was I working on seven regular programmes a week, but also from time to time took part in short series of a current affairs nature. I was obviously of value to HTV and I was looking for some recognition of this. I knew that Bruce was on staff and was also earning more than I was. I desperately wanted security and plucked up courage to ask that I should either be put on the staff payroll or have my contract salary substantially increased. Neither request was granted.

I wasn't sure whether my request fell on stony ground because I'd upset someone in the top hierarchy at HTV. There had been a black-tie dinner at the studio, after which I was invited for coffee by one of the management. I assumed the invitation was to take coffee in his office and discuss my request. Instead he asked if I would give him a lift to the hotel in which he stayed during the week, and we'd have coffee there. Bristol is hilly and the hotel was on a split level. I parked the car and we entered the building at basement level, taking the lift to the ground floor and the coffee shop. There were many members of HTV staff in the bar and they saw the two of us together as my 'host' went to reception. He collected his keys and I felt uneasy. Uneasy, not because I couldn't deal with the situation but because it was one in which I didn't wish to find myself. What could I do? Yes, we could discuss business in his room but I'd rather have had the discussion in the lobby. Suffice to say, I didn't stay long, took the lift to the basement by-passing the ground floor, and drove home ready for an evening out with a friend.

The next morning, gossip was rife in the studio. Because I hadn't been seen leaving, the HTV staff made a very wrong assumption. I was furious. I don't mind being hung for what I've done but not for what I haven't. I immediately went to my news boss, Ron Evans, and told him the whole story. Of course, he believed me but there was nothing we could do to scotch the rumours, especially as the gentleman in question had something of a reputation.

I wasn't actively looking for other work, but Fate stepped in and played a hand. First of all I had a phone call from Terry Dobson, the editor of *Pebble Mill At One* – a popular lunchtime magazine programme transmitted from the lobby of the BBC building in Birmingham. Terry wanted me to join the team and was prepared to come down to Bristol for a meeting. I also had an offer from BBC Scotland to join Donny B MacLeod (who also worked on *Pebble Mill*) and Derek Cooper (a well-known wine and food connoisseur) in presenting a new series called *The Food Programme.*

I haven't often been 'head-hunted' in my career, but it is an extremely flattering experience. If people other than your current employers want you, you have value and worth. It was heady stuff. Money didn't really enter the equation. Terry was offering £1,000 a year more than HTV, but it would necessitate my having to stay in Birmingham during the week. He was prepared to pay expenses for a short while and then I was on my own with travelling and renting somewhere, so the extra cash would be eroded.

Terry Dobson took me to lunch at Harvey's in Bristol and at the end of lunch I was in a huge dilemma. Would I give up my relatively safe existence at HTV and go for exposure on a programme that went out nationwide? Perhaps it was a feeling that I was taken for granted at HTV despite the good ratings and the ever-increasing popularity of *Women Only*. Perhaps there was a subliminal feeling that I might make 'the big time' with national exposure. I really can't be sure.

I left HTV in June and was gratified to read a piece in the local press entitled 'Hard to replace'. A 'spokesman' for the company indicated that I had an excellent rapport with the viewers and for the time being they would be trying out new faces and I would not be replaced for some time. It may have run its course, as programmes do, but *Women Only* didn't survive for much longer than a year after I left.

During the summer of 1976 I was busy filming inserts in Scotland for *The Food Programme*. I remember my very first encounter with the gentle Scottish lady who'd originally phoned me at HTV. Jeannie Hodge is one of the world's really good people. She'd had polio as a young girl and needed a calliper on one leg. This didn't stop her from working like a Trojan and getting about like a whirling dervish. She was also one of the most efficient production assistants you'd ever hope to meet. Everyone loved Jeannie; her warmth and her smile lit up everything around her and nothing was ever too much trouble. Jeannie met me at Glasgow Airport and we drove north for a couple of hours to Loch Crinan. We liked each other immediately and as we drove, she filled me in on the programme.

I'd never been further than Glasgow and found the scenery on our journey north quite breathtaking. We arrived at Crinan and I hardly had time to unpack my case before changing and being rushed up onto the hotel roof to start filming. The roof was flat and the surrounding wall had crenelations resembling a castle. With filming, one is always at the mercy of the weather and as it was in our favour, Mike had decided to shoot. I was to interview a chef about the secrets of a dish called Scallops Henry Morgan. The scallops were cooked in Veuve Cliquot Champagne and nothing less would do. I have to say, the finished dish was splendid but I'd rather have drunk than eaten the champagne! So there I sat in solitary splendour, scoffing the scallops, against the backdrop of the most incredible sunset as the sun sank over the loch.

The next day, we drove to the Galley of Lorne to do a piece about the Black Velvet Festival. This was an excuse for a feast of oysters washed down with Black Velvet, which is Champagne and Guinness. Again, what a waste of Champagne. But it was great fun and I remember getting sunburnt. Sunburn in Scotland! When the sun shines on the West Coast of Scotland, it beats many a Mediterranean hot spot. When the proceedings were well underway, the Laird of the surrounding area tapped the microphone and drew our attention. He gave out some rubbish about an explosion in the area. We thought he'd either indulged in too much Black Velvet or had sunstroke. However, when we returned to our hotel at Crinan, we were amazed to see the pier, perfectly symmetrical when we'd left in the morning, was now leaning at a crazy angle. The story was that some fishermen had dredged up an unexploded shell in their fishing net. As there was no bomb disposal team in the area, the navy came to the rescue. They carefully transported the shell from the fishermen's net and slowly lowered it down over the side of the pier. Telling all the bystanders to take cover behind the sea wall, they detonated the shell. (Even I know that explosions magnify in water.) The pier creaked, groaned and slid sideways and a local wag stood up and asked the commanding officer if his name was Captain Mainwaring of *Dad's Army* fame.

The Food Programme was partly looking into the way foods were raised, produced, or made, and partly us eating our way around hostelries of Scotland from the highest to the lowest. When we visited restaurants, Donny and Derek were the most superb company as both were good raconteurs and very witty. We had some great times together and the two of them often made my face ache with laughter. How I wish I'd had a small recording machine to make a collection of their stories. I think they used to try and out-do one another in making me laugh. At other times, we'd be off in different parts of Scotland filming inserts for the programme. I remember one of Donny's on the making of black pudding. It's a dish I don't particularly like but, after seeing Donny with his arm up to the elbow in blood, it put me right off.

I did some filming with Bird's Eye in Norfolk. You wouldn't believe the precision that goes in to picking a crop of peas at just the right time. Men with walkie talkies are all over the place; it's like a scene from an American movie. The whole process of harvesting is run like a military operation. There is a count-down to 'action'. At the designated moment, huge machines swing into life harvesting the delicate crop without damage. I couldn't believe it when I saw a baby rabbit come out through the threshing arm, obviously frightened but unscathed. As it had been separated from its mother and was too small to survive on its own, I insisted that we put it in a box and, at the end of filming, visit the local vet. Whether the vet found it a home or gave it a chop behind the ears as we left, I don't know, but I felt I'd done my bit for nature.

We devoted a whole programme to the way the wealthy Georgians ate and dressed. The venue was Rothay Manor at Ambleside in the Lake District. Bronwen Nixon, the proprietress, regularly held evenings where the guests would dress in costume appropriate to the period of the food they would be consuming. We filmed all the preparations in the kitchen during the day and I couldn't believe the richness of the food, nor the quantity. Items such as sugar demonstrated that you were a man of means, and the desserts were among the most sickly I've ever encountered. I wasn't surprised to learn that the women wore little velvet patches on their faces to hide their spots. In the evening, I was kitted out in Georgian dress and sat and dined with the other guests. In the course of conversation I learned many things, including the fact that you can always tell whether silver is Georgian by its warmth. Georgian silver is pure, and soft and warm and velvety to the touch. Later silver is mixed with different alloys and definitely has a much colder feel to it. Bronwen was a lovely hostess and, despite catering for three dozen people, was totally helpful during all the filming. Some years later, I picked the morning paper off the mat and was reading the front page as I walked back to my kitchen. There was a report of a murder in the Lake District, and as I read on, I was horrified to discover the victim was Bronwen.

By the autumn of 1976 I was working on *Pebble Mill* from Monday to Thursday, sometimes flying up to Scotland on a Friday for filming and studio recordings of *The Food Programme*, and sometimes getting back to my home in Bristol for the weekend.

My colleagues on *Pebble Mill* were all easy to get along with. Initially, Terry Dobson had looked upon me as a replacement for Marion Foster, but she had become popular with the viewers and a decision was made to use the two of us. Donny B MacLeod (he was referred to in his native Scotland as Donny B) I already knew and liked and the other members of the team were David Seymour and the strikingly handsome Bob Langley. Bob tended to be given all the outdoor material. David was our intellectual, Donny got many of the book reviews and most of the personality interviews and we two women were interchangeable. We were definitely at the bottom of the pecking order.

Marion and I got on well together and, as both of us had to maintain homes in London and Bristol respectively, to economise we joined forces and rented a one-bedroom studio apartment. The deal was we alternated having the bed one week and the put-u-up the next. The British appear to be reticent about discussing money matters but after a while the two of us discovered that we were being paid almost half what the men were getting. As if that weren't bad enough, Donny was flown down from Aberdeen weekly and both he and Bob were put up in the Strathallen Hotel at the BBC's expense. This wasn't the first and certainly not the last time I encountered sexual discrimination within the television industry. Did the hierarchy assume most of us had husbands to keep us and we were only working for 'pin money' with no need to earn a proper living? After a few months, Marion and I took a brave pill and, feeling there might be safety in numbers, the two of us had a meeting with Terry in which we pointed out the injustice of our salaries compared with those of the men, plus the fact that we had to run our homes and pay for accommodation in Birmingham. Mr Dobson's answer: 'Ladies, if you don't like it, there's the door.' There was nothing we could do about it. Terry was the boss and what he said went. So we stayed.

From every angle, *Pebble Mill* was not an easy programme on which to work. For a start, it was transmitted from the big glass lobby of the studio complex. This made it notoriously difficult to light. The poor old lighting men would set the programme at around 10 a.m., when the world was grey and they needed every light they could get. By the time we went on air, the sun would break through and we would be sweltering under the over-bright lamps. On one occasion, Marion's hair was singed by the heat! We worked in temperature extremes. One minute you'd be baking hot inside, then you grabbed a coat, and ran round the back of the building to do a gardening piece or a programme link. The lobby was long and narrow and often you'd be halfway through a piece to camera on autocue when the camera would start to recede as it was pulled down to the other end of the 'studio'. I made a golden rule that my script was always to hand, even if I had to sit on it, so I wouldn't be left high, dry and stranded. I didn't bargain on it ever being eaten! I once had to do an item in the *Mill* 'garden' with three goats. They will eat anything – and they did; my script.

Everyone had to work hard. To fill an hour every lunchtime is no mean feat. The researchers worked flat out and often didn't have time to check out the guests adequately, or even make sure that a story would 'stand up'. The format of the show was: transmission at 1 p.m. followed by sandwiches and a glass of wine in a large room adjoining the editor's office. After the guests were despatched we had the programme meeting for the following day. I was always grateful whenever I was given a book review. Though I am a fast reader, I find it impossible to spot read so there was no quick option for me. I like to be thorough and didn't feel I could conduct an interview authoritatively with a writer if I hadn't done him or her the courtesy of reading the work in full. Often it was necessary to burn the midnight oil.

Sometimes there was a time restraint and it was impossible to do justice to a book. Then I would have to rely on the researcher's notes and line of questioning. This happened to me with the late Robert Morley. I asked a question and was very sweetly put down by him. The question was a nonsense and it showed I hadn't read the book from cover to cover. However, he was very forgiving and asked Terry Dobson's permission to take me to lunch. Had I asked, I doubt that an assent would have been forthcoming but Terry couldn't easily say no to Robert and off I went to lunch in Birmingham. I felt very honoured and it is one of many treasured memories from half a lifetime of interviews.

The actor Frank Finlay was in Birmingham playing Henry VIII in a Leslie Bricusse musical called *Kings and Clowns*. He was my guest for the programme and on visiting him in his dressing room, I was staggered when he warned me he might dry up. I truly believed he was joking. He was a star of stage, no stranger to television cameras, used to memorising scripts and coming under scrutiny from the audience. How could this confident man possibly suffer from nerves? But he did. A glazed look enters the eyes of one about to dry up. Having been warned by Frank, I recognised the signs, made a joke about it, got around it, and the interview proceeded to the satisfaction of all concerned – I think!

David Soul, from the American cops and robbers series *Starsky and Hutch*, visited the studio to promote his latest single. I didn't know a singing voice was one of his attributes and must say was pleasantly surprised not only at his vocal ability but at his courteousness.

I was warned that the actor Robert Hardy was tricky to deal with. All I can say is that he gave me a lovely interview and was utterly charming. I know I'm not a highly intellectual interviewer but in so many of the autographed books from my days at *Pebble Mill*, guests have commented on my ability to put them at their ease. To do this, you have to be familiar with your subject matter so that with a structured line of questioning, you gently lead your guest into portraying themselves in the best light. I may not always have achieved it, but I believe the interviewer should fade into the background, giving centre-stage to the guest. I did care about my guests and never wanted to see them 'stitched up'. I've had many a heated discussion with researchers and producers over not being tough enough with a guest. That isn't my way and that is why I could never be an aggressive current affairs or newspaper journalist. I don't like strangers intruding into my life and I won't do it myself. *Do as you would be done by.*

Some of the guests left me with distinctly unpleasant memories. I found the French singer Charles Aznavour fell far short of his reputation for Gallic charm and I found Andrew Lloyd-Webber a little difficult to handle. Andrew and his cello-playing brother had brought out a record called *Variations* – jazzed-up versions of many familiar classical pieces. Why I'd been given the interview, I don't know. Marion was the music expert on our team but that day she had been given a fashion interview. I know quite a bit about fashion and had been given the music piece. It was perverse, as we were both struggling. I am always happy to admit my ignorance of a subject and did so with Andrew and Julian, asking for their guidance so that the interview would be favourable to them. Julian was charming, kind and helpful, Andrew less so. It pains me to have to pay a lot of money to see his shows but then he is highly creative even if he isn't, in my opinion, an agreeable person. Sometimes problems arose because of the entourage surrounding the major stars. Once you got through the 'minders' many of the stars themselves were normal, approachable and very nice.

Sometimes the researchers would brief us as to how awkward, difficult or unpleasant they'd found our potential guests. You'd be prepared for the worst and then find an absolute pussycat. Perhaps it's because people get wound up before an appearance on television and it brings out their prickly side. I know I'm at my most aggressive when I'm wrong-footed or out of my depth.

One of the most embarrassing interviews I ever had to do was with the singer Andy Williams. He was in England for a concert tour and to promote his latest recording. But the main reason everyone wanted to interview him was because his ex-wife had been accused of shooting her lover, and as Terry Dobson despatched me to London, I was left in no doubt as to the line of questioning required. I was distinctly uncomfortable.

I presented myself at the reception desk at the Dorchester Hotel in Park Lane and asked to be put through to one of Mr Williams' aides. All knowledge of a pre-arranged interview was denied. We didn't have mobile phones in those days, so I had to queue and wait for one of the public ones in the hotel lobby. Obviously phone calls flew back and forth and finally I was told that Mr Williams would do the interview and I was to wait for him in reception. About half an hour later he arrived with a young woman draped over his arm! In the taxi going to the sound studio at Broadcasting House, I simply couldn't find a way around asking him the personal questions I'd been ordered to put to him. It was doubly difficult because of the young lady accompanying him. When we got to the studio, in desperation I owned up to the fact that my editor had given me instructions and I stood to lose my job if I didn't carry them through. Mr Williams acted like a true gentleman and did answer the awkward questions although, understandably, he was very guarded. It wasn't the best interview I've ever done, but I kept my job!

It was a joy to me to be able to interview so many people I admired and whose work I respected. But the highlight of my time at *Pebble Mill* was when I was alone in the office waiting for my guest of the day, the actor and film star Jim Dale. Donny McLeod, who usually did the major personality interview, was fog bound in Aberdeen and couldn't get down for the programme. One of the researchers came to the office and, as I was the only interviewer around, said, 'Jan, would you mind doing an extra interview today. The guest is Omar Sharif.' Mind! You must be joking. You couldn't see me for dust as I belted down the corridor for the pre-recorded interview. I had no research notes, but had read his autobiography *The Eternal Male* a few weeks earlier. Omar is a self-confessed gambling addict and needed to raise finance, so he did promotional work for board game manufacturers. Obviously the games had to be mentioned but I was let loose to interview my all-time heartthrob. I'd sat through *Lawrence of Arabia* and *Doctor Zhivago* so many times and leaned heavily on questions about the two films. Omar was everything I'd ever imagined and more; a total gentleman with the most mesmeric eyes and the sexiest voice imaginable.

He also came out with some rather surprising statements. He said, 'I don't want to be a film star any more . . . it gets in the way of a private life. I have no girlfriend, family or wife.' Mind you, he did appear to go on enjoying a bachelor existence and dated some beautiful women although I don't think he ever married again after the divorce from his first wife. He also gave his explanation of why men prefer the company of men: '. . . they (men) remain children and don't mature and become adults so they like to sit and talk to other men.' He's got something there – I also feel that in some ways men never grow up – women are a much more mature breed.

Because the interview was pre-recorded for transmission the following day, I was given that day off. When I got back to the studio, one of the researchers casually announced, 'Oh, by the way Jan, Omar Sharif phoned up to talk to you after the interview went out yesterday but we told him you'd got a day off.' Curses. It would have been lovely to have had a lunch date with him but by now he was far away on his promotion tour and

I would imagine never gave the interviewer at Pebble Mill another thought. Still, meeting him was a magic moment and I've got his book autographed, 'To Jan, with my love, Omar Sharif'. He could simply have put 'Best Wishes'! He didn't have to put 'love', did he?

As well as coping with our workload, we also had to deal with the requests, which came in thick and fast, for one or other of the team to attend a fête, a gala dinner, a charity event. Often the invitation would contain the line, 'We would only need Donny/Bob/David/Marion/Jan for half an hour.' What so many forgot was the travel time. We tended to keep our acceptances to within a reasonable radius of the *Pebble Mill* studios or to the area of our main domicile. One of the requests came from Leicester and it was to be judge on a Coal Board competition for their Annual Coal Flame Queen. The venue was a Holiday Inn and on arrival I noted how refreshingly different and pleasing was the decor in reception. On being greeted by the PR woman for the hotel, I made a complimentary comment and was told the designer was at the hotel that day and asked if I would like to meet him. I really didn't want to, but having made the comment it would have seemed churlish to refuse. And so Ezra Attia entered my life.

CHAPTER EIGHT

BBC RADIO 2

Ezra was an Israeli with a fiery temper. He was dark haired with brown eyes and exotic good looks. I should have read the warning signs when we were first introduced but, as so often in my life, I was blind to the staggeringly obvious. He was a total flirt and was used to getting his way with women. Our relationship was never anything but stormy and, from my point of view, very disruptive. We didn't even speak the same language. Although his English was extremely good, he was not familiar with its nuances. I remember one day uttering a throwaway remark about some decision we had to make and said, 'Oh well, beggars can't be choosers.' He saw red and shouted at me, 'I am not a beggar.' He had an air of mystery about him, hinting that he was engaged on some sort of secret business and could be recalled to Israel at a moment's notice.

He would sometimes come to my home in Bristol at weekends and at other times, I'd visit him at his apartment in the Holiday Inn near Heathrow. We had virtually nothing in common and my friends didn't feel comfortable with him. That should have made me start questioning our relationship, but it didn't.

We had only been dating for a few months, when he announced that he wanted me to meet his family and that we would be going to Israel for a visit. It had never entered my mind to go there and the prospect was exciting. Once I got over the initial shock of armed soldiers all over Tel Aviv, being

119

frisked when you entered most buildings, and seeing the beaches being swept for mines, I enjoyed the holiday very much. Like most things, you get used to this 'siege' mentality and within days I wasn't bothered by it. Ezra took me to Jerusalem but, as he wasn't really interested in its history, I don't think I got to see nearly as much as I should have done of that fascinating city. Bethlehem was very commercial but, despite this, I experienced a sense of awe when taken to the shrine that purports to be the actual birthplace of the Christ Child.

The Dead Sea was an amazing experience. You really cannot sink in it. In fact, you can't even float on your stomach; if you try, you automatically turn turtle and end up on your back. If you get any water in your mouth, it is excruciatingly bitter. When you get out, you must take a shower or the mineral salts dry into a crust on your skin and cause great irritation. While we were in the area, we visited Masada, the ancient mountaintop fortress on the western shore of the Dead Sea. The day was blisteringly hot, but I was determined to visit a site of such historic interest. Masada was the last Jewish stronghold during a revolt in Judaea in AD 66–73. Besieged by the Romans for a year, nearly all the inhabitants killed themselves rather than surrender. Today the site is an Israeli national monument.

I really liked Ezra's mother and sister, who welcomed me with open arms despite my being a Gentile. Ezra's father had died many years previously. I rather suspect his mother wanted grandchildren and didn't ever think her son would settle down, so I was a welcome diversion. I believe religion sits more lightly on the shoulders of a great many Israelis than it does on the traditional Jewish person. I felt they were Israeli first and Jewish second. They were fiercely nationalistic.

When we returned from Israel, Ezra started making plans to move out of the hotel into his own apartment. By this time we were engaged, but the relationship was a stormy one. Heaven alone knows why I took the drastic step of selling my house in Bristol. It represented my security. But I was supposed to be getting married and moving into Ezra's beautiful apartment in

Top left: My father – Ivan Terrence Atkins – aged thirty. (I think he looks like the film star, Richard Todd.)

Top right: My mother – Hazel Louise Haysey – aged 21. Isn't she lovely!

Far left: Me – wide-eyed and innocent.

Far right: With my sister, Gillian Penelope. You can see she is a little tinker.

Below left: With Daphne and David Manly. Such was my puppy love, I dug worms for his fishing expeditions. Ugh!

Below right: With Mummy on her seventieth birthday – she's still beautiful.

1963: Modelling in New Zealand.

Above: 1963: Continuity announcing for the NZBC in Wellington. (The 'Galloping Gourmet' – Graham Kerr – is in the background.)

Left: 1963: Myrrhine in *Lysistrata*, Wellington, New Zealand.

Above: Newsreading for Channel Ten-10. Will you look at that microphone!

Right: Eloise in the Palace Theatre production of *Diplomatic Baggage*, Sydney, Australia. (With some of the extra pounds picked up on the Young Elizabethan Tour of the outback.)

Far left:
Metamorphosis!
After my car accident
(1967).

Left: Feline company
on a *Women Only*
programme, HTV
Bristol.

Above: Members of the Oxford
Playhouse under Frank Hauser's
direction (1968). From left:
Stephanie Beacham, Georgina
Ward, Nigel, me, Maggie Jones
and Joan Peart.

Left: I may be smiling for the
Press but all I wanted was a 'get
me out of here' ticket home –
I was so nervous.

Above: In the News Studio at the time of the Iranian Siege (1981). Please note the sumptuous News Desk!

Right: My Eric. (Red Arrows Familiarisation Flight, 1983.)

Proud mother with son.
(Jonathan, 1981.)

Below left: Patrick, Jonathan and me – our son was an absolute joy.

Below: Jonathan at 21 – he is a great chap and has the most beautiful smile.

Above: HTV days: Kate Adie, Don Mon, Michael Dennison and me. Don't ask what we were doing – judging something, I think.

Left: Pebble Mill: Donny B MacCleod, Marian Foster, Bob Langley, yours truly and David Seymour. They were a great bunch with which to work.

HTV's *Women Only:* With George Melly in his 'deckchair' suit.

Above: As a patron of the Duke of Westminster's Christmas Appeal (for the homeless), it was my task to host the Prime Minister, Margaret Thatcher. I met her many times and have the highest regard for her.

Left: Fooling around with the Goodies – or at least two of them!

British Broadcasting Corporation, Broadcasting House, London W1A 1AA
from the Chairman, George Howard

20th May 1982

My dear Jan

I think you must be collecting a record number of awards this year! Anyway, congratulations on the one you received this week from the Writers Guild of Great Britain.

I imagine you'll be collecting for another in September

Love

George.

Miss Jan Leeming,
c/o Man.Ed.Tel. News,
Room 6202,
Television Centre.

Left: George Howard, Chairman of the BBC, appeared to be a champion of mine. Sadly he died young and he wasn't around for me to turn to in 1987.

Above: Prince Charles, in his role as President of Business in the Community, shares a joke with me at the Cutler's Hall, Sheffield (November 1988).

Left: Royal Variety Performance (1985): HM The Queen, Michael Aspel, me, Russell Harty and Rolf Harris.

Right: With Jill Dando at a charity function for the Bone Marrow Trust.

Below: I sent this photo to Sir John and asked him to autograph it for me.

Below right: This letter, from Sir John Gielgud, was one of over 2,000 I received after the mugging in 1987.

Bottom: BBC Glasgow: with Paul Coia, Caron Keating and Eamonn Holmes, presenters on *The Garden Party*.

SIR JOHN GIELGUD

Feb. 17. 87.

Dear Miss Leeming

I was most horrified to read of your dreadful experience though relieved to see you looking comparatively like your usual self. I do hope you will have no ill results and that your weekend attackers may be brought to book. Don't dream of answering this brief note, but after our meeting at Lady Beaverbrook's I couldn't resist sending you a line of sympathy and appreciation.

Most sincerely,

John Gielgud

From left: With the Duchess of Gloucester and lovely Gina Fratini at a charity function.

Angela Rippon and myself: she was probably giving me advice – she is much wiser than I am.

19th February 1985

Jan Leeming,
▓▓▓▓▓▓▓▓▓▓
▓▓▓▓▓▓▓▓▓▓
▓▓▓▓▓▓▓▓▓▓

Dear Jan,

Sunday February 10th, Main Evening News 14.1 million, third equal in the BBC charts. Congratulations, keep up the good work.

Yours sincerely,

Ron Neil

DAILY MAIL

New girl Jan in the BBC news

By MARTIN JACKSON
TV Editor

BBC Television has signed up another girl newsreader, just 24 hours after Fran Morrison made her debut on BBC 2's Newsnight.

She is Jan Leeming, a Radio 2 disc jockey, who has been presenting the early hours programme You and the Night and the Music. She begins a four-month TV news contract on March 1. She will read the 7.30 news bulletins and late night summaries.

DAILY STAR

FRIDAY, FEBRUARY 1st, 1980   8p   Printed in London   (10p C.I.s, Eire)   ★

HOT NEWS!
Angela signs off at the Beeb

Jan . . . stepping in as newsreader

Angela . . . six months off the screen

By BRIAN WESLEY

BBC glamour girl Angela Rippon signed off as newsreader for six months last night — and handed over to another pretty face.

The latest recruit is 27-year-old Jan Leeming, who will deliver some of the shorter bulletins on both BBC channels for four months this summer.

At tea time last night Angela read her last news until the summer.

But dark-haired Jan is not replacing her, the BBC insisted yesterday.

A spokesman explained: "Angela is on the second year of a two-year contract, under which she reads the news for a year and spends the rest of the time working on other radio and television programmes."

Stint

Jan, a divorce, is on holiday in France and has not been told her temporary assignment has been confirmed.

She is currently an announcer and late-night disc jockey on BBC Radio 2.

But she will be best known to television viewers for her three-year stint as one of the interviewers on the Birmingham-based lunchtime magazine, Pebble Mill at One.

This week Glasgow-born Fran Morrison made her debut as news-reader-cum-reporter on BBC 2's late-night current affairs show

Examples of press coverage during my early days newsreading for the BBC.

Masterminds' Kate (left) and Jan

Salute these siege girls

AFTER all the tension of the brilliant BBC1 live coverage of the Iran Embassy siege was over, I suddenly realised that the whole thing had been "masterminded" for our screens by two girls—on the spot reporter Kate Adie and newsreader Jan Leeming.

Congratulations, ladies. It was a very difficult job extremely well done.

(Mrs) J WHITWELL, Leicester.

DAILY Mirror

Wednesday, July 2, 1980   10p

The job's yours, Jan

By KEN IRWIN

VIEWERS' favourite Jan Leeming has landed a regular TV newsreading job with the B.B.C.

She was given a two-year contract yesterday after a successful trial run.

For the past four months 26-year-old Jan has been filling in for Angela Rippon, Richard Baker and other news-readers while they took holidays.

Viewers were impressed by her style.

Alan Protheroe, editor of BBC-TV news, said last night: "We have had

ANGELA: "Different."

a very good public reaction to her appearances.

"Her voice is exactly right and she has a very good personality."

Delighted Jan said: "I don't see this as a Women's Lib thing. I think I'm quite different from Angela and Anna Ford.

"I don't see the day when TV will have only women newsreaders. But it is nice to be taken seriously and prove that you can do a job—just as well as men."

While Jan will now be a regular reader, Richard Whitmore is to combine newscasting and reporting work.

Shake-up on the Nine O' Clock News

29.6.81

LEEMING . . . WEEKENDS **BAKER . . . EARLY EVENING** **STUART . . . MIDDAY**

By CHARLES CATCHPOLE

THE BBC is planning a big shake-up of its TV news readers.

Some of the most famous faces on the Nine O'Clock _____

Stuart, TV's first black woman newscaster, who joins BBC TV from Radio Two in August. The BBC's midday bulletin is also likely to be _____

Left: Drama on the *Nine O'Clock News.*

Below: For once the papers got it right. I hadn't been informed. It seems 'par for the course' these days.

LONDON NEW STANDARD 30.6.81

Newsreader Jan 'not told of shuffle'

by Sue Summers

NEWSREADER of the Year Jan Leeming has not been consulted over plans to use her for weekends only in the big reshuffle of BBC Television news.

Her hu____ announcer___ today: " I___ out of the ___ " She ha__ body abou__ lined what__ nobody ha__ is what w__

" And Jan hasn't told them what she wants to do either."

Miss Leeming, who has been on two months' maternity leave, returns to the BBC on Friday.

Leaked

The man behind the changes — the new editor of BBC TV news, Peter Woon— said today ___ to Miss Leem-

from Alan Protheroe six months ago, is planning a complete reorganisation of the BBC's news bulletins.

They are considered rather staid by Corporation executives.

Details of his plans have been leaked to Fleet Steet in an anonymous letter headed on BBC TV News paper.

The changes include plans _____ bulletin to have _____ newsreaders. ___t some of the ___s will move __O'Clock News _ill disappear

JAN LEEMING

Left: Typically 'over the top' emotive headlines. No one was ecstatically pleased but we weren't working ourselves into a frenzy.

FURY OVER THE BBC'S 9 O'CLOCK SHUFFLE

By PETER BOND

TOP BBC TV newsreaders **Richard Baker** and **Jan Leeming** are to be **sacked** from the **Nine O'Clock News.**

The axe will also fall on four other big-name presenters of the programme — Kenneth Kendall, Peter Woods, John Edmunds and Richard Whitmore.

Last night anger erupted over the sacked six, who are victims of a major shake - up of BBC news bulletins.

Jan Leeming—named Newsreader of

ANOTHER Sun EXCLUSIVE

the Year just a few weeks ago—is said to be bitterly upset.

The attractive 39-year-old returns to television on Friday after having a baby.

Both she and Baker will stay with the BBC as newscasters.

Demotion

But colleagues see their removal from the No. 1 bulletin as demotion. The reshaped Nine-O'Clock programme—to start in September—

Continued on Page Two

Jan Leeming . . bitterly upset

Top: With Bob Whitting at the Hairdressing Function for which he took me from 'mouse brown' to blue black with aubergine highlights! (New Zealand, 1962.)

Top right: How fashions change! It isn't quite all hair – there's a shadow on the photograph.

Above: Bob leaning on a car – I don't think he could drive.

Below: My lovely friend, Michael Laurence (Australia 1966).

Right: A publicity photo of Michael that I couldn't resist – doesn't he look like George Chakiris, the American actor who starred in *West Side Story*?

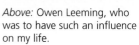

Above: Owen Leeming, who was to have such an influence on my life.

Left: 1961 and marriage to John Staple. Our best man, sister Mandy, John, the reluctant bride and Gillian.

Above: With Hayo in Australia – two very happy people.

Right: Marriage to Patrick Lunt (Ledbury, Hertfordshire, 1980). Dress by Gina Fratini – off-the-peg!

Above: Jeremy Gilchrist (inset). 1972 and our wedding
reception at home in Bristol. Another Gina Fratini dress,
which I wore to Ascot oodles of years later.

Left: Penn Church. Blessing service for the wedding to
Chris Russell (1977). (Now, I can see the body language!)

Above: Outside the mairie (town hall) after our wedding in Alleins, Provence. From left: Mireille Loisin, Eric, me, Owen Leeming, Mark and Caron Steenson and my son, Jonathan.

Below: The looks of love.

Highgate. I was splitting my life between Birmingham, Bristol and Highgate and it was very wearing.

I enjoyed most of my work with *Pebble Mill* but I didn't relish the outside jobs in the winter. I have poor circulation and feel the cold badly. My fingers go white and I lose sensation in my toes. When you are that cold, it is difficult to function properly. We had one particularly sadistic director on the programme who'd be sitting comfortably in a warm production cabin while directing the poor interviewer to re-do a shot over and over again. The worst experience of all was the Boat Show at the NEC. Poor Marion nearly drowned in one of the lakes. Then it was my turn. I was doing a piece to camera from the prow of a boat (a gin palace, to be exact!) and was made to do it again and again as the boat moved round in a circle under the waterfall in the middle of the lake. When the director finally called a wrap, my waterproof clothing had actually stuck to the prow where the moisture from the fountain had frozen between my behind and the wooden deck. I took forever to thaw out and the pain that comes as circulation returns to one's digits was excruciating.

It was coming up to the end of the *Pebble Mill* run and the long summer break. Terry Dobson wanted to see me and I thought it would be to discuss the next twelve-month contract. Was I in for a shock. Terry told me he was not renewing my contract but complimented me on my professionalism. I felt, from what he said, that he didn't like me. To use a vulgar expression, I was totally gobsmacked. I thought I'd been doing a good job but obviously not good enough. Perhaps my personal angst, over the difficult relationship with Ezra, had affected my performance. The news shattered me.

I was given an unexpected couple of days off and, being very upset, went down to the flat in Highgate, looking for a sympathetic shoulder to cry on. Ezra wasn't expecting me and, as I hung up my coat, I saw a pair of woman's boots and a decidedly feminine umbrella in the cloakroom. He had some plausible story but it really was the thin end of the wedge for me. The writing was on the wall. I was being let down on all fronts and found it very difficult to return to *Pebble Mill* and concentrate on work for the last few weeks of the run.

Recently I came across an old newspaper cutting in which it was stated that I would be leaving *Pebble Mill* and that the editor, Terry Dobson, said the parting of the ways was 'an entirely amicable arrangement'. I can assure you it was anything but, and I've often wondered how and why I got on the wrong side of Terry. I am not a 'Yes' girl or the sort of person who will allow myself to be pushed around. If I think I have right on my side, I will stand up for myself. After years of making the same mistake, I now realise you should keep your head down, do your work and make as little fuss as possible. That way you'll stay in a job!

I was working very hard and the emotional strain of my relationship with Ezra was taking its toll. As a freelancer, you can never afford to turn down work – not that I would have wanted to, in most cases. The gardener on *Pebble Mill* was a lovely chap called Peter Seabrook and I was invited to join him in presenting the *1978 Chelsea Flower Show*. It was a real treat to be able to see and film exhibits with no crowds around. Even on Members' Day, I find the show too crowded for my liking and no longer attend.

When *Pebble Mill* came to an end, I had no choice but to go to Highgate. My house in Bristol had been sold months earlier in anticipation of a long-term relationship with Ezra. That was now looking less and less likely. Our relationship was little short of disastrous. Within a couple of weeks, and while he was watching a World Cup match on television, I packed my belongings and left. I now think of that episode as funny, but it wasn't at the time. Ezra was so glued to the television, he was totally unaware that I'd gone. Men!

Initially I went to stay with a girlfriend, but it was only a temporary solution. I was at rock bottom: no home, no job and only a few thousand pounds' profit in the bank from the sale of the house in Bristol. And then a fairy godmother came to my aid in the shape of my father's sister. My Aunt Marjorie had been widowed a few years previously and, when she heard of my plight, offered me a home for as long as it took to sort my life out.

I really enjoyed my months with her. It was lovely to have someone mothering me, cooking for me, and someone to laugh with at the end of the day. Looking for work is a soul-destroying business for anyone but, in the cut-throat world of broadcasting, it's even worse. I wrote dozens of letters to television and radio companies and received very few replies.

Auntie Marjorie and I were sharing a bottle of wine one evening when the phone rang. Among the many letters I'd written asking for work was one to BBC Radio 2. The phone caller was Jimmy Kingsbury, who was in charge of the newsreaders and continuity announcers for the station. He invited me to an audition the very next day.

I passed the audition with flying colours and was offered a one-year contract in London. I didn't mind working on radio rather than television at all and was absolutely delighted to have a job. As continuity announcers, our job entailed making the announcements between programmes, reading the news bulletins on the hour and spending one working day a week writing and recording the 'trailers' for future programmes. We worked on a shift system, which could be early morning to lunch time, lunch time till mid-evening or mid-evening until close down.

Sometimes we'd be rostered onto a late shift with an early one the next day. This necessitated staying in the Langham, which was a far cry from the luxury five-star hotel it is today. When it belonged to the BBC, it comprised offices, studios and a corridor given over to very rudimentary accommodation. The rooms were large and cold, with floors covered in linoleum. There would be a washbasin, a mirror and a bed that looked as though it had been requisitioned from the army. On the first occasion I had an 'overnight' I was horrified to discover that the bathroom facilities were at some distance from our rooms. Some years previously, I had become worried about an aspect of my health and in the course of investigations it was discovered that I have three kidneys. It isn't quite as uncommon as one would think, but unless you have any trouble with them, you are not likely to find out. Because of this situation, I need to visit the loo more frequently than most and it makes outside filming a nightmare for me if there are no 'facilities'. At the Langham, I really didn't want to be padding around in my night-attire, especially as some folk were quite convinced the place was haunted. I don't know whether the guys did it to wind us up, but we were often regaled with tales of ghostly 'sightings'. I didn't like my nights in the Langham, not least because the beds were so uncomfortable and I could never get warm. The only advantage to an 'overnight' was breakfast in the canteen. Terry Wogan always poked fun at the liquid refreshment which was, admittedly, awful, but the cooked breakfasts were superb.

The late seventies saw the rise of the 'personality' DJ on Radio 1 – people such as Tony Blackburn, Dave Lee Travis, Simon Bates, Andy Peebles and Noel Edmonds. The latter used to delight in trying to make me 'corpse', a theatrical term for sending you up and trying to get you to laugh when you shouldn't. He wouldn't do it if there were really serious news but if the mood was relatively light, you never knew what Noel would come out with when you handed back to his programme. Eventually a missive came from on high instructing him to cease this frivolity! Nowadays, banter and repartee appear to be actively encouraged, almost overdone. Everything has become too matey for my liking.

Life was beginning to stabilise and to be fun again. I was negotiating to buy a small house in Buckinghamshire not too far from my mother and sister. I'd been approached by Bryan Skilton, a colleague from my Bristol BBC days, and asked to front a new series of programmes to be recorded in Plymouth. *Zodiac and Co.* had an interesting format. Very often with a new idea, a series will have a local showing. Then, if it is successful, it might go nationwide. This was the hope with *Zodiac*. However, to begin with, it was only for transmission in the West Country and our guests had to either live in the area or have an association with it. The programme comprised a team of an astrologer, a graphologist and a palmist. Julia Parker, whom I knew well from *Women Only*, was our astrologer. In advance of the programme, she would be given the guest's birth date, time and place; Albert Hughes, the graphologist, would receive a sample of handwriting, and Lori Reid, our palmist, got a palm print. The three team members would have to reduce their deductions to one and a half minutes on camera, in which they delivered their findings about the guest. The guest would remain in a room hidden away from the panel, but a camera would record their reactions, which were shown to the audience at home. After the prognostications, the guest would join me and the team to discuss the findings.

It was amazing how accurate the team could be, often seeing facets to the guest about which the public were completely ignorant. One of the biggest surprises was John Cleese. Our experts saw his other side, a morose one, and when he came on stage to meet the panellists, he admitted that they had seen sides of him that were hitherto unknown and that their assessments were perfectly accurate.

After several series *Zodiac and Co.* did get on to network television. The format was changed, so was the panel and the presenter became Michael Aspel. Of course, I was upset that I didn't transfer with the programme but if I had to lose it to anyone, I can't think of anyone better than Michael, whom I like and admire greatly. I felt the changes in the programme format were not for the better, however, and the show was to have a very short life.

Apart from its stars, in my opinion the BBC will always find ways of getting more work for less money out of everyone. In 1979, BBC Radio 2 was about to become a round-the-clock-operation. Who would want to do the graveyard shift? No one in their right mind, or at least not unless it was for a lot of money. The decision was made that for three of the night-shift hours a programme called *You and the Night and the Music* (YATNAM) would fill the gap. It was to be fronted by the already existing announcers, of which I was one. Although I was delighted to be getting some experience presenting a show, we had almost no say in its content. And as for needle-time (what was paid to record companies for the use of their music) forget it! If my memory serves me correctly, we were allowed to play about three tracks in three hours, for which the BBC would have to pay. The rest of the music was either out of copyright or paid for in a package.

However, I wasn't going to let this small hurdle deter me and offered to present a series looking at the old Hollywood musicals, of which I was a great fan. Titles such as *Seven Brides for Seven Brothers, Oklahoma!, Carousel, Flower Drum Song* and *Fanny,* filled me with enthusiastic joy. With so little needle-time, I was left to tell the story with the most sparse of musical illustration, but I read up on the stories, the production and the stars and wrote myself a reasonable script. We built up a dedicated audience for the *YATNAM* shows and each of us had our own followings. I remember Sheila Tracey, who'd been a member of the Ivy Benson all-female band and obviously had a preference for the big band sound, gained an audience of long-distance truck drivers and was their 'pin-up'.

Our regular listeners were insomniacs, shift workers, old people and many who were simply lonely in the wee small hours of the night and listened to the radio for comfort. I feel radio is a much more intimate medium than television. It is just you through the microphone communicating with the audience. In television there are so many people manning cameras, lighting, sound and running around all over the place, real intimacy is impossible.

I enjoyed my *YATNAM* nights but physically found them a total killer. It can't be easy for any human being to work through the night, as it goes against our circadian rhythm, but at least if you get a run at it, a few weeks on and a few weeks off, your body can make an effort to adjust. We didn't have this luxury and were mixing night shifts with every other shift. I, for one, cannot sleep to order. I rarely managed to get to sleep before going onto the *YATNAM* shift and know I looked a wreck in the morning. The show was on air from 2–5 a.m. Often I'd be sitting in Broadcasting House reception waiting for my car home (the one luxury we were afforded) when Dave Lee Travis would enter the building. He usually made some appropriately dismissive remark as to how awful I looked. But as we were friends, I forgave him. And he was correct.

Although I enjoyed my radio job, I couldn't see it going anywhere and was always on the lookout for other opportunities. My sister worked in the Maidenhead area, where she was constantly rubbing shoulders with personalities such as Terry Wogan, Ernie Wise and Mike Parkinson. In conversation with the latter, she mentioned my experience and my desire to move on. Mike very kindly agreed to meet me for lunch to see if he could give me any helpful advice. Part of success in the world of broadcasting is to have a good agent. It is a vicious circle: the artists need an agent to help them succeed and the agent doesn't really want the artists until they have succeeded and are making money, preferably lots of it. So how do you break into the magic circle? Mike was with the extremely prestigious agency International Management Group (IMG) run by Mark MacCormack and originally set up to foster the interests of international sporting stars. They had branched out and opened an entertainment arm, of which Mike was a client. He was a good host and made helpful suggestions about the way forward in my career, but in no uncertain terms told me that his agents wouldn't be interested. I simply wasn't *big* enough and certainly didn't have the income to attract them. A few years later, their tune was somewhat different.

John Dobson had come back into my life for the occasional date and I also went out with several other interesting men. I was earning a living and enjoyed the work but didn't like the night shifts. My body says it needs to be tucked up in bed getting at least eight hours sleep, not trying to keep awake with cups of black coffee. So once again my yearning to be back in the sunshine of Australia came to the fore.

Michael Laurence and I hadn't kept in regular touch and because of his peripatetic life as an actor, chasing work and living in flats all over the place, I was never sure whether I had an up-to-date address for him. I reckoned that he might still have the same agent and rang her in Sydney. She told me where he was working and I phoned the studio straight away. We were able to talk and I asked if I could come and stay. His letter to me a few days later expresses his feelings accurately: knowing Michael I could hear his voice coming off the airmail paper ...'If the Pope himself had rung me I couldn't have been more surprised. When they told me there was a call for me on the studio phone, my first reaction was one of mild irritation. I thought "I wish people wouldn't ring me when I'm taping a show". Then BAMBAMALIKAZAM-WHOOSHWHEE AND POW! You'd have to be kidding wouldn't you?? After ... many years ... suddenly a phone call. My darling I couldn't be happier ... more delighted ... wonderfully surprised ... and just plain knocked out.' He went on to say that I could stay with him while finding my feet and yet again offered to pull out all the stops to help me get work.

It was May in England and winter in Sydney and as I wanted to visit in the Australian summer, needed to save the money for the fare, arrange leave with the BBC and fulfil several work commitments, we decided that I would plan my trip for September. I was very excited at both the prospect of returning to Australia and seeing Michael. A lot of water had gone under the bridge since his proposal of marriage and then his subsequent backing away from the prospect, but I still had a soft spot for him and, if I were honest, had a small hope that we might rekindle the flame between us.

I have an entry in my diary round about this time that says, 'Resisted temptation to fall for the charms of Patrick Lunt.' Patrick and I had been colleagues for almost a year and were often on the same shifts together. He would be in the News Suite (a grand name for a room no bigger than ten feet by ten feet) and I'd be in the Continuity Suite (which was bigger because it housed a large console and had to have room to accommodate guests) or vice versa. So we'd get plenty of time to chat. It also helped to keep you awake on the night shifts if you had someone to talk to.

As I was planning to go back to Australia, there was no way I wanted to become involved with anyone. Besides, I was having a pleasant time going out with different men, not being involved and preferring to keep it that way. There's definitely safety in numbers. Looking back on my diary I now see that Patrick's name was appearing more regularly than that of anyone else. He took me to the airport and I commented on his clean-shavedness, expressing my preference for his beard.

I left England on the evening of 4 September, arrived in Sydney at 7 a.m. on the 6th and the diary entry indicates that I was on the beach before midday with Michael and his little dog Biddy. At this time in his life, Michael had abandoned the acting profession and was writing scripts for film and television, so he was much more his own boss. He was able to make time to be with me. When he had to attend work meetings or go to the studio, I took the opportunity of catching up with people I hadn't seen since leaving in 1966. My first port of call was Carla Zampatti. She was already well on her way to phenomenal success in the fashion industry. Even though Hayo had been dead for thirteen years, we talked about him and again she stressed that he really had loved me, despite his roving eye. All those years later, it was still a comforting reassurance.

I also caught up with Kit Moore. I'd met her at a party in Sydney in the sixties and will never forget the amazement we both felt when we saw our host's bath full of ice and oysters. The expense in England would have been prohibitive but in Australia it was on a par to offering smoked salmon – good but not quite in the caviar class! Kit was a BBC-trained make-up artist who had come out to Australia on a £10 Migrant ticket. She was exceptionally good at her job and was doing very well. A couple of years after our initial meeting, Kit had returned to England for her marriage and asked me to be a bridesmaid. We'd lost touch in the intervening years but now we had a chance to renew our friendship. Kit had four children and a beautiful home with horses in the paddock and a swimming pool in the garden. She also had her career and on the surface appeared to have everything one could wish for. Not long after that, her marriage disintegrated and she was faced with the usual problems accompanying a break-up – the drastic reduction in one's standard of living, the downsizing, having to work full-time and still concentrate on rearing a family . . .

Michael hadn't seen his mother for a while and decided to drive up to Queensland for a visit. When I lived in Sydney, I'd had neither the time nor the money to go north, so the trip was very exciting. The route is beautiful and in parts you drive alongside the Pacific Ocean. Michael's mother, Jo, and I took to each other immediately. I suspect she hoped her son might at last be considering settling down. However, I knew differently. The few days we'd had together in Sydney had established that our relationship was to be purely platonic. This was Michael's choice. I make no bones about the fact that I still cared for him and had hoped the flame between us could have been fanned into something bigger, but it wasn't to be. This didn't stop us having a good time together.

Jo lived just south of Surfer's Paradise at a place called Tweed Heads. In England we have British Legion clubs; in Australia the equivalent are Services clubs. I couldn't believe my eyes when I read that Howard Keel was to be performing at the Tweed Heads club and begged Michael to take us. I was a great fan and had watched every musical he'd ever been in. We went to the show and I plucked up courage to go backstage. Howard Keel is a very big man – he is very tall and well built and his voice has so much resonance it makes you shake. He was pleasant and charming and chatted to me for ages. I came away clutching his autograph and became an even greater fan than I'd been before.

We returned to Sydney where Michael had lined up a few interviews for me, the prime one being with his uncle, Jack Gully, who was a senior executive with the ABC. Jack knew my work from the sixties, liked me and offered to find me a job. There was one big snag. I had to come back to England in order to get a work permit. It couldn't be done in situ.

My holiday was nearing its end and Michael declared that I couldn't possibly leave Australia without experiencing the Eighth Wonder of the World – The Sydney Opera House. Richard Strauss's opera *Salome* was being performed for a week and that's what we saw. I don't remember much of the opera but the Opera House was quite an experience. It is probably sacrilegious to say it but I wasn't impressed. Perhaps it is because it has enjoyed so much hype over the years, perhaps I am too much of a traditionalist, but it wasn't to my taste.

I have now known Michael Laurence for almost forty years and for most of that time he has been seeking spiritual peace. He has followed many different paths and in 1979 was very taken up with Buddhism. Just before I left, he took me to visit a friend, a Thai Buddhist priest who lived in a very ordinary 'semi' on the outskirts of Sydney. The holy man had a prayer room with a large table simply covered in Buddhas – large Buddhas, small Buddhas, whole Buddhas and Buddha heads. The faces were multi-racial, some Chinese, some Indian, some Thai. It was a beautiful display and I commented on it, singling out a particularly beautiful and benevolent Thai Buddha head. We took tea and when the time came for us to depart, the priest handed me the Buddha head I had admired. Naturally I declined his offer but Michael explained that this would have been a rudeness: 'Buddhists attach no importance to worldly goods and to make a gift of this possession is a blessing to him.' I was covered in embarrassment but thanked him profusely and left, clutching my Buddha head and wondering how on earth I was going to carry it home.

It proved impossible to pack and as it was quite heavy, I decided I'd have to carry it on to the aircraft as my hand luggage. That Buddha head has had pride of place in my home for more than twenty years. Not only do I get a feeling of serenity from the beautifully carved face but I remember the selfless offering of the priest who gave it to me.

CHAPTER NINE

PATRICK AND JONATHAN

I was sad at leaving Michael and Sydney. The tears had started to well up as we kissed goodbye in Departure, but Michael said, 'Darlin' don't worry, you'll be back so soon and time will go so fast.'

I returned to a busy schedule. There were more recordings of *Zodiac and Co.* and I was doing the occasional TV appearance for a current affairs programme called *Midlands Tonight*. I felt quite honoured when I received a request to work on the *Miss World* programme. Well, not exactly to work on it, but to lend a helping hand. My role was to undertake the dummy run of interviews with the contestants, to make them feel at ease before they were asked questions by the show's compere, the Gallic heartthrob Sacha Distel. It was the kind of request I and, I'm sure, most of my colleagues have received often throughout our professional lives. Invariably, there's no fee involved but one is told 'It will be good for your career!' or 'Would you do a pilot programme for us? Of course, there's no fee, but if the idea gets taken up by the network, you will be considered as the presenter.' I'm fairly sure there was no fee on this occasion and I know I was told it would be good for my career and, of course, I was flattered to be asked even though I wouldn't be part of the broadcast transmission.

The whole evening was jinxed. The sound engineers went on strike and the programme wasn't transmitted on television.

132

Despite this, I worked like mad trying to put the contestants at ease. It is not a simple feat to undertake interviews with people from different cultures who don't fully understand our customs and language and I certainly couldn't communicate with them in their mother tongue. Because of the language barrier there are only a few standard questions one can ask and I asked them. I did my bit and then left the Albert Hall to go to the celebration dinner at the Grosvenor Hotel in Park Lane. Patrick Lunt was my partner for the evening. Because of the strike there was a natural pall over the occasion and then a Spanish waitress, who had been bolshy from the moment we sat down, spilled a load of gravy down the back of my evening dress. So, an event to which I'd greatly looked forward turned turtle. But the worst wasn't over.

I woke to find that I had inadvertently become the centre of a major row. One paper carried the headline 'Miss World Fury – Never Again vows Sacha'. Sacha Distel had apparently taken umbrage that I had asked the girls in rehearsal the questions he planned to ask them on the actual show. Sacha said, 'I had been rehearsing for three days, working myself to death. Then this girl [me] came along and interviewed the girls. Her interviews were before mine and made me look a fool asking the same questions.' I think he had seriously missed the point. I was only the warm-up artist and was never going to appear on television. Mr Distel had been introduced to me several days prior to the show and I'm sure would have been made aware of my role. Julia Morley, the show's organiser, went on record as saying, 'No disrespect to him, but the whole plan was in the script, which he had three days before the show. I'm sorry if he didn't read it.' Looking back, I think he was fed up that the strike prevented the show from being transmitted and had to vent his spleen on something or someone, so I got it in the neck. All I got for my pains were some column inches in the newspapers and a boss (Jimmy Kingsbury) who took a very dim view of the adverse publicity.

I was taking positive action over obtaining a work permit for Australia and had got as far as having a medical when events began to overtake me. Before I'd gone on my Australian jaunt, I'd written a letter to the Editor of BBC Television News. I'd been on an evening shift at Broadcasting House and was watching a late evening news bulletin. I found myself thinking, 'I can read news as well as that person, maybe even better, so why don't I go for it?' I'd nothing to lose, so I wrote a letter requesting an audition and heard nothing. Then months later, when I'd forgotten about my application, I received a phone call requesting me to turn up for an audition at Television Centre on 13 December. I mention the date because thirteen is supposed to be my lucky number.

I was nervous but had the benefit of experience with newsreading and have always been a good sight reader. There were a few tricky pronunciations – such as 'Deng Xiaoping', which isn't difficult when you know how – and they tested one's ability to ad lib for the occasions when video inserts and films didn't appear when and where they should. Everyone was very friendly and told me how well I'd done. I went home and heard no more.

I'd been spending quite a lot of time with Patrick Lunt. He'd met me at the airport on my return from Australia and had regrown his beard for me. We were growing closer and I was sure this was the correct way to fall in love. Not the immediacy of a 'coup de foudre' but a friendship that grows into mutual love and attraction. I was torn. I was certainly beginning to fall in love with Patrick but I really did want to go back to Australia. I made an assumption, and without discussing it with Patrick (big mistake), I thought I would be able to convince him to move with me to the Antipodes. So our affair progressed and it was decided that we'd spend Christmas together. We were both working over Christmas itself but had a couple of days off afterwards and planned to spend it with his parents in Ledbury.

Ronald and Veslemoy Lunt were very welcoming hosts. As Ronald was a canon of the church I was nervous of meeting him because of being a divorcee. But Ronald was non-judgmental and we took to each other instantly. Veslemoy was doubly welcoming because she felt she already knew me, having been an avid viewer of the *Pebble Mill* programme. Veslemoy is Norwegian, so our late Christmas was celebrated in the Norwegian manner. Patrick's mother is a very good cook and we experienced the festive season in a totally different and very enjoyable way. I'd taken both my dogs with me, which was chancing my luck a trifle as the Lunts had a Norwegian Buhund. Fortunately, the dogs were amicable towards each other, so a good time was had by all.

On our way back to London we got caught in a flood. It was quite frightening to watch the water level in the car slowly mount. I was fairly sure we wouldn't drown and the only damage would be to the car but I was worried about the dogs panicking at the water. Then I saw the dogs' eating and drinking bowls – quite large because they were big dogs – and began to bale out the flood water through the window, which I was able to wind down. I am a strange creature in that I worry myself silly about situations before they happen but when faced with an emergency, I'm the one who is as cool as a cucumber and can usually deal with most exigencies. My presence of mind, coupled with my calmness and practicality in dealing with the situation, so impressed Patrick that he proposed to me!

I had been financially independent since leaving school at seventeen and a half, and had reached a stage where I owned my own, heavily mortgaged, home and had never looked upon a man as a meal ticket, but I have to admit that I want to love and be loved in return. I don't feel my life is complete without a partner. So what was I to do? I so much wanted to go back to Australia and yet was frightened of being on my own. My biological clock was ticking away and an extremely presentable, kind and loving man had asked me to be his wife. I accepted Patrick's proposal and we started to plan an April wedding.

Then an event occurred that was to turn my life upside down. It was 1 February 1980 and Patrick was with me at my house in Hedgerley, Buckinghamshire. The phone rang and a male with a Birmingham accent said, 'Is that Jan?' to which I replied in the affirmative. I thought it was a Roger, a close friend of Patrick's, and was about to hand the phone over to him when the voice continued, 'How does it feel to be stepping into Angela Rippon's shoes?' 'Oh, come on Roger, stop messing around, what on earth are you talking about?' I said. A very peculiar conversation ensued in which I still thought I was being sent up by Roger, something of a practical joker. Then the caller said, 'Well, if you don't believe me, go out and buy a morning paper.' The caller was a reporter from a Birmingham newspaper and I never did find out his name.

I raced across the road to the village shop and sure enough my picture was on the front page of two tabloids, with more pieces inside others. The *Daily Star* headline read, 'Hot News! Angela signs off at the Beeb'. As is the way with grabbing headlines, the substance of the story was slightly different. Angela had a contract with the BBC to read news for a specified number of days and then was free to go off and pursue other programme interests. She had not 'signed off'. But where did I fit in?

I phoned the BBC and asked to be put through to the Alan Protheroe, Editor, Television News. His PA told me he wasn't there that day and asked if she could help. When I explained my total ignorance of what was going on, she enlightened me. My audition had been well received and it had been decided to 'borrow' me from radio. I was not a replacement for Angela but a stand-in for Richard Baker, who had been given a three-month sabbatical leave period. Amidst all the negotiations, no one had thought to tell me. In an organisation that is all about communication, no one had communicated with me!

Communication or no communication, I was delighted. My newsreading duties weren't to begin until late March. As Patrick and I had planned our wedding for 10 April, I had to let the news people in on the secret and beg a couple of days off. The weeks flew by. Patrick had bought a house in Hackney requiring an enormous amount of 'doing up' and financial outlay, and I had my little home in Buckinghamshire, which was 'liveable in', so the decision was made to sell Patrick's place and live in mine. With all the moving and preparations for the wedding, my news debut was soon upon me.

Fortunately, I appeared to go down well with the public and the press and flattering comments were made. However, I was only on loan from radio to television and didn't harbour any great hopes that the position would be made permanent. News of our impending marriage had been 'leaked' to the press, much to our chagrin. I was advised by the BBC Press and PR Department to give the story to one gossip columnist in order to throw the others off the track. The Hickey column in the *Express* was chosen and given the details all except for the date. That was the deal and I'm glad to say we did manage to keep it a secret.

We married in Ledbury at what is reputed to be the oldest register office in the country – the Tudor Council Chamber. It was a beautiful venue and we walked from there up the cobbled street to the church, where Patrick's father carried out a service of blessing. We had a small reception in The Feathers inn, went off for our wedding night at Castle Combe – the setting for the film *Doctor Dolittle* – and a few days' honeymoon in Paris. Then, it was back to work for both of us.

By May I was halfway through my 'attachment' to television when the Iranian Embassy in London, close to the Albert Hall, was besieged and hostages taken. I was on duty that day and even 23 years later I can recall the tension. It was no ordinary day, as programmes were constantly being interrupted for updating 'news flashes'. I had to be in the studio on 'permanent' stand-by. It was extremely difficult to leave the desk even to visit the Ladies. Six days later I was on duty again when the seige ended. It was horrific and dramatic.

When the Embassy had been seized, most of the hostages were Iranian staff with a few civilians who'd been there for visas. In the intervening days, five hostages were released after negotiation, including a BBC Producer, Chris Kramer who had fallen ill. On the sixth day, the terrorists declared that, if their demands were not met, a hostage would be killed every half hour. Sadly they kept their threat. Shots rang out and a body was tossed onto the pavement outside the building. At this stage the situation was no longer tenable and the SAS went in.

There was an explosion – we heard a voice say – *that was a bomb* – and shortly afterwards flames began to lick around the windowsill and reach up to the sky. Afterwards we learned that the SAS had entered the building, killing three of the terrorists, another went to hospital and one was in police custody. What I found particularly sad was that at one stage the gunmen had issued a message saying, 'We're sorry . . . tell the outside world we're sorry'. But they were terrorists and as the then Home Secretary, William Whitelaw, said on television: 'We are not prepared to tolerate terrorism in our Capital City . . .' All the action taken was with the full cooperation of the Iranian government. The gunmen had hand grenades and the SAS had no options.

Kate Adie did an extremely good job with her unfalteringly calm commentary and in the upper echelons of the BBC it was considered that both Kate and I had done well. My future was beginning to change almost imperceptibly.

I am extremely grateful to the viewers. All their kind comments and letters about my prowess as a newsreader were beginning to have an effect and my handling of the siege set the seal on matters. I was offered a year's contract to read news. The BBC has three levels of employment. You are staff, with all the security and pension rights that a staff job affords. Then there is a staff contract, which is midway between being staff and being on a contract and offers some security of tenure. Then there is the least desirable option (in my opinion) and that is a contract. If I accepted the year's contract then I had to give up my 'staff contract' status with radio. It was all heady stuff and there really was no choice. I went for the 'big time', accepting the insecurity of a contract.

Around that time, Desmond Wilcox phoned to let me know that his agent, Richard Armitage of Noel Gay Artists, was interested in talking to me and a lunch date was arranged. The Chief Press Officer, Peter Rozier, informed me in no uncertain terms that the BBC did not take kindly to agents and that it would be in my best interests not to get involved. I duly phoned Richard and made some lame excuse not to meet him.

The result was a financially poor one for me. With no one to fight my corner, I moved from my radio job to television news for a salary increase of £500, taking my annual income to £10,000 per annum. I mention this amount because, not only was it tens of thousands less than magazines and newspapers inferred I was paid, *but for that sum I signed away my right to privacy forever*. I was given a one-off sum of £500 to help with wardrobe and that was the sum total of my 'dress allowance' for seven years at the BBC!

However, a lack of privacy was not at the forefront of my mind at the time. I was having a ball. The press appeared to like me and I was in demand. In June I was thrilled to be asked to review the fashions at Ladies' Day at the Ascot Races. Eve Pollard (now Lady Lloyd and married to an ex-editor of the *Express*, Nick Lloyd) was heavily pregnant and couldn't fulfil her usual role as commentator. She was extremely kind and offered to meet and give me tips on how to do the job. Despite the help, I was extremely nervous and didn't know what on earth I could wear. Competing with the Ascot Ladies in their designer clothes and hats was out of the question, so I went the other way and chose simplicity. Funnily enough I was photographed in my outfit and the picture appeared among the best dressed in the *Daily Telegraph*. I was wearing the simple organza dress in which I'd married Jeremy, topped off by a straw hat that had cost me a few pounds. I trimmed the hat with some blue roses, which I think were the most expensive part of my ensemble. I must have been the most inexpensively dressed female Ascot had ever encountered.

The BBC crew looked after me well. It was my first meeting with Desmond Lynam, who was also very helpful. I felt a man's perspectives on ladies' fashions were good ones to follow. Des and the crew were full of helpful suggestions as to which outfits caught their eyes. I took note, inwardly digested the information and regurgitated it over the airwaves. The day was a bit of a blur, with me running every which way. Live broadcasting is always difficult but when you've got to cope with the crowds, the weather, running large distances between interview venues and remaining cool calm and collected, the job is even more demanding. I got through the ordeal and can't have done too badly because they didn't sack me!

I'm often asked about stories that I remember from my BBC News days. I suppose I remember the dramatic stories that tugged at the nation's heart. I remember when Keith Barron was reporting on the famine in Ethiopia. It was the early eighties and before the emergence of Electronic News Gathering (ENG), which is instantaneous reporting. The film had come in, was rather long and was still in the editing stage when I went into the studio for the news bulletin, so I had no chance to view the finished story. The editor warned me that the ending of the filmed piece was rather disturbing, but nothing prepared me for the emotion that was evoked by Keith's excellent reporting and feel for the story. The piece ended with an emaciated child 'keening' (rocking back and forth and making wailing noises) and Keith's voice over the report indicated that by the time we in England saw the film, this poor child would be dead. I was unprepared for the ending and had a hard job to speak because of the lump in my throat.

I remember the IRA bombing of Harrods, on 17 December 1983. I had put in for a day's leave to attend some function or other, but someone had messed up the leave forms and the department head insisted that I came in to work. The story was even more horrible because it was happening right on our doorstep – not in Ireland. The fatality and casualty numbers were changing by the minute. At one stage it was thought around forty people had died, although this wasn't broadcast because of its non-verification. Eventually, the number of people who lost their lives came to far less than this but there were many casualties. The whole day felt surreal and it was hard to remain unemotional.

I also recall the occasion of an earthquake in South America and though hundreds lost their lives, it was the story of one little girl that I can't forget. She had been trapped by some fallen masonry and thick mud was oozing around her. The rescue teams fought valiantly to free her but they took so long, the poor little girl died before they could pull her free.

In the first few days of the kidnapping of Terry Waite, the Archbishop of Canterbury's special envoy, in 1987, we stayed on after the final scheduled news bulletin in case of fresh news 'breaking'. This had been going on for a while and when it came to my shift on Saturday, we were kept at the studio until gone 1 a.m. I had to go home and do a quick turn around to be back in the studio on Sunday morning to record a programme called *News Review*. That night we were told to be on 'stand-by' again. By this time Terry Waite had been missing for many days. I stood up to the news editor and said words to the effect … 'This unfortunate man is either dead by now or we won't hear of him for a very long time. Haven't you got homes to go to and do you really think the public are staying up to all hours waiting for news?' I was not popular for voicing this 'sacrilegious opinion', but my words proved true and Mr Waite wasn't heard of for about another year and a half.

To me, reading the news was a job. I felt privileged to be doing it, but it was a job and I had a home to go to and a family to care for. I wasn't a 'news junkie' – I didn't eat, sleep and breathe the news, and at the end of my shift, I didn't go to the bar, but headed home to my loved ones.

Richard Baker returned from his sabbatical. In 1954, Richard and other stars of the day, including Jack Hawkins, and television's Macdonald Hobley, were attending a charity cricket match in Woolwich. As a shy twelve-year-old, I had queued to get their autographs and here I was sharing an office with Richard and the other newsreaders. Sometimes I felt like pinching myself to establish whether I was dreaming. Although I'd been taken on as a stand-in for Richard and was to have been restricted to the lunch-time and six o'clock news bulletins, by June it was decided that I could read news in the prestigious nine o'clock slot. Things were going from good to better. I was also being requested to appear on other television programmes and corporate companies were asking for my services. I presented conferences, product launches and award ceremonies for just about every major company and corporation you could think of – Boots, the Post Office, British Gas, the Wellcome

Foundation and Apple Computers to mention just a few. I had no idea how to charge myself out to these companies or for these events. I needed an agent and decided to phone Richard Armitage regardless of the BBC advice. We met for lunch and I became a client of the Noel Gay Organisation. But the financial dye had been cast and he was not able to drive up my salary appreciably.

Clothing was a problem. Not only did I have to dress appropriately for the news but I had to find outfits that were right for corporate work and also a fair amount of evening wear. When I first signed my BBC TV contract, I was given a few hundred pounds' allowance, but that didn't continue. I had to fund everything out of my salary and, although I was able to buy from some designers at cost, my bills were large. If you wear the same thing over and over you receive criticism and if you have an ever-changing wardrobe you still receive criticism. In my early days at *Pebble Mill*, I'd worn a dress of which I was particularly fond and which I'd worn often at HTV. A woman viewer wrote and complained that '... as my licence money is putting the clothes on your back, I'd like to see you in something different'.

Not the Nine O'clock News enjoyed enormous popularity in the 1980s and it was considered an honour to be taken off on the show. I remember getting a phone call from a friend one evening: 'Are you watching *Not the Nine O'clock* – if not, switch it on fast, you're on.' I used to wear some plain and, I thought, fairly innocuous gold hoops. Pamela Stephenson had latched on to these and as each edition came and went my earrings got bigger and bigger until she was wearing enormous shoehorns down to her bust. She also parodied the way I held my script while reading news. The first time I watched the programme with 'me' on it, I dug my fingernails into the palm of my hand so hard they left marks. After a few programmes, I could see the funny side of everything and when asked to actually appear on the show, accepted readily. Pamela was taking off both myself and Angela Rippon and was dressed in identical clothes. We appeared next to her and the studio audience gave marks out of ten for her performance. She sent me a very large pair of earrings that Christmas and a lovely letter in which she thanked me '... for all the many hours of hard work you've put in helping to make me famous'.

Although things were going so well at work, Patrick and I both wanted children and as I was in my late thirties, we couldn't afford to waste any time. Despite loving my job and feeling that I'd actually achieved something in my career, my desire for a child was paramount and if it curtailed my career, then so be it. We'd only been married a few months when I became pregnant. Because of my age and because there was Down's syndrome in my family, I decided to have an amniocentesis test. This detects Down's, spina bifida and hydroencephalus. Down's syndrome is not hereditary, but you have to be a specially blessed person to cope with it. I'd seen my uncle and aunt bring up their Down's syndrome daughter in a wonderfully loving environment but instinctively felt I had not been blessed with the patience required for this kind of selfless devotion.

Along with the results of the amniocentesis comes the sex of your offspring. I have a sister and a half-sister and had always wanted a little girl. When the envelope arrived containing the results of the test, I toyed with it for ages. What would we do if the result was a positive one? However, I opened it and sighed with relief. Our baby showed no signs of deformity and it was a boy. I was thrilled. All thoughts of a girl were forgotten. I sank to my knees and thanked God that our child was going to be all right. We didn't want anyone else to know the baby's sex, so when my mother asked in what colour she should knit baby clothes, we said 'Lemon'.

I managed to keep my pregnancy a secret for a surprisingly long time. It was only the perceptive eyes of the wife of a newspaper editor who noticed my dress looked a little tight around the bust. Enquiries were passed on to the BBC Press Department. Bob Dulson, from Press, was soon on the phone to me. With a chuckle in his voice, Bob said, 'I've just taken a call asking if you are pregnant – ho-ho.' He was staggered when I confirmed that it was true.

I had a wonderful pregnancy up until my birthday. We were moving into a slightly larger apartment to accommodate our baby and the move was designated for 5 January. I'd been invited to a luncheon in London and Patrick encouraged me to go but I felt mean at leaving him to cope with everything. So I stayed at home and worked like a Trojan. That night I was on duty at Television Centre. I remember feeling very uncomfortable but put it down to having eaten something that disagreed with me. The next day I was rushed into hospital with a threatened miscarriage. Within an hour of my admittance, the news hounds were at the door. I couldn't believe it. My baby's life hung in the balance and someone had tipped off the papers.

I remember the lovely nurse who admitted me, Jeanne Tozer. She threw open her arms, cradled me in them and said, 'Go on, let go, have a bloody good cry.' While I lay there worrying about losing our son, I wondered if I was experiencing God's justice for the sin I had committed over twenty years previously. I was wired up to all sorts of machines and thanks to the gynaecologist and the lovely staff at the Princess Margaret Hospital in Windsor, our baby pulled through. However, I did wonder whether all the stress would have an effect on our unborn child.

In February, when I was six months pregnant, I was asked to appear on *The Russell Harty Show*. The way it was put to me was that Russell and I were going to do a double act at the piano, which would have been fun and acceptable. By the time the whole thing had taken off, I was required to sing a song solo. My voice isn't bad, but it isn't that good, and I had reservations about making a fool of myself. Being a great lover of the show *The King and I,* I chose to sing 'Hello Young Lovers'. It is one thing to sing well in the bathroom, quite another to sing on television! The press reaction was mixed but all in all, it was an enjoyable experience, and one day I will pluck up the courage to watch the video!

In April 1981, I was presented with the Television and Radio Industries Award for Best Newscaster. It was a fun event and made even more amusing by the fact that the sponsor of the newscaster prize that year was a firm called

Bulgin and, as my colleague Richard Baker commented on presenting me with my prize, I certainly was that! George Howard, Chairman of the BBC, sent me a congratulatory telegram of which I was very proud.

Jonathan was born on 18 May. Patrick was with me during most of a long and difficult labour but I was determined to have the baby as naturally as possible. It was only after about eighteen hours that the gynaecologist said I would have to have help. I begged him to let me have one last try – so I was given a caudal block, which partially anaesthetised my lower half, and not long afterwards Jonathan made his entry into the world. I wondered why he wasn't given to me straight away and didn't realise he wasn't breathing. He had to be given an injection to kick-start him into life but then he was fine. I cradled him for a while, during which time we both billed and cooed over him with me declaring I wanted another baby immediately! I was totally overwhelmed by the cards and presents sent by the viewers. So much love and work had gone into making shawls and matinée outfits. The shawls were lovely, many of them so fine they looked like cobwebs. One viewer, Mrs Joyce McCallum, sent a beautiful christening outfit that she had made especially for Jonathan. It was exquisite.

Patrick and I had been told that one of the best investments at the time of a birth is to pay for a maternity nurse for a couple of weeks. We heeded this advice and despite the hundreds of applications for the job, managed to choose the loveliest girl from Durham, Judith Allan, who turned out to be worth her weight in gold. Childbirth is exhausting and when you are an elderly prima-gravida (medical jargon for an older first-time mother) it certainly knocks you for six. Judith came to the hospital when Patrick collected me and totally took charge of everything practical without excluding me from the precious bonding I wanted with my son. I wish we could have kept Judith as our nanny but she was dedicated to looking after newborn babies and their mothers, and we simply couldn't persuade her to stay.

Not being on staff at the BBC, and therefore not entitled to six months' maternity leave, I took the minimum time off but while on leave got a call from a friend at work. She warned me that my job was hanging in the balance because there were going to be big changes. Yet again the organisation that is built on communication had failed to adhere to the common courtesies and let me know about those changes. It was only then I remembered a meeting many months previously, before Jonathan was born. I'd met Patrick in the BBC Club at the Langham and a slightly inebriated man approached us. He challenged me over the fact that I wasn't a journalist and in his opinion, only journalists were capable of delivering the news. I heartily disagreed, not realising that this person was the new Television News Editor and oh boy, was he going to make changes! In 1980, I had resigned from the NUJ, partly because I was no longer actively reporting and interviewing and partly because I was at odds with its very left-wing bias. I was actually advised to resign by the Treasurer and to rejoin later if my working conditions changed. My rash decision to leave the NUJ precipitated my dismissal from the BBC some years later, or was used as an excuse!

Because of the changes, Richard Baker, Kenneth Kendall and myself were under threat. In the end, it was decided that we would be taken off the prestigious *Nine O'clock News* and relegated to the early evening or the weekends. Richard Armitage told me that my 'bacon' was saved by the fact that I appeared to be popular with the public and the BBC could hardly get rid of someone who had just won an award and also given birth to a baby. According to Richard there was also considerable support from some high-powered business-men in the City. Public sympathy was on my side as well, so I kept my job.

I couldn't put the situation any better than Esther Rantzen did in her autobiography. She wrote: 'Somewhere in the BBC machine, is a steel ruler, designed to rap its staff over the knuckles whenever they risk feeling confident, or heaven forbid, loved and respected. The ruler swings like a pendulum. You're reaching great heights? Fine. This will teach you how far you can fall. Smack. Let's see you scramble out of that one.'

In my day the BBC hierarchy actively disliked publicity surrounding their 'personalities'. They didn't like the attention Angela got when she showed her legs on the *Morecambe and Wise Show* and they certainly didn't approve of the attention I was getting. There wasn't much I could do about it. Attitudes have changed a great deal – attention brings ratings and nowadays the BBC appears to court these figures as much as the other channels.

One Friday evening after work, and about a year after my relegation to weekends, I went to visit a sick friend in the Royal Free Hospital at Hampstead. On leaving her, I pulled into a nearby petrol station and was amazed to see my boss, the News Editor, being asked by a police officer to get out of his car. I could see that he was the worse for drink and for a second, the nastiest part of me wanted to 'shop him'. But I couldn't do it and instead rang a friend in the BBC PR Department to alert them so that they could be on the offensive with the newspapers. I got my reward a long time later when the boss saw me at a function and quite shyly thanked me.

Although I was none too happy about working every weekend, in the long run it turned out to my advantage. We often picked up our biggest audience share of the week on a Sunday evening. This meant that a large number of businessmen were home watching television and that, in turn, led to requests to do corporate work (hosting conferences, product launches etc.). The weekend was to have been shared between Richard Baker, Kenneth Kendall and myself. Richard decided to leave and concentrate on programmes in which he could use his extensive musical knowledge. Kenneth was close to retirement and had always wanted to run an antiques shop, so he left and did just that. Thus, after a short period, I was left to man the weekends single-handed.

Because of the expense of moving house, our lovely baby and paying a nanny, we weren't going to have a holiday but I had returned to work a little too soon after the birth and was feeling exhausted. Patrick arranged an inexpensive fortnight in Crete. We weren't expecting five-star luxury for two-star prices, but when we arrived in the middle of the night, we found ourselves in a 'villa' that was little better than a double garage with a filthy cooker and pillows so disgustingly stained and smelly we had to put our beach towels over them in order to use them. The place was absolutely appalling and though we complained bitterly to the rep, nothing was done to alleviate the situation. As chance would have it, on our return I was invited to write some travel articles for a new magazine. I wasn't to be paid to visit any exotic spots, but to write about places I'd already visited on holiday. I was very complimentary about the island and the holiday in general but didn't mince my words when it came to our accommodation. Much to my surprise it elicited a letter from the owner of a chain of five-star hotels who expressed his regret at the accommodation we'd encountered. He made a very generous offer that if we provided our own travel and paid for our board, we could have a room in his beautiful Elounda Palace Hotel in Crete the following year.

In November I received an invitation to visit my very own RAF station – Leeming. Patrick and I were flown to Leeming from Northolt and spent the day at the base. It was a fascinating look behind the scenes and I was given a flight in a Bulldog piloted by the station commander, Group Captain Brian Batt. Many years previously I'd been sent to do an interview at RAF Chivenor. At the time Chivenor was facing one of its many proposed axings. I had to interview the commander, who arranged for me to be flown in a Hunter jet. The Hunter could only go through the sound barrier by taking a dive and the pilot didn't warn me what the G-force would feel like. I remember an elephant sitting on my lap and a great desire to be sick. All I could concentrate on was not throwing up in front of the squadron leader. Fortunately, the Bulldog at Leeming was a training aircraft and didn't do anything amazingly ridiculous. I was allowed to take the controls in the sky, and again on the ground when they let me get behind the wheel of one of the station fire engines, and actually drive it. It is a weird experience to have all the weight of a full tank of water behind you if you've never driven anything other than a small car. Patrick and I had a great day. So many lovely things were happening in our life, it felt too good to be true.

Although we were working part of the time, we had our first Christmas with Jonathan. He was only seven months old, but we had great fun decorating trees and packing presents for him.

The new year got off to a 'cracking' start for me, with the much-documented and oft-repeated 'Exploding Light Bulb' incident. It was 2 January and I was presenting the very short mid-afternoon bulletin, which came at half-time during the Saturday sport. I had just read a story about the IRA when there was a loud bang. I thought I'd been shot. I hadn't, but I was showered with molten glass from a 625 watt quartz iodine bulb, which had exploded. The glass narrowly missed my face and landed on the seat very close to my posterior. But in true theatrical tradition, I brushed myself down and kept on reading. At least the BBC had the decency to compensate me for the burnt clothing. I've lost count of how often that piece of video has been shown on television and even found its way onto a BBC video called *Mis-takes*.

One of the mothers who had been in the same ante-natal class and given birth at the same time as me, had moved to Hong Kong and invited Patrick and myself out for a holiday, an offer that we gratefully accepted. We were due to go in March and, just before our departure, Richard Armitage told me I'd been chosen to present the Eurovision Song Contest for 1982. I was absolutely thrilled – and very worried. Katie Boyle had presented the show for years and was fluent in French. Although I had a passable accent, there was no way I could call myself fluent. Because of the staging of the show, it would be impossible to use autocue. So, packed in my luggage was a script, which I spent most of the holiday learning!

When the well-known designer Gina Fratini discovered that I bought her clothes from time to time, she invited me to come to her premises in London to see her shows and order direct from her at wholesale prices. It was a nightmare finding enough clothes for my television appearances, functions etc., so an offer like that was very much appreciated. We had become friends and I'd been buying from her for a decade. I naturally assumed that I'd be able to choose my Eurovision dress from her collection. Wrong. Although the BBC had never provided me with a wardrobe, on this occasion they insisted that my dress should be designed in-house. Apparently their thinking was that, as the show would be seen by an audience of over 350 million people, one designer should not be given such prominence. I suppose they saw it as advertising.

They really were a funny lot. They had the same attitude when a nursery wished to name a rose after me. It wasn't allowed because the hierarchy decided it was too commercial. Instead of taking the line that every time people saw the rose they would think BBC Television News, they took the opposite view – that when people saw me they'd think of the rose. Stupid, isn't it? I did end up with a petunia named after me, but I think the poor little thing died without trace in an 'onion patch', as I've never seen it for sale.

Eurovision was scary and exciting. I felt enormously honoured to be presenting it and very worried about measuring up to the job. There were all the technical things that could go wrong and, of course, there was Terry Wogan. You never knew what he would say to send you up. As it turned out, he was on relatively best behaviour and the show went without a hitch. But I was so nervous, I wrote in my diary ' … my kingdom for a rail ticket back home.' My efforts in learning the script paid off because so many people believed I was talking off the cuff. They didn't realise the blood, sweat and tears that had gone into the performance. Katie Boyle did know what went into a live programme of such magnitude. She very generously sent me a good luck telegram and after the show sent a lovely letter of congratulations.

The year 1982 was a charmed one for me. I became a panellist on a television quiz show initially called *Top Secret* and then renamed *I've Got a Secret*. It was not unlike *What's My Line*, which had enjoyed huge success decades earlier. I was awarded the Television Newscaster Award for a second year running, but had been in Hong Kong at the time. It was handed to me in the newsroom by the weekend news editor. I was surprised at the jealousy around me. One correspondent commented that it was all right for me to be sitting around in a cosy studio picking up awards when they were out risking life and limb. You pay your money and you take your choice. I did the job I was paid to do and had no desire to cover myself with medals at the front line. Years later that correspondent was showered with awards.

On Jonathan's birthday, 18 May, while presenting the prizes at the Pye Colour TV Awards, I was taken completely by surprise when the tables were turned on me and I picked up the Television Personality of the Year Award. You don't enter yourself for these awards. They are done completely behind closed doors and the results are decided by the votes of the viewers.

Sundays were relatively quiet days at Shepherds Bush. Not a lot of programmes were staged and the News was one of the few 'live' areas at Television Centre. The RAF aerobatic team The Red Arrows came on a visit and, as there was very little action, I was roped in to meet and talk to them. They were a highly charismatic bunch of men and their leader, John Blackwell, extended an invitation for me to fly with the team during one of their practice days. I did eventually get a flight with the team, but not for almost a year.

June saw the tercentenary of the Royal Hospital, Chelsea, and I was asked to narrate and do the interviews for the celebration programme *Boys of the Old Brigade*. History is one of my great loves and doing the research was a pleasure rather than a chore. I'll always remember the programme, not only for the wonderful old pensioners I spoke to, but for the area in which we had to work and from where I did the commentary – the Gentlemen's loo near one of the gates. The chaps were still using it and we had to ensure there were no flushes at certain moments in the recording!

A week later Patrick and I were invited to the closing ceremony *Beating the Retreat,* at which we were introduced to Prince Charles. It was the second time in a month that I had had the honour of meeting the Prince. I really feel for the royals, who have to make endless small talk with all manner of people. They are damned if they are starchy and damned if they are not. I think the Prince was attempting to be informal with me, because he grinned and said, 'We'll have to stop meeting like this or people will talk.'

In July, the veteran broadcaster John Snagge invited us to accompany him to Henley. It was a miserable day weather-wise (perhaps if they moved Henley and Ascot to different months, the organisers might score better with the climate, because it always seems to be raining). Jilly Cooper wrote that it was so wet it should be rechristened Duckley. She also singled me out for attention, commenting on the Gina Fratini outfit and hat I was wearing. Again it was my Jeremy wedding dress, which by then had been in the wardrobe for years.

John invited us back to his house for a drink. He offered sherry and poured it into a whopping great glass. I'm not over fond of the beverage and certainly couldn't cope with the amount he poured. At one strategic moment, when he'd left the room, I'm afraid I poured it into his aspidistra. Unfortunately, on his return, he noticed my empty glass and refilled it. I wonder what happened to the plant?

Shortly after Henley we took off for a holiday in Norway, where Patrick's mother had a small cottage by a lake. It was a primitive weekend and looking after a baby still in nappies wasn't easy. But we enjoyed the experience enormously and spent time visiting Patrick's relatives.

For our second week we moved down to an island in the middle of the Oslo Fjord. To me, Norway was a country of snow, rain and very little sunshine, so I couldn't believe the super weather we were experiencing. The heatwave had its downside, though. When we reached the island we found that water was in very short supply, which again made it difficult coping with a very hot baby and his needs. Patrick had to row to the mainland every day to fill up with water and on one of his expeditions I was doorstepped (if you can be on a remote island) by some Norwegian journalists wanting to talk about Eurovision. How they had discovered we were there I'll never know, but then the press are like that. They turn up when you least expect them and always when you don't want them.

Most of the BBC's natural history programmes emanated from the Bristol studios, so their Wild Screen Awards were to be held in Bristol. I was invited to present them and was doubly delighted because of my love for Bristol and the chance to catch up with some friends. At the party afterwards I bumped into Terry Dobson – he who dumped me from *Pebble Mill*. He had the cheek to put his arm around my shoulder and suggest he was responsible for my 'success' because of not renewing my contract. He hadn't experienced the financial and emotional worry I'd had for months after leaving Pebble Mill!

November saw Esther Rantzen, Gloria Hunniford and myself on stage at Drury Lane. We were part of the Royal Variety Performance. Our party piece was 'Anything You Can Do, I Can Do Better' from *Annie Get Your Gun*. Gloria had trained to be a professional singer, so why it fell to me to hit Top C in the song I simply don't know, but we had an enormous amount of fun rehearsing and performing.

I looked at the video recently and was amazed at the applause we got for our number, especially after my high note. The audience was probably as surprised as I was that I hit it. The whole evening was dedicated to 'The Magical World of Musicals'. Perhaps it is because of my partiality to the old Hollywood musicals but I thought it was one of the best Royal Variety programmes in an age. Howard Keel sang 'Oklahoma!' superbly and once again I made a point of talking with him. I'm sure he didn't remember me from Australia, but he was polite and gracious.

The year wasn't all sweetness and light. I had been the butt of some fairly bitchy comments in the press, ranging from attacks on my over-inflated salary to my performance – all from female journalists, of course. The funny thing is that most of the journalists who were bitching were earning vastly more than I was, or any of my colleagues were. In certain areas of journalism, the money is phenomenal. It's rather like television – some are paid ridiculous money and others plod along, working hard and living from hand to mouth.

I have a theory that most of the female journalists wanted our jobs and indeed several did end up working on television. One of the most cutting remarks was made in an article in which I was being upbraided for inferring that feminists took the dignity out of being a woman. I was reminded that I should be grateful to these feminists to whose actions and to whom, indirectly, I owed my job. Sorry, I disagree. I was working my corner way back in the sixties, when no one stood up for women, and getting where I got to came as a result of sticking with a notoriously insecure and fickle profession and working hard. The writer started her article with the words 'Newsreader Jan Leeming has been speaking *what passes for her mind* on the topic of Women's Lib.' I will champion the *rights* of women but I will not burn my bra and become a man-hating feminist.

In the midst of all my work fulfilment and happiness, there was a very worrying development. There were cracks in my relationship with Patrick. He appeared to be distancing himself from me and I made a diary entry towards the end of 1982 expressing my hurt that we didn't share the same closeness. Perhaps he was finding it difficult to cope with my apparent success. Most men don't like being in the shadow of a woman and my career was certainly on a rising path. But we had our gorgeous little boy, from whom we both derived so much joy, and life was very good. 'It will sort itself out in time,' I thought. It did, but not in the way I had envisaged.

Although I had, quite rightly, to ask the BBC for permission to do outside work, they were usually fairly good at assenting. They had a few bees in their bonnets about areas in which I couldn't work. To my surprise, building societies were seen as political, so they were on the 'No-no' list. But permission was readily given for me to present a conference for the Crown Paints Group. Sue Lawley had worked for Crown for several years and she was their first choice again. However, she had another commitment and they approached me.

So on 10 December 1982, I drove the short distance from my home in Stoke Poges to Marlow for a preliminary meeting. And there I met Eric Steenson.

CHAPTER TEN

ERIC

Eric shouldn't have been at that meeting. Crown had just taken on sponsorship of Liverpool Football Club and chosen 'Team Work' as the conference theme. As guest speakers they had invited Bob Paisley, manager of the club, and Ian St John. Liverpool's colour is red, so who better to make up the guest team than a member of the prestigious Red Arrows. As leader of the Arrows, the invitation went to John Blackwell. John, whom I'd met in the spring, was too busy to attend and sent in his place a new member of the team, Squadron Leader Eric Steenson, Manager of the Arrows. I remember thinking he had lovely eyes but immediately put him down as 'married with two teenage children'. (He was married, but with very young children.) The meeting progressed with a certain amount of banter and me saying that I liked men in uniform. We had lunch and went our separate ways. I didn't give Eric another thought.

Patrick and I were both working over the holiday period but we had Christmas morning with Jonathan and all the excitement of watching a toddler dive into his presents. He had so many, not only from the family but also from listeners and viewers, that we rationed him to the main ones on Christmas Day and then two daily until they ran out. He was kept busy well into the new year. After the present opening, we went off to work and my mother took charge. My mother was a very large part of Jonathan's life. Nannies simply hadn't worked out.

This was partly because of where we lived, which was rural and offered no nightlife or entertainment to a nanny on her time off. Also, although we were happy to give a nanny more than two days off during the week because she was needed at weekends, most girls wanted their weekends off. After a series of nannies, we decided that the constant change was not good for Jonathan and as my mother had recently retired, only lived a few miles away, and was itching to look after him, that was the course we took. She looked after him for years and chauffeured him around when I couldn't, so a very close bond grew up between Jonathan and his Nanny.

The new year was upon us and off I went to Brighton on 4 January for the Crown Paints Conference. We were to stay in the Metropole Hotel and I was given the Marie Antoinette Suite. We were rehearsing on 5 January and I was standing in the draughty wings of the set when I became aware of someone standing next to me and a voice said, 'You're cold. Here, have this' and Eric draped his sweater over my shoulders.

My friend from Granada days, Sue, lived close to Brighton. Although she was Jonathan's godmother, we didn't get to see each other very often because of work commitments and distance. It was an ideal opportunity to catch up on family news and and she came to the Metropole for lunch. Eric happened to walk through the dining room, saw us and joined us for coffee. After he'd gone, Sue, who is a very forthright Northern lass, said, 'He's interested in you', to which I retorted, 'Rubbish, besides we're both married.'

After we'd finished rehearsals, the Crown people took us out for a meal and as it was my birthday, a cake had been ordered. Eric and I were at opposite ends of the table but I was aware of him looking at me several times during the evening and at one stage he blew me a kiss.

The conference was staged on the morning of the 6th, followed by a lunch. There was to be a gala dinner in the evening, so the afternoon was free time. The delegates were thinning out and Eric had come to join our table. We were immersed in conversation when I realised that the waiters wanted to clear away the dishes. Not wishing to put them out, I suggested to the few left at the table that we could continue our conversation in my suite over a cup of tea. The other delegates had things to do, but Eric accepted my invitation.

We were talking quite animatedly when he suggested that he'd like to ask me a personal question. I replied that he could but reserved the right to refuse if I thought fit. It was an odd question. He asked if lots of men chatted me up. 'Of course not,' I replied. 'Besides, I'm married.' He hadn't touched his tea, but I didn't realise he never drank the stuff.

I needed to go into the other room for something and when I returned he was standing by the window. It had snowed the previous day and after the snow Brighton was now grey and wet with an angry sea. I joined him at the window and was about to say, 'Question asked and answered, perhaps it's time to leave', when his arms were around me and he bent down searching for my lips. A disjointed voice, mine, was heard saying, 'Are we going to behave like adults and go our separate ways or ...' It was the 'or' and neither of us could help ourselves.

This is where you get the 'dot, dot, dot' in the story. Eric carried me into the bedroom and I can only say the afternoon was magic. It was as if we had known each other all our lives. We also talked a great deal! We felt elated and guilty at the same time but both of us were sure we could handle the situation. I'd no intention of messing up my marriage, even though I was worried about the strained relationship with Patrick, and I certainly didn't want to do anything to damage Jonathan's security. Eric talked very fondly of his wife but inferred that their relationship had lost its edge through no fault of hers. Where had I heard similar words before? *But we thought we could handle the situation.*

The gala dinner was difficult for both of us – acting like strangers but having shared an intimate afternoon and longing to be with each other again. We spent that night together and still *thought we could handle the situation.* Who can handle the situation when two people fall in love, or lust? I'm sure the initial attraction between most men and women is a sexual one based on pheromones. How else does one explain the attraction to one person and not to another? I can meet a man and sense his sexuality but if it is not the right man, it does nothing for me. I'm sure the same is true for a man. He too can feel a woman's sexuality but unless the pheromones are in tune, nothing happens. If the pheromones are in tune and you are fortunate, a love grows and develops into mutual understanding and companionship, which again grows and develops into a long-standing relationship and friendship. Well, our pheromones were working overtime and it was hard to say goodbye to each other. We made no plans to meet again.

In early January, I was engaged to present the *Miss UK* programme in London. Eric had to be in town at the same time and we arranged to meet for dinner. That night he told me he loved me and I told him not to be ridiculous as we didn't even know each other. But how do you quantify love? Where and how does one draw the line between sexual attraction and love? I believe they are totally intertwined.

Life was full and Patrick and I were about to move house. We'd found a modern, four-bedroom detached house in Penn, near Beaconsfield in Buckinghamshire. It had a good-sized garden, suited our budget and would give us a great deal more space. I very much wanted a companion for Jonathan, but I don't believe in shoring up a marriage with a child. Our relationship was rocky and another baby wasn't the answer. I was worried about the move because it would stretch our finances greatly. However, we decided to go ahead with the project.

At this time I was working hard on a book. In 1982, just about everyone was writing books on exercise and fitness. Because I was winning awards and popularity polls, I was approached by a publisher. The assumption was that with the wave of popularity I was enjoying, anything I wrote would have a good market. But a book on exercise didn't appeal at all. Firstly, I am not an exercise freak and wasn't prepared to write about something I didn't adhere to. The editor persuaded me to have lunch and while I was talking myself out of a book on exercise, I was talking myself into a book on tips for the busy working woman. At lunch I'd been asked questions about my beauty routine. In common with most, the editor assumed I had a barrage of make-up artists, hairdressers and wardrobe advisors at my beck and call. When I confessed that I had to do it all myself, ran a home, shopped, cooked and had a small child, the emphasis on a publication shifted. The project, titled *Simply Looking Good*, was to be a book about how to make the most of oneself on a tight budget and with very little time.

I'd done all the research and needed some sustained peace in which to put the whole thing together. I rented a cottage for a couple of weeks in order to write. It also presented an opportunity for Eric and me to be together. I am an incurable romantic, so is Eric, and we had a couple of memorable meetings at the cottage. I don't know how he felt but each time we said goodbye I felt as though part of me had died. I couldn't see our relationship going anywhere and could only see hurt for both of us but I was powerless to do anything about it. I didn't have the strength to walk away and nor did he.

I felt very bad about my infidelity but justified it to myself because of the widening gap in my relationship with Patrick. Apart from the fact that we had difficult work schedules so being together for quality time was a problem, I began to realise that, except for our work, we didn't have much in common. I like to entertain people to dinner parties; Patrick was just as happy going to a pub for a few beers. I suffer from sinus problems and the smoky atmosphere in pubs always adversely affects me. I can't cope with the noise level and basically am not a pubby person. Patrick is sporty, musical and has a good voice. He liked to sing in choirs. He was quite happy for friends to drop round unannounced, stay drinking and if necessary fall asleep on the floor. I am completely wrong-footed if I haven't prepared for visitors. I suppose Patrick is a far more laid-back, casual person than I am. The gap was widening.

We moved into our new house in Penn on 2 February and two days later were off to Atlanta. I had met our American host at a charity function a couple of years previously. When he brought his wife over to England, we met for a dinner and got on well together. Helen Barnett was a beautiful woman, both externally and internally, and I quickly became very fond of her. Jack had asked Patrick and I to do some voice work for him and our 'fee' was a holiday in Atlanta. I thought the break might bring us closer together, but it didn't.

In April, I received my promised invitation from the Red Arrows. The Arrows were allowed to fly a guest once in their season and the guest then wrote a piece to be used in the following year's programme. I asked whether Patrick could also be given a flight but this proved impossible. However, he did accompany me to Scampton, where the Arrows were based. As Manager of the Arrows, it fell to Squadron Leader Steenson to play host and we were invited to stay at Eric's quarters.

On arrival we had to wait at the gatehouse for him and as he came cycling up to us my heart gave a leap. This was going to be an impossible situation for both of us. I have a diary entry which says that, 'it was unadulterated hell sleeping under the same roof as Eric but not being together' and adding, 'Patrick showed his usual lack of interest.' It was also a difficult time because I found Eric's wife, Robin, totally charming and liked her immensely, which made me feel even worse.

The next day was flying day. After I'd been kitted out, with great difficulty because I'm quite small, I had to go for a familiarisation flight. This was to ensure that I wasn't going to pass out, freak out or be sick when I came to fly in their practice display. Eric was given the job of taking me on the flight. It was a wet and grey day as we took off in Eric's Hawk. We flew close to Castle Howard, where I'd been a guest a year previously attending a pre-Eurovision function. It was great fun to see it from the air and despite the weather I was thoroughly enjoying the flight when Eric put the plane into a climb. We rose higher and higher and suddenly broke through the cloud base into brilliant sunshine. It was magical and made even more so when he said, 'I love you' at 500 m.p.h. What were we going to do? All we could do was wait and see what happened. Neither of us wanted to hurt our families, but anyone who has ever been madly in love will know that the feeling is almost like a sickness. You require such enormous strength to break away and neither of us had it.

Although the Red Arrows can display in some adverse weather, there are some conditions where it is impossible. After my familiarisation flight, I spent the rest of the day in the crew room waiting for the weather to break so that I could fly with the team in their practice display. The weather didn't oblige and John Blackwell indicated that I'd have to come back later in the season and try again.

Not long afterwards, Judith Allan, who had been my maternity nurse and with whom we'd kept in touch, was getting married. I was making the journey by train because of needing to return to work the next day and Patrick, who had a few days off, was bringing Jonathan to the wedding by car. He was also going to travel on to Lincoln and drop our son off with Robin. She'd heard that we were having trouble with Jonathan's potty training and, as he was about to go to nursery school, it was a necessary prerequisite. She offered to have him for a few days and see if she could work her magic spell, as both of her children were trained from an early age. I ask you, what a situation!

While Patrick was with Robin in Lincoln, I went back to the rented cottage to put the finishing touches to my book. Eric was able to spend a couple of days with me, which was bliss. We weren't able to meet that often, but whenever I had to do a corporate job and stay away for the night, Eric would try and join me. On one occasion he arrived late afternoon and I left him in the room while I went down to the corporate dinner. At the end of the evening I had a very difficult job persuading my hosts that I was perfectly happy to walk back to my room unaccompanied. I had to, as I didn't have the key. We didn't know where our lives were going or how our affair would resolve itself. And life went on, getting more and more complicated by the minute.

I was, happily, busy with work. Apart from my weekend newsreading, I was a regular panellist on *I've Got a Secret,* hosted by Tom O'Connor, and was being asked on to other programmes, such as *Blankety Blank,* as a guest. I'd never watched the show until invited to appear on it and had my private opinions about it and its host. After I met Les Dawson, I did a complete volte-face. What an intelligent, multi-talented and kind man he was. I became a devoted fan then and there.

In August I was able to take advantage of the postponed flight with the Red Arrows. They were having a 'family day' when they displayed on home territory at Scampton. I hadn't had any qualms at all about flying with the team, only a feeling of intense excitement. Then, after I'd been kitted out with my flying gear and G-suit (a harness that automatically inflates and deflates to counteract the effects of gravity) I was taken to an aircraft hangar and introduced to the complexities of an ejector seat. John Blackwell was with me and said, 'If you hear me say, "Eject, Eject," you pull this lever and don't ask any questions.' Suddenly I realised that there was a slim chance that things could go wrong. Up till then the invincibility of the Arrows had never been in question in my mind. However, I was there, committed, kitted and nothing was going to spoil the day. It has gone down as one of the most memorable experiences of my life. I can't tell you how honoured I felt to be up there in John's lead aircraft, experiencing the intricacies of a full-blown display. It is impossible to describe the elation of being as close to a bird as possible, to feel the pull of gravity and witness the amazingly close proximity of the other aircraft as they went through their routine.

At the end of the month there were some more recordings of *I've Got a Secret* and the tables were turned on me. I was reasonably good at guessing the answers in the programme but was completely foxed and came out with some comments which, in context, were hilarious and I couldn't understand why the audience were laughing so much. The secret was our guest was the engineer who had serviced *Jan Leeming's Hawk* – the plane John Blackwell had flown in the display at Scampton. Eric was a long-standing friend of the show's producer, Tim Marshall, and had been invited to the recording. On the video,

I can still pick his laughter out from that of the rest of the audience. Little did anyone realise that we had our own secret!

I was still going back to my hairdresser Jean in Bristol for the major jobs, like cutting and colouring, and did my hair myself the rest of the time. Jean had known me for a long time and had been through all my ups and down with me. She is an incredibly wise person and, being in the hairdressing trade, is also an immensely good amateur psychologist. Most women confide in the person to whom they entrust their crowning glory. Jean knew about Eric and the state into which I was getting myself over all the uncertainty in my relationship with Patrick. She knew an extremely gifted clairvoyant and thought it would be a good idea if I paid her a visit. I was so desperately mixed up and unhappy, I would have gone to a witch doctor if it had been suggested! Jean arranged an appointment for me with Kwesi. I had imagined a wizened crone looking like Gypsy Petulengro (one of the earliest astrologer/clairvoyants) with a head scarf and a crystal ball. Kwesi was my age, dressed quite normally in a suit and was immediately friendly and welcoming. She was a white South African brought up in Durban who spoke fluent Zulu, having been raised among them. Kwesi is Zulu for 'Morning Star'. I have to admit that I was slightly sceptical until she said there was someone in my life with a name like 'Derek' and told me that my marriage was in trouble. I am positive that Jean hadn't told her anything about me and her revelations continued to amaze. She assured me that Eric and I would eventually be together.

The editor who had commissioned *Simply Looking Good* had left the publisher, Arthur Barker, and the book looked like biting the dust. A new editor arrived and gave my book the go-ahead. But I got wind of the fact that they were going to publish with black-and-white illustrations. How ridiculous can you get? A book on make-up and fashion with no colour. I opened my big mouth and said that if the publication went ahead I would pay for the colour out of my advance. And that's what happened!

I had seen some excellent photographic work at an exhibition in The Theatre Royal, Bath. Edward St Maur was the photographer and I suggested him to my editor. He perused Edward's work and approved of my choice. In August, I went down to Jean's to have my hair done for the photographic session; Eric was able to get away and we met in Bristol just prior to the session. Edward was lovely to work with and managed to capture all manner of expressions. Looking back, there was one particular shot where he asked me to think of someone I loved. I can still read that look in my eyes twenty years later.

Although I'd expressly aimed my book at the busy woman with a very limited budget, it was published at the same time as books by beauties such as Sophia Loren and Joan Collins. So how was my work going to compete with theirs? It didn't. Other than the advance, minus the money for the colour photography, I didn't make anything out of the book but, nearly twenty years later, it's still being borrowed from libraries, which is something of a compliment.

We had a family holiday planned in Crete, taking up the generous offer proffered two years earlier by the owner of the Elounda Palace Hotel. I was hoping that the time together with Jonathan might serve to lessen the developing distance between Patrick and myself. We obviously took great joy in our little boy's appreciation of sun, sea and sand but the holiday was not a success. Patrick went off on his own a great deal of the time and when I caught some mystery bug and was raging with fever for a couple of days he virtually ignored me. At the end of our fortnight he told me he was going to leave me after the holiday. Although I no longer loved him, I was desperately worried about the effect on Jonathan and also very concerned about the future on my own. However, we came home and nothing happened, so I wondered if there was still a vague chance that we could come to an arrangement. But he moved into the spare bedroom. The marriage was definitely over.

In September, I was invited to present the Bi-Annual Achievement Awards Conference for IBM. Not only was it a prestigious job with a very good fee but the venue was Cannes. It mystified me how they could afford to take hundreds of the

workforce abroad for a 'jolly', but it was explained that to hold
it in Cannes, out of season, and chartering a whole aircraft, was
cheaper than staging the affair at hotels in England. I had never
stayed anywhere so palatial as the Carlton in Cannes. They
allocated to me an incredibly grand suite and I felt like a queen.
They were a lovely group of people to work for and everything
was done to the highest standard. The 'personality' guests were
Lord Lichfield and Benny Green, the comedian. Janet Brown,
who did a wonderful impersonation of Margaret Thatcher
amongst other famous names, was to be the star of the gala
dinner cabaret.

I had such a fun time, that engagement is forever etched in
my memory. Lord Lichfield had been delayed in England and
didn't arrive in time for the scheduled dinner, when we were all
to be briefed. As a matter of courtesy the dinner was aborted
and it was arranged that we'd have sandwiches in my suite
when he did arrive. Although I'd met royalty and other high-
ranking people in society, I'd never had to entertain a member
of the aristocracy or sustain conversation. I was very nervous.
As it turned out my nervousness was quite unwarranted.
Patrick Lichfield is not only a delightful person but he is
incredibly funny and, when he did arrive, proceeded to
entertain the assembled IBM hierarchy and myself way into the
small hours of the morning. I only wish my memory were good
enough to relay some of the tales to you, but I know I'd miss the
punch lines. Not only did I enjoy the luxurious surroundings of
the Carlton but we were all taken out to one of the most famed
restaurants in the area, the Moulin de Mougins just outside
Cannes. I'd never experienced food like it.

In October Eric rented a canal boat for a few days and we
spent time together. We were moored near Oxford and took a
trip down memory lane by going to the Elizabeth, where I'd had
my first restaurant dinner with my then BBC boss, Dr Archie
Clow. They still served the trout dish on rectangular plates!

The strain of Patrick's impending departure, the uncertainty
over the future and the impossibility of our situation were
taking a toll on both of us. In November, Eric and I agreed to

part for a trial period. It was incredibly painful and I phoned Kwesi for help on many occasions. She kept assuring me we would be together but I couldn't see a happy conclusion to the whole sorry saga. I am not mistress material. I want the man I love to be with me full time. Eric loved his children, his wife and me. I made it clear I couldn't accept a life with him on a part-time basis.

Our parting lasted six weeks and the separation was unbearable. We met again just before Christmas. Patrick was definitely moving out and was actively looking for somewhere to live. Strangely, under the circumstances, we had a good family Christmas arranged around our work commitments. My father and stepmother and one of Patrick's sisters visited us over the holiday and outwardly all seemed normal, while underneath was total turmoil. We hadn't said anything to our respective parents and family about the impending break. We had told no one because of fear of the press intrusion. And then it happened. First of all there was a press enquiry on 2 February. On the 4th a representative from the *Mirror* was on our doorstep and we despatched him. Patrick and I were still living under the same roof, so who snitched on us is a mystery. Patrick had obviously had to negotiate rented accommodation and sign legal forms, so whether the leak occurred there, we don't know. On 9 February, we were warned by the BBC Press Office that the story was about to break in the papers the next day. Hasty phone calls were made to our respective parents, who were dumbstruck.

I have a diary entry that says the press besieged us from 9–13 February, which means that for the four days we had members of the press beating a path to our door. We disconnected the bell and still notes were pushed through asking for 'just a picture' or requesting that we 'deny the story'; others offered us money for an exclusive. I remonstrated with the reporters on our doorstep and said, 'This is a personal and private matter and I wish you to respect our privacy.' I was staggered when a reporter replied, 'Wrong, Miss Leeming. You are public property.' We refused to talk to any of them.

On Saturday 11th, I had to go to work. In retrospect it's all rather funny but at the time we didn't see it in a humorous light. We couldn't get out through the front gate because of press, so we negotiated with our next-door neighbours. We propped up a ladder and I went over the dividing fence into their garden. Then the neighbour drove out of his garage, with me lying low on the back seat. Patrick drove out of our house and the press didn't follow him because they were really after photos of me. Our neighbour Peter drove to a rendezvous point and transferred me to our car. So far, so good. We had phoned the BBC and a side gate was going to be open for easy access – except it wasn't and, while we were negotiating to get in, we were photographed looking duly stressed and angry.

To give you an idea of what the press get up to, one picture and story was published in the *Mirror* and in the corner was the caption 'Mirror Picture Exclusive'. The picture had been taken months previously – the three of us were standing at the back of the house in summer clothes with leaves on the trees. They also stated in the article that within hours of the split being announced I 'was reading the 5.40 p.m. news on BBC 1 as if she hadn't a care in the world'. Life has to go on in the midst of personal hurt and I had to continue to earn a living. If I'd been a weeping mess they would have criticised me for that too. You simply can't win. Anyway, by the 13th the press had bigger fish to fry and we were left alone.

Something happened at that time which made me deeply suspicious of people. I'd told a few of my newsroom colleagues about my escape over the neighbour's fence and to my horror it was reported a few days later in the *Sun* – 'Jan Leeming's *tales* of SAS-style escapes from her Tyler's Green, Bucks, home are beginning to *bore* chums at the Beeb.' I was immensely hurt at the betrayal. I'd told the story once only to a group of five people. And then I remembered Angela Rippon's last words to me when she left the BBC: 'Don't say anything upstairs that you wouldn't want to see in print. They'd sell you for a pint of beer.' I didn't believe her at the time but, sadly, she was absolutely correct. I viewed those people and everyone else with deep suspicion for the rest of my time at the BBC.

There was another nasty article in which my sister was misquoted in a very hurtful manner. She rang to let me know that she hadn't said what appeared in the papers – something about me being bossy and in control. As I was beginning to get used to the machinations of the press, I gave her the benefit of the doubt and assumed she'd said something that had been twisted to make a good headline and story. If I hadn't adopted that attitude it would have driven a wedge between us which might never have healed. I know I made the right decision. Gillian spent money she could ill afford in challenging the paper but the power and money of the newspaper giants is such that you have to be mega-rich to take them on.

People must have wondered what was going on. Despite all the press coverage, Patrick remained at our home for another month. I asked him to reconsider but he wouldn't and I have to say I think he was correct. We weren't right for each other, our interests were diametrically opposed, and a break was inevitable, whether it came sooner or later. I felt so sorry for Jonathan and was determined to keep as much of a friendship with Patrick as I could for our son's sake.

Shortly after this I was sitting next to Michael Caine at a BAFTA awards dinner. Michael commiserated with me over the press intrusion I'd gone through and declared that he'd experienced the press all over the world and the British were the worst. What is it about journalists that they have to write so negatively? Actually, it is probably an extension of a British attitude summed up in a story about an American and an Englishman at a bus stop. As a Rolls-Royce goes gliding past, the American says, 'Gee, if I work hard, maybe, just maybe, someday I'll have a car like that.' The Brit says, 'Why has he got a Rolls-Royce and I have to travel by bus?'

I had been invited to launch an exercise routine, which was to benefit a charity. The gentlemen of the press asked me to don a leotard. I refused, because I didn't think it was in keeping with my image as a newsreader. The next day I was attending a private function at Lewis's in Manchester. A request was made for me to go into the body of the store and serve customers. I love chatting to people and was always mindful of the role the public had played in my popularity. However, I was concerned about endorsement of a product and politely refused. This was blown out of all proportion. I'm pleased to say that not only were there letters of support in the press but when I got to the office at the weekend there were dozens of sympathetic letters there too. One lesson I have learned over my years in television is that you simply cannot please all of the people all of the time. I used to get dozens of letters every week and answered all of them, sometimes personally typing them and, if there were too many, using the services of the newsreaders' secretary, Lydia Ryder. I could scribble a few notes on a post-it, attach it to the correspondence and know that Lydia would make a good letter out of my thoughts.

Most of my mail was a delight. Viewers would identify with me over many areas, like being a working mother, and they'd share their experiences. Others would ask me for advice. Some would admire my hairstyle and clothes while others would criticise me. I would get conflicting letters in the same mailbag. My pronunciation was sometimes taken to task. One letter was from Sir John Colville, who had been personal secretary to Sir Winston Churchill. He told me I was his favourite newsreader but please would I pronounce 'controversy' correctly. If you look in the dictionary you will find that both 'controversy' and 'controversy' are thoroughly acceptable. However I felt that Sir John must know what he was talking about and changed my pronunciation to controversy – only to receive more letters criticising me for the new mode of delivery.

I actually spoke to John Humphrys about it and he laughed, saying, 'When you are in Wales if you pronounce a word one way it will offend those from North Wales; conversely, pronounce it differently and you'll alienate the South Wales people.' So you can't win, even over words!

There were fan letters and the odd smattering of nasty ones, always unsigned. I received some very ugly and disturbing mail from a crank but, after letter two, I recognised the handwriting and threw them in the bin without opening them. I didn't think of taking them to anyone. In the millennium year I read that dozens of women, predominantly actresses, had been deluged with mail from this same person over a period of 25 years. There was an extensive police investigation but the perpetrator was not caught.

Because of the inclemency of the English weather, the Red Arrows decamp to Cyprus around mid-March each year for a month of aerobatic training to perfect their display for the new season. Eric visited me before his departure and promised he would make everything all right for us. Ten days later I received a 'Goodbye Jan' letter. I couldn't believe it. He argued that I needed someone who could financially take care of me and that, though it was breaking his heart, he really felt I'd be better off without him. Reading between the lines, I think it was the enormity of the decision he had to make that was frightening him. I had told him I would not and could not be 'mistress material' and he knew that having me meant the end of his relationship with his wife and not living permanently with his children. He really did try very hard to do the honourable thing and end our affair.

We'd been lovers for over a year and now, just when it looked as though we stood a chance of being together, it was all over. I accepted his decision and crawled into a hole of misery. The only things that kept me going were Jonathan and the need to earn a living. I always had the ability to put my problems to one side whilst working and this is what I had to do now. I felt numb but life had to go on and I tried very, very hard to put Eric out of my heart and mind.

On the 26 March there was a message on the answering machine in which he told me there'd been an accident and, although the pilot was alive, he wouldn't be able to continue the season. This meant that a new pilot would have to integrate with the team, necessitating them staying longer in Cyprus. What I didn't know, until I received a small parcel, posted in England, was that Eric had come back to sort out some arrangements. The parcel contained a piece of jewellery. Eric had copied the 'J' from my handwriting and a Cypriot goldsmith had turned it into a brooch. It came with the briefest of notes sending me all his love. I was shocked that he had been in England but hadn't contacted me and felt that his goodbye letter was definitely meant for real.

I had to go to Morecambe to present a fashion show for the Estée Lauder Organisation and took the opportunity of staying with Sue in Leeds. Sue had known about Eric and myself for a long time. Apart from Jean, she was my only other confidante and, as a straight-talking and very sensible woman, I valued her advice. Although he hadn't contacted me when in England, Eric had spoken to Sue and told her he was really trying to sort himself out. She sensed how much we cared for each other and felt there was a fifty-fifty chance that he would come back to me. I didn't, and that evening I had far too many brandies, tore up his photograph and burnt it.

I threw myself into work and a social life. I'd met Lord Buxton through a charity function some years previously and he came onto the scene and took me out to lunch and dinner a few times. I found him fascinating company and I think he liked me too, but I was aware he feared that our friendship might leak to the press and be totally misconstrued. He was a widower but as a peer of the realm and close to the Queen, he had to be careful of his image. A newly separated, still-married news-reader probably didn't fit the bill.

I kept myself feverishly busy trying to hide the hurt and the heartache. I gave dinner parties like they were going out of fashion, and reconnected with Richard Wade from *Tom Tom* days. We'd had the occasional lunches over the years and there was a definite attraction there, although he was such an academically bright man he frightened me. I was also being wooed by letter. An American professor doing a course at Edinburgh University took a liking to me. He told me all about himself, sent a photo, sent flowers and I was seriously tempted to meet him. It was extremely good for my battered ego. I was doing a reasonable job of convincing myself that losing Eric was all for the best when I got a phone call.

It was 11 May and the phone woke me. A very strained voice said, 'I'm yours, if you want me.' I got the strength to tell him that though I loved him very much, I simply couldn't go through any more emotional turmoil and it really was best for Robin, him and me, that we never saw each other again. He rang me so many times that day but I adamantly refused to see him. Finally, in the evening, he extracted a promise to meet him next morning on my way to work, just to talk!

I can still remember that meeting in the lay-by off the M40. I'd not seen him for almost two months and, though my love hadn't diminished at all, I couldn't cope with any more hurt. I repeated that it was best we stayed apart. I left him in tears and drove to work feeling totally wretched. Richard rang me and I broke down and cried, remembering the look of devastation on Eric's face when he realised I meant what I said. He phoned several times that day and finally I agreed that he could come to the office after my shift and we would talk again. FATAL. Of course, he came home with me and from then I knew I was losing the battle with myself. He told me that he'd tried to make a go of things with Robin but it just wasn't working and he was making plans to separate.

In June, my much-loved standard poodle, Fleur, died. I'd lost little Sheba while Patrick and I were still living at our previous home. Life was in such chaos, I couldn't think about having another dog although I missed the companionship a great deal.

Eric came down to see me as much as possible but I still didn't believe we were going to be together. All three of us were under great strain. We weathered the storm somehow and rather like the time we flew out of the clouds and into the sunshine, things did look brighter and it began to look as though we had a future. We even planned a holiday at the end of the Arrows season in October.

The autumn was busy for me because of the publication of *Simply Looking Good*. Although the book wasn't a raging financial success, it did briefly top the best-seller list and I thoroughly enjoyed the promotional tour, which ranged from book signings in shops, to radio and television interviews. I was invited back to the *Pebble Mill at One* programme and was highly amused at the coincidence of the Red Arrows being on the programme the day before me. Eric asked Paul Coia who were the guests for the following day and my name was mentioned. Paul rather dismissively said, 'She's coming on to talk about a book but it was probably ghosted for her.' Absolutely not, I did all the research and writing with no help from anyone else, until it got to the editing stage and then it wasn't altered very much.

The Late Late show in Dublin made a request for me to appear and talk about the book. Of course, the publishers were delighted and readily agreed, so off I went. Little did I realise what a trap I was walking into. One of the other guests was Robin Knox Johnston. He told me that when he saw the way Gay Byrne was treating me, he was just about to come back onto the podium and rescue me, when the interview was brought to a halt. In the green room before the show, the researchers had been all sweetness and light and asked questions about the book in order to brief Mr Byrne. He wasn't in the least bit interested in publicising my book, it was merely a pretext to put me in the hot seat over my marriages. It was highly embarrassing, but I thought I behaved in a dignified fashion until I returned to the green room when I was, I think, justifiably angry. Nothing untoward had happened on screen but to read the newspaper reports you'd have thought we'd had fisticuffs on air with headlines such as 'Jan Leeming in chat-show fury'. That's the press for you.

The icing on the cake for me was my very own Foyles Luncheon. The late Christina Foyle started the luncheons in 1931 and mine was the 521st and was held on 19 September. Miss Foyle had very kindly invited me to many of her luncheons and they had always been most enjoyable. I was always a guest on the top table and sat next to some highly interesting characters over the years.

I don't remember much about the lunch, as it all came and went in a haze. I'm always terribly nervous at having to give speeches, especially when there were such distinguished guests on the top table with me. It was daunting to have to speak in front of newsreading colleagues from the other side – Pamela Armstrong and Carol Barnes – and to perform in front of such seasoned broadcasters as Mike Parkinson and Esther Rantzen. However, Christina wrote me a lovely letter and I still find it hard to believe she said my speech was, 'one of the best we have ever had'. Either she was being incredibly polite or I must have been in overdrive. I would have anticipated the Foyles Luncheon speakers, as authors and wordsmiths, to have ranked far more highly than myself.

As the time came for Eric to separate from Robin the tension was almost unbearable. I felt sure his love for the children would hold him back and he'd let me down as he had done several times before. But they'd sorted out the domestic arrangements and Robin had opted to move to a house Eric bought for her in Abingdon. He moved into the Officers' Mess for the last few months before he left the RAF.

In October we had our holiday in France. Owen was in a relationship with a Parisienne. Mireille worked as a child psychologist in Paris and, though she obviously loved Owen, was not prepared to live in Provence all the time, nor to live on a next-to-nothing income. Owen had to think about working full time again and had moved up to Paris to be a translator with the OECD (Organization for Economic Co-Operation and Development). So his house at Alleins in Provence was empty and he generously offered it to Eric and myself. We couldn't go anywhere publicly so the offer was readily accepted. In order to avoid the press, I flew to Paris and Eric took my car across on the ferry and drove to Paris. We met up at the airport and went to stay with Owen and Mireille for a couple of nights before driving south to Provence. Mireille was a joy and we took to her immediately. I think the feeling was reciprocated and that both of them liked my Eric.

I couldn't believe how lucky we were. It was a perfect holiday, perhaps one of the best we ever had. Provence is superb in the autumn, when most of the tourists have left and one can see the sights in comfort and still enjoy warm sunshine. We explored the area, which is rich in history. The place we found most enchanting and which was to become precious to us was Les Baux, which I had visited with Owen over a decade earlier.

It was still warm enough to eat al fresco. We ate in, we ate out, and we made love – so much so that at one point Eric suggested that I occupy myself with reading a book. The only non-French volume in Owen's bookcase was *Fanny Hill*. It was an extremely sensual novel and I don't think that's quite the sort of book Eric had intended for me to read! We were so very, very happy. Our most memorable day was visiting Fontaine de Vaucluse in the Lubéron. The town is at the source of the Vaucluse river, which gushes out of a massive cavern in the limestone hillside. The Italian poet Petrarch lived and wrote there and the whole place just emanates romance. I remember we chose to eat Canard au Poivre sitting out at a restaurant overlooking the water wheel and fast-flowing river. I've been back there so many times and I always see the two of us sitting at the same place, eating what seemed to us like a five-star Michelin meal. It could have been cheese on toast and we would have thought it wonderful.

On our return there was a really weird piece about me in the *Daily Express*. The Hickey column had a large headline: 'Riddle of Jan's "publicity baby"'. I wondered if they knew something I didn't! I certainly wanted Eric's child, but the subject had not yet been raised between us. The article inferred that after the launch of my beauty book, 'the publishing world was licking its lips at the idea of a money-spinning follow up'. Hickey claimed that he had a memo in which it was suggested I should produce a second child to coincide with publication of a beauty guide to pregnancy. According to the article, I liked the idea and negotiations were taking place with a book publishing company. This was news to me, particularly since Patrick and I had separated months earlier. Where do they get these stories?

Eric was to leave the RAF in early January but, as his working life was winding down, he was able to come and visit most weekends. Of course, I had to work but it was wonderful coming home to him. My house was only half an hour from Abingdon, so when he came on a visit he would go across to see his children. I still worried that he wouldn't come back and I know it was a very difficult time for him too. But he had taken a long time making up his mind and he was now sticking by his decision.

We spent our first Christmas together in 1984. Well, at least we woke up in the same bed, though I had to go to work and Eric went to see the children. But we were together, very much in love and so hopeful for the future.

CHAPTER ELEVEN

LEAVING THE BBC

Eric officially left the RAF on 3 January 1985 and immediately stepped into a job in the civilian world. The communications company Maritz, which had staged the Crown Conference in late 1982, had been impressed with Eric and had offered him a job. It was flattering to be told that they would wait for him to finish off his tour of duty with the RAF and an enormous plus was that they were based in Marlow, just down the road from my home.

Richard Armitage had realised a dream and was restaging the musical *Me and My Girl,* written by his father under the pseudonym of Noel Gay (the name of Richard's agency). Robert Lindsay took the lead and a rising star played the love interest. That rising star was Emma Thompson! We received an invitation to the opening and the first night party. We'd had two years of 'kissing in the shadows' and had been living together for four months. The press were bound to find out about us sooner or later so we decided to take our chances and attend the show and party as our 'coming out'.

Me and My Girl was a great show and the applause and myriad curtain calls told Richard he'd backed a winner. So we all trooped off happily to the after-show party. The story line was 'rags to riches but marries true love from the East End of London', so the theme of the party was market stalls serving bangers and mash, with the odd pearly king and queen circulating for good measure. It wasn't long before the photographers started circling around Eric and myself. We divulged nothing and next day the gossip columnists were asking who was the mystery man in my life. Needless to say, it didn't take them long to find out. In a way we were relieved and it now meant we could go everywhere together as a couple.

A few weeks later we were invited to the film première of *Carmen*. At the after-show party we were introduced to one of my favourite film stars and some press photographers took photos of the three of us. I was so upset when the article appeared and found they'd cut Charlton Heston out of the picture!

A few days later I received a lovely note from the new News Editor, Ron Neil, offering congratulations on the viewing figure for the Sunday evening main News – 14.1 million. When Ron was head of the new Breakfast Television Show, he tried to poach me from the News. It was an offer I didn't even have to think about twice. My eighteen months in radio, working totally anti-social hours, had taught me what I could and couldn't do. There was no way I could have worked that early morning shift. Besides, I wanted a life with Eric and didn't wish to be in bed at eight o'clock each night.

I didn't socialise much with people in the News Department. This was for many reasons, but partly because of working odd hours – also, most of them lived in and around London and I didn't. Esther Rantzen and Desmond Wilcox had been very kind and supportive at the time of the break-up of my marriage to Patrick. They'd had me to their home and taken me out and I wished to reciprocate. But who could I invite to partner them? I then discovered that Ron and Esther had worked together and hadn't socialised in years. I invited Ron and his wife and the Wilcoxes. The evening was a success and I shan't forget, as I was halfway between the dining room and the kitchen, hearing Ron praising my work to the point that I felt embarrassed. But things change!

In July there was an invitation to take part in a charity event at the Albert Hall. The charity was Cruise, which looks after widows and orphans from the armed forces. The Queen was to be in attendance and one of the main performers was Sir John Gielgud, whom I admired enormously. I don't know whether I was more excited about meeting Sir John or the Queen or performing in the Albert Hall, but it was a memorable day.

Not long after that I was fortunate to be invited to a dinner with Lady Harlech and met Sir John again, in a much more convivial atmosphere. I'd been a regular participant in the annual *Story of Christmas* performed in St George's, Hanover Square. We had prestigious guests each year and the event raised hundreds of thousands of pounds for the Duke of Westminster's Appeal, which benefited the homeless in London. Lord and Lady Harlech supported the charity and I'd met them many times. Sadly, I was on duty the day we carried the story of his death in a car crash. It's difficult enough having to read unpleasant stories but when you know the person or people involved, it is almost impossible. I'd written a letter of condolence to Pamela Harlech and some time later received the invitation to dinner.

On the work front, I had to pinch myself. I was in demand for corporate work and the BBC were good about giving me permission to do most of the jobs. I'd never have dreamed I would be meeting and wining and dining with so many interesting people, such as Sir John and Charlton Heston. But into every life some rain must fall and life was far from perfect at home. There was no problem with the love Eric and I felt for each other, but outside influences were having a bearing on us. Eric's children, Mark and Caron, came to stay every second weekend and these visits were difficult. Naturally, they felt awkward with me and probably, understandably, resented me. I began fully to comprehend how awkward life must have been for my own stepmother. Jonathan was being difficult and, when all five of us were together, the tension in the house was palpable. Eric was also finding it much more difficult to adapt to civilian life than he'd expected. We both felt that Maritz had put him in the wrong slot. Eric had spent a large proportion of his service life instructing young pilots. He was an ace award-winning aerobatic pilot and the teaching of cadets came naturally to him. Instead of joining the training arm of the company, he was put into sales. Eric was not a salesman and the role sat uncomfortably with him. He also caught some mystery virus, which laid him low for weeks.

In July we took the children on holiday to Brittany. I think they had a lovely time but it nearly finished us off as a couple. We were both protective of our own children and any small hiccup between them developed into rows between us. Matters were not helped by the fact that after a wonderful babyhood, Jonathan had become a difficult young boy. Anyone who has experience of step-children and step-parents will fully understand all the problems that come with the package.

We were so wrung out when we got home that we planned to take another holiday later in the year without the children. A person we knew had contacts in Mauritius. It sounded as good a place as any and we made arrangements to book a villa by the sea. We were met at the airport by the villa owners, an old Chinese lady and her son and daughter, driving a beaten-up old car with the springs showing through the upholstery. It was a long and very uncomfortable drive up to the north-western end of the island. The state of the car made us wonder what the 'villa' would be like. It was a sizeable distance and across a main road away from the sea and the cooking facilities were filthy. The family waited for us to give our approval. It was growing dark, we had two large suitcases and, if we refused the villa, where were we going to stay for the night? Then Eric said, 'We can't possibly stay here. I'll pay them off and we'll just have to find something else.' They charged us an exorbitant sum for the taxi ride, but we were glad to see the back of them.

We must have struck a comical picture, wheeling our cases along a main road with very little in the way of human habitation. We did eventually come across a motel that had a vacancy sign in the window. It was dark by now, so Eric decided we'd book in and he'd go looking for something better in the morning. The accommodation was quite primitive and our room had a corrugated-iron roof, which didn't appear to be attached to the walls as birds were flying in and out under the eaves. In the morning we went to breakfast and on our return, the pillows were covered with bird droppings. I'm so glad the little feathered creatures hadn't wanted to relieve themselves in the night.

I was left to look after the cases and Eric went off foraging. He came back a couple of hours later driving an open mini-moke and beaming. 'Damn it,' he said, 'we're here now so let's melt the plastic.' The hotel into which he'd booked us was vastly more expensive than our rented villa would have been, but at least it was right by the sea and also had a swimming pool. One of the first holiday-makers we bumped into at the Merville was a journalist from the *Daily Express*. We kept a wide berth!

We had a good holiday, aside from one big problem. I desperately wanted Eric's child. Apart from loving him to bits and wanting our child, I wanted a companion for Jonathan. I believed that having 'our' child would provide a bridge between 'his' children and 'my' child. Also, the biological clock was clanging. I was 43. Many a night, we'd sit up late discussing the issue. Eric definitely didn't want another child. He was worried about my age and felt that, if we had an offspring, it would mean his children being pushed further out of his life. We were at a total impasse.

At Eric's suggestion, I had changed agents. There had been some communication problems with Noel Gay Artists and Eric had approached IMG on my behalf. They appeared keen to take me on as a client. We took Richard Armitage to dinner and told him that I would be leaving the agency. He bade me a very fond farewell, wishing me great good fortune. I believed there was no ill will. Clients often change agents and agents like to take on new blood. I liked Richard very much indeed and respected him enormously, but he wasn't looking after me personally, as I had hoped, and there were several elements in the agency with which I was unhappy.

Whilst a client I'd been a recipient of much of Richard's bounteous generosity. He lived in a beautiful old house at Great Dunmow and every summer threw a huge party for his clients, friends and business associates. Richard knew everyone there was to know in the field of entertainment and the parties were totally star-studded. The format was to arrive for lunch, after which those who wished to could play cricket against the village team. If you weren't a cricket aficionado (and I'm definitely not – in my book, it's like watching paint dry!) you could swim or just loll about in the extensive grounds. In the evening there would be a cold buffet in the village hall and Richard would stage entertainment, usually featuring up-and-coming young artists he'd taken under his wing.

I went to three of these events but the one I remember most was when Andrew Lloyd Webber and Sarah Brightman put in an appearance. They arrived by helicopter and instead of being driven from the field and up the lane to Richard's house, someone had organised a 'bridge' across the small stream so that they could walk directly into the grounds. The bridge was little more than a couple of planks of wood. Sarah trotted across very daintily and Andrew slipped and fell with both legs straddling the plank. Ouch! Remembering his rudeness to me in the *Pebble Mill* days, I am ashamed to say that I smiled broadly. But then so did a lot of other people! Sarah was lovely.

In November, once again I was invited to take part in a Royal Variety Performance for The Queen. The theme was to be 'The World of Film Musicals'. I was teamed with Michael Aspel and Russell Harty to perform the song 'Triplets' from the MGM film *The Band Wagon*. The triplets sang '... *we do everything alike, we look alike, we walk alike, we talk alike and what is more, we hate each other very much* ...' The three of us, dressed in frilly nighties and bonnets, sang the song carrying huge lollipops and teddy bears. We had so much fun together. Russell died not long afterwards, which makes the memory particularly poignant.

Whether it was the power of IMG or the fact that I'd worked so many times over the holiday period, I actually got leave for Christmas Day 1985. We had the three children for presents and lunch and then all three went off to Robin and Patrick. Eric and I had often daydreamed about the other two falling for each other but were surprised that it had happened. We weren't sure when it had begun, but we were pleased that they had found happiness together. We rather suspected that it was Jonathan's need for potty training that had kick-started their relationship, when Patrick had dropped him off with Robin following her very generous offer to see if she could help. Many months earlier, when I'd been making arrangements with Robin for the pick-up of the children, she'd told me that in a way she was grateful for what had happened. Eric had, unwittingly, dominated her life to the point where she felt she'd begun to lose herself and now she was more able to be, and do, what she wanted.

On looking back at cuttings I was surprised to see that in his *Diary of Resolutions* for 1986, Nigel Dempster referred to me as his 'favourite newsreader', because this didn't save me from coming in for 'stick' from time to time in his column. (My New Year resolution was not to make any. 'Invariably I break them after a few months and then I get depressed at my own failings,' I was quoted as saying and it is true, so I've made none since.) As his 'favourite newsreader' I was surprised to read in his column about 'Jan Leeming's Knight on the town' in which I was purported to have been out with a certain married man, which was completely untrue. I knew the gentleman through charity work and he and his wife had been to my home for dinner, but I had never otherwise socialised with him. I was totally incensed at this erroneous journalism and rang up the 'Knight' to ask what procedure we should take. I was told that his PR department would deal with it and they said it was best not to draw attention to the story. I was also concerned at what his wife might have thought. Some years later I found out there was a double and she had been 'seeing' the Knight in question. That could account for the advice I was given.

The year progressed with a mixture of newsreading, corporate work and functions to attend. Over my newsreading years I had from time to time been invited to BBC dinners on the sixth floor of Television Centre. The sixth floor was where the great and good had their offices. I'd sat next to Lord

Snowdon at one of them and got on very well with George Howard at another, at the time he was Chairman of the BBC. In May I received an invitation to one of these dinners from the Director General, Stuart Young. Among the guests were his brother, Lord Young, who was Secretary of State for Employment in the Tory government, Christopher Benson from MEPC and Chairman of the Docklands Development Corporation, whom I'd met several times at the annual Westminster Christmas Appeal functions, and David Hatch, Controller of Radio 4. There were other guests and talk turned to left-wing bias within the BBC. I was asked my opinion and, despite the BBC being my employer, did not hold back with my views, which I thought were genuinely sought. I definitely saw bias in the newsroom, both in the writing and the way videotape was cut. With what I said I stepped unwittingly into a minefield and may have cut my own throat.

In June came a completely unexpected invitation to attend Wimbledon. I was offered two seats in the Royal Box. I don't play tennis but enjoy the game and was highly honoured at the invite. One of the girls with whom I had shared a house in Australia was coming over for a visit and, knowing she was fanatical about tennis, I proffered the invitation to her. We attended lunch and were about to take our seats when I realised that the hem of my skirt had come undone. It was too far gone for a pin to do the job. I asked one of the lady members of the armed forces, who was on duty, if she could help. She found me a small sewing kit and I spent the first ten minutes of the game surreptitiously repairing the hem with the largest stitches I could manage. Sarah Ferguson was in the front row and when she appeared on the lead page of the *Telegraph*, my skirt was in the background! Jan, my friend, was beside herself. She thought all her Christmases had come at once. Not only was she at Wimbledon but she couldn't have dreamed of better seating arrangements and the Australian tennis star, Pat Cash, was on centre court.

One of the most unusual invitations I ever received came one day when a call was put through to the Newsreaders

Office. The caller was a gentleman who said he worked for and was phoning on behalf of the Sultan of Pahang to invite me to dinner. I really thought this was some joke. I'd never heard of Pahang and couldn't believe a Sultan would invite me to dinner. Anyway, after duly checking out credentials, and insisting that a paper invitation was sent, I discovered that everything was bona fide. I asked for the invitation to be extended to Eric, which it was. We had a most entertaining meal in The Grosvenor House Hotel in London. The Sultan was absolutely charming, very down to earth and there were other interesting guests at his table. Some time later the Sultan's 'gofer' rang again and said I was invited to Pahang to attend the wedding of one of the Sultan's sons. I would love to have gone but Eric was not included, so I turned down the invite! Pity, I'm sure it would have been the experience of a lifetime!

The year brought some highly enjoyable events. Eric and I met Princess Alexandra at the Bond Street Tercentenary Ball. I've met her many times over the years and she remains my favourite royal person – so kind, warm and unassuming. BBC Radio's 'hairy monster', Dave Lee Travis, published a book of female personalities revealing their finer points or phobias. Called *A Bit of A Star* we were photographed either doing something or showing something we liked or disliked about ourselves. Joanna Lumley, who doesn't like her hair, allowed Dave to snap her in a bald wig. She still looked gorgeous! The diminutive Lynsey de Paul always wanted to be taller and Dave featured her being stretched on the rack. Eric thought my mouth my best feature, so Dave photographed me with my hand around a glass, incongruously padded, to protect my lips. There were many highly entertaining and innovative photos in the book and I still enjoy looking through it.

The most traumatic event of 1986 was losing our baby. Eric had finally been won over to the idea of having a child and shortly after stopping the contraceptive pill, I became pregnant. I wanted our child so much, I really didn't care if it cost me my job. The climate was changing slowly but I still ran the risk that in my position and unmarried, a pregnancy could have brought about a termination or non-renewal of my contract.

At ten weeks I went to the John Radcliffe Hospital in Oxford for a scan. When Eric had moved in, he bought me a standard poodle to replace my lovely Fleur. Some animals loathe travelling but Kiri revelled in it and always tried to become a passenger, whether I intended to take her with me or not. As I was leaving the house she dashed past me and headed for the car so I took her to Oxford with me and left her in the car park with the window of the car slightly open.

I can still hear the operative's voice, cold and unemotional as she ran the probe over my abdomen and said, 'There's nothing there ...' I went icy cold and waited, waited for her to say she'd made a mistake. But she hadn't. I went back to a side room and the gynaecologist came to see me. He was so kind and compassionate as he explained that, though I showed all the normal symptoms of pregnancy, I had what is called 'a blighted ovum'. He explained that I would naturally miscarry in the next few weeks, but gave me the option of having a D and C (dilation and curettage procedure used to clean out the womb) there and then. He left me for a while to think about what I wanted to do. I couldn't bear the thought of waiting for a miscarriage and opted to have the D and C.

I was left to recover for a few hours, during which time there was a terrible thunderstorm. Kiri was so frightened of thunder that she would find me and cower under my chair and there she was in a car, with the window open, and a storm raging. Just before I left the hospital, the gynaecologist returned and advised me to take precautions for a couple of months but after that there was no reason why I couldn't conceive again and have a healthy pregnancy. I cried quietly all the way home.

Thank goodness Eric was back from work early that evening. We sat on the sofa and wept together. I never got pregnant again. My Catholic upbringing reared its head – I felt the inability to have the child of the man I adored was again atonement for the sin I had committed all those years ago.

In August, we took the children to Brittany again. Owen drove from Paris to have a meal and stay with us. Eric had a small lump-sum gratuity from the RAF and, as it was not enough to buy a holiday property in England, we were thinking of somewhere in Provence. This would not only give us a foothold in an area we both loved, but would enable us to have inexpensive holidays with the children. Owen promised he would keep his ear to the ground for properties coming on the market in his village of Alleins.

A few weeks later, he phoned to let us know there were several places for sale, mostly big and old and not considered desirable by the younger generation, who wanted modern houses with all modern conveniences. But we didn't mind as we weren't going to live in it full time and could see ourselves lovingly restoring a property over a period of years. We decided to pay a flying visit to Provence over the late August Bank Holiday weekend and Owen lined up some viewings. The properties weren't ideal but they more or less fitted our price bracket. I offered to make up the difference and pay the notary's fees and the deal was struck.

When I got back, Ron Neil, the News Editor, wanted to see me. I couldn't imagine what for. I worked weekends and never got to see the editorial staff at all. The long and the short of the matter was that it had been decided not to renew my contract. I was given some cock-and-bull story that the format of the news programmes was to be changed and I wouldn't fit the bill. To be honest, I was getting fed up with weekend working for several reasons. Jonathan was now at school, which meant I didn't have the time with him midweek anymore. Eric worked Monday to Friday and with me working weekends, our social life was almost non-existent. I had been thinking of asking for a change to my duties or coming to some arrangement, but Ron's announcement came as a bolt from the blue.

I was still topping polls and appeared to be popular, so I challenged his decision. He told me he thought my performance was not as good as in the past. I know a bad workman blames his tools but I did feel there were some mitigating circumstances, if indeed my work was faulty. We had a weekend editor of whom as a person I was very fond, but he'd had a heart attack and on his return to work appeared to have lost his edge. Items were dropped, changed, altered, moved around the bulletin with monotonous regularity. It appeared to me that weekends were used as a training ground for staff, from directors through to floor managers. Often there were breakdowns in communication and information wouldn't be relayed to me, changes would be made, hard copies of scripts wouldn't make it to the studio and I'd be left coping with an almost illegible flimsy copy. I was doing my best against difficult working conditions, so perhaps my performance wasn't as good as it had been.

I was informed it would be convenient for me to stay on until the Easter of 1987 and a half-year contract would be drawn up. Frankly, I wanted to tell him where to stick his contract but the old insecurity raised its head and I kept quiet. Besides, six months would give my agent time to sort out other work.

I couldn't help wondering if my departure from Richard Armitage's Agency had anything to do with the decision. Richard and Bill Cotton (Managing Director, BBC Television) were bosom-buddies and a word from the latter could easily have destroyed my career. I thought back to the time when Richard admitted that the approval of some high-powered City businessmen had kept me in a job when the then news editor wanted to get rid of any of us who weren't journalists, regardless of how good we were or how popular. Also, I realised I'd been stupidly frank about the left-wing leanings in the BBC and the news room in general.

One very interesting facet to the whole business was that my agent told me that the BBC would prefer it if I made no waves and that if I didn't 'there would be other work' for me. It was rather like a veiled threat. I argued with James Kelly, my representative at IMG. I wasn't going to scream and bitch about the BBC, but I did want the public to be aware of what was going on. I had not been with IMG very long. They were big and powerful and I was leant on to keep quiet.

Against my better judgment I bowed to James' wishes. Later, I wondered whether James had horse-traded my interests against those of another.

The BBC, in common with most large organisations, will always have its moles. Someone had slipped information to the press and there were many requests for 'my story'. Eventually, James decided to give the story to Lynda Lee Potter with the proviso that a representative from IMG was on hand to help with any awkwardness. Lynda is a very fine and accomplished journalist and, although she agreed to the condition, soon managed to get rid of the minder. She can be very hurtful and she can be very supportive and my files include articles written by her where she's veered from supporting me to attacking me. In general I have a lot of respect for her and was longing to tell her the total truth. Lynda didn't realise it, but her headline did me a deal of harm with regard to future work. The front-page caption read 'Jan Leeming quits the BBC for love', and inside the paper was the story of our 'love swap'. Years later people who employed me for corporate work told me they thought, at the time, I'd left with a golden handshake, that Eric earned pots of money, and that I didn't need to work. Eric was not on a large salary and was supporting Robin and his children. I was paying the mortgage and the bills on our home, so work was essential.

It amuses me how papers do a story to death. Two days after our front-page story, Robin and Patrick were approached by the *Mail* to give their version of the 'love swap' for a show business exclusive. They were offered a chauffeured car to London, a champagne dinner and a fee. They told us about it so that we could vacate the house and not be bothered by any more journalists. They had a good dinner and gave their story, which didn't denigrate anyone. In fact, Robin even commented on how down to earth I was and that I had helped her with the washing up! However, they were told the story wasn't salacious enough so there'd be no fee, just the dinner and champagne. But the story was printed anyhow and the next day a cribbed version of the *Mail* article appeared in the *News of the World*.

I received many supportive letters from the public, but the one that I treasure most was from a clergyman, the Reverend Malcolm Perkins. We have remained in contact and I don't think Malcolm would mind my sharing his letter with you. He wrote:

> As one of your T.V. audience admirers, may I just say how happy I am to learn that you and Eric are in love with one another and to wish you both a long time together and a lot of real happiness.
>
> Life, I know, has been very hard for you at times, you have had to weather a lot of storms and have come through with a smile. Indeed you have had more than your fair share of hurts and disappointments. I so so hope that you will be very happy and feel loved and secure. Although I have never met you, I think you are a lovely person and you will be missed by a lot of people on the T.V. screen, including me! God Bless.

I was so very touched by his words, especially as he was a vicar. It put the hurtful letters and newspaper articles into perspective. You can't please all of the people all of the time and there will always be those who stand in judgment on others even though they don't know them.

Now that I had no steady job I wanted us to back out of the French house purchase. Having got the bit between his teeth, Eric decided that he would take out a fixed-rate mortgage for ten years to cover the shortfall of £18,000. So we paid the notary's fees and began our 'Years in Provence'.

That Christmas, the BBC wanted to make everything look cosy and I was requested to do some publicity. If it had been with anyone other than Les Dawson, I would have told them where to go, but I'd fallen under Les's spell and happily agreed to pose with him for the papers. He was dressed in a Santa outfit and was supposed to be kissing me under the mistletoe. As usual, he was pulling silly faces. I took my mother to the photo shoot and she was thrilled to meet Les and be photographed with him. And I worked my last Christmas and Boxing Day on BBC Television News.

In February 1987, I became a Freeman of the City of London. Apart from giving me the right to drive a flock of sheep over London Bridge, this is an honour in title only. But I did feel honoured and derived great pleasure in being able to ask my mother to the celebratory luncheon. She had never attended a function like it and was tickled pink by the whole panoply.

At Television Centre, all the newsreaders shared an office, as rarely were two of us on duty together. Our room was next door to the office of *John Craven's Newsround*. During the week, we would have to take the long route down to the News Studio but at weekends we could take a shortcut through the *Newsround* office, which was empty. It was Sunday, 15 February. I'd read the early evening news, had something to eat and was in the office answering correspondence from viewers. It was nearing time to go down for the next bulletin and as it was to be the last for the evening, I packed up my briefcase in order to take it with me to the studio so that I could go straight home.

As I opened the connecting door between our offices, the light from my office fell on three figures. I can't remember exactly what I said but it was something like, 'What are you doing here. Can I help?' I felt a tug at my shoulder strap and something was sprayed in my face. I must have opened my mouth to scream because the substance went over my tongue. I stumbled back into the light of my own office but momentarily couldn't remember the phone number of the Newsroom. I ran down the stairs and along the corridor to the Newsroom in a very agitated state.

Shock was setting in and I remember beginning to shake. A friend of mine, floor manager David Gold, sat me down and cradled my head against him. My hair was damp from the substance sprayed on me and, whatever it was, it also affected David's hands. They weren't exactly burnt but they came up red and were very sore. It was decided that I should be taken to the nearby Hammersmith Hospital.

The news was read by Chris Morris. Someone must have informed the press even before his appearance, because by the time the ambulance reached the hospital, there was a posse outside the entrance and we had to go in through an emergency exit. I was taken into Accident and Emergency, which was – amazingly – empty.

A male nurse told me to get onto a bed and then a saline solution was played over my eyes to neutralise whatever had been sprayed into them. I was wearing a thick sweater with a polo neck. The water was running over my face and into the sweater. It was getting wetter and wetter and I was getting colder and colder and decidedly uncomfortable. I asked the nurse if I could take my sopping wet sweater off and have a robe.

Then a diminutive female doctor came to see me. She decided I needed a saline drip. I may not have been sparking on all my marbles but I was feeling relatively OK and just wanted to go home. Also, I have wobbly veins and it is almost impossible to get a needle into them. I did not want to be put on a drip. The poor doctor prodded and poked for ages and then she hit an artery and blood spurted all over the cubicle. That had to be staunched and fastened with a large bandage and I still didn't know if she'd got the needle in properly to administer the saline solution. The hospital staff wanted to keep me in overnight but I adamantly refused. I simply wanted to go home to my own bed. At about 1 a.m. I was allowed a release. The saline solution had soaked the bandage and I don't think much had gone into me. My arm was swelling up from the puncture in the wrong place. The staff were very kind, but I was only too glad to leave the hospital.

Eric couldn't come and collect me as there was no one else at home to look after Jonathan and we could hardly call my mother in the middle of the night. Eventually my agent, James Kelly, turned up and drove me home. We got back at around 2 a.m. and, to my amazement, there were a few members of the press outside the house. James told them I'd nothing to say, would not give an interview and needed to go to bed. By that time, adrenalin and everything else had kicked in and I was wide awake. I felt dirty and violated, so I had a bath and washed my hair to get rid of the noxious substance. Sleep eluded me and by 6 a.m. the press were on the doorstep, in droves. Again I had financial offers for my story. I declined.

The headlines on the Monday tabloids were unnecessarily lurid. The *Sun* carried 'My Hell' in two-inch high letters and, on the Tuesday, the *Express* had a story on page 5 with the headline 'Jan tells of terror raid at the Beeb'. All I can say is that the experience was very unpleasant but it was neither a *Terror* raid nor did I refer to *My Hell*. The press use such emotive language, they don't leave themselves anywhere to go when there's a real tragedy or emergency.

As most of the papers had carried the story of the mugging we couldn't see what more could be said. Eric told the doorstep reporters I had nothing to add to what they already knew so standing outside in the cold wasn't helping anyone. They just wouldn't go. Then the News Editor, Ron Neil, rang and asked me to give an interview to one of our own people. I didn't want to but he suggested that, if I did, there would be nothing else for the press and they would leave us alone. I chose Bill Hamilton, whom I liked and respected, and the story was carried on the BBC news that evening. The Beeb gave the story to ITN news but, somewhere along the line, I was accused of profiting out of the experience, the inference being that I was paid for the story.

Anne Robinson took a swipe at me and suggested that she'd seen my bed covers before . . . 'I think she's worn them to read the news'. Apparently several readers complained about her uncharitable remarks. A week later, she carried in her column, one of the letters from an angry reader which started, 'Dear Ugly Mug . . .' and went on to express the hope that she got mugged, as it might improve her face. The writer and friends had also declared their intention to give up buying the *Mirror*. I can only take my hat off to her for having the bottle to publish such an uncomplimentary letter. But then Anne is a strange mixture, as are many female journalists. She will tear you to shreds one week and champion you the next.

Anne wrote a lovely piece a couple of days after I left the news. She poked fun at my hairstyles, but it was gentle fun. She said she thought women changed hairstyles as they changed lovers and assumed I had a string of them. She also took Eric and myself to task for having said we couldn't marry because we couldn't afford to. For one thing she'd got my salary wrong by almost £100,000, quoting it as £120,000 when I was actually earning £23,500 and Eric was on less and keeping his family. The mortgage rate was extremely high and we were not awash with money. Unfortunately, our society doesn't appear to encourage marriage and we were better off, tax wise, staying unmarried. But she entitled her column 'Farewell to a TV Newsreader with heart ...' and for that I was grateful. Thank you Anne.

On the afternoon after my attack, I had a visit from the police. They brought along some 'mug-shot' books. I don't have the best of memories for facts and figures but I do have a sort of 'photographic' memory for faces, places and things. The difficulty lay in the fact that there were only two books, one for Caucasian faces and the other for Afro-Caribbeans. I had only seen one youth clearly and he was obviously of mixed race. However we got a reasonably accurate picture and when the detective came back into the bedroom and saw it, he knew immediately who they were looking for – a young chap who was continually in trouble.

There is always a silver lining to a cloud. I was sent so many flowers from friends, viewers and well-wishers that the hall, sitting room and dining room resembled a flower shop. Eventually the florist suggested drawing up a credit book and letting me have arrangements as and when I wanted them in the future. That credit lasted for months. When I returned to work, there were over two thousand letters of sympathy. I couldn't possibly answer them all, nor could Lydia. I had a hard job to persuade the News people to send an acknowledgement to these viewers. After all, they were our viewers and it was a small and courteous public relations exercise. Finally a very nice standard letter was sent out.

I had stated publicly that I was all right, only a little shaken, and therefore would be back at work the following Saturday. I underestimated the shock factor – my arm was bruised black and green from the wrist to the elbow from the hospital treatment and it hurt a great deal. I really wasn't feeling up to work. Ron phoned to say that the *Wogan* programme had made a request for me. I didn't wish to exploit the incident, but Ron wanted me to comply.

I did appear on the programme and was very surprised that Terry didn't come and say hello personally. After all, we knew each other and frequently met at functions. He'd often poked fun at me through his radio programme, criticising my clothes etc. I took that in the spirit in which it was intended, as gentle fun. He sent a researcher to get the details but was kind and sympathetic in the interview.

He asked me if the news affected me. It did greatly. During my years reading news, it seemed the world was all doom, gloom and destruction. 'Good news' isn't 'News' in the Newsroom, so we get a seemingly relentless litany of the wrongs of the world and few stories about the good in it.

I don't like seeing myself on television, so most of the recordings of my work have remained unwatched since the day when were made. To check facts for this book, I had to watch a few like *Eurovision* – very dated and embarrassing – and the *Wogan* show. I couldn't believe the applause, cheers and whistles that greeted my entrance onto the latter.

There was a lot of discussion about security at the BBC. Actually, in my opinion, it was a joke. At the front of Television Centre it is like Fort Knox. Richard Baker, Paul Daniels and I have amusing memories of us, the employees, being refused admission by new and officious commissionaires. But at the back of the building it was a leaky sieve. All my assailants had to do was shin over the iron railings and get in through the scene dock, or the Outside Broadcast Bay, where the cars were constantly coming and going. In fact, when they were caught, it was discovered that they'd regularly got into the building, usually at weekends when fewer people were around, and freely roamed, taking anything portable and saleable from open offices.

On my first day back at work, Eric accompanied me. Lightning was hardly likely to strike twice in the same place but it did give me a secure feeling, knowing he was there. When I signed off, I added a simple thank you to all the kind people who'd wished me well. I got reprimanded for it and even that got into the papers.

Less than a fortnight later I was stricken with Mumps Meningitis. At first, the doctor thought I had flu. I have never known such pain in my head – I thought it would burst. When my temperature reached 105 degrees, I was admitted to hospital in a state of delirium. I can only think that, in my debilitated state over the mugging, I'd caught mumps from Jonathan. He had it so mildly, it hardly affected him. I was in hospital for a week, during which there was the tragedy of the Zeebrugge ferry disaster. I watched it on the television in my room and was somewhat grateful I wasn't on duty over that period.

After my mugging I'd had a letter of sympathy from Sir John Gielgud. Encouraged by the contact, and the fact that we'd also met socially a couple of times, I was bold enough to invite him to dinner. I am a reasonably good cook and enjoy entertaining but get slightly phased when dealing with people who are used to staff. However, I went for it and proffered the invitation, which he readily accepted. Sadly the hospitalisation put paid to the dinner party and, though we tried to reinstate it several times, we never managed it, due to his work commitments, but I have got and treasure six letters from him.

As the time approached for me to leave BBC News, I was surprised to receive, what to me, were offers of large sums of money for my story. I didn't go hawking my story around Fleet Street as claimed in Nigel Dempster's Diary. So much had already been written about me, I was very surprised that any paper wanted more. James Kelly advised me that stories would be printed anyway, so I might as well accept the money and have some control over the serialisation. The *Mail* approached me first through a letter from Diane Hutchison. The *Mail* had invariably been fair to me, and as I knew Diane, I was happy to go with them. Diane and her husband had been on holiday in Crete at the same time as Patrick and me and we'd spent some convivial evenings together. She didn't write any stories after the holiday and I felt I could trust her.

James Kelly had a particular association with David Wigg, the showbiz writer of the *Daily Express*. In the end James prevailed and the story went to the *Express*. David was a delightful person by whom to be interviewed – gentle and probing but not unpleasantly so. We had a good rapport and I hope the *Express* were happy with what they got.

The people at the *Mail* were obviously miffed at not getting the story, so they sent Diane to Paris to nose out 'my secret'. That secret was Owen Leeming. All those closest to me knew about Owen, including my bosses at the BBC. Whenever I'd been asked about my name, I replied quite truthfully that I'd taken it by deed poll. Why did I need to reveal more details of my life than were necessary? The paper must have spent a lot of money because Diane was despatched to Paris and a reporter in New Zealand was sent sleuthing around there. The big joke was that Owen was in constant touch with me by telephone and the whole thing had overtones of a farce, with Diane stuffing notes through the mailbox in his block of flats. To leave the block you exit by a basement car park, which comes out into a different street, so Diane didn't succeed in contacting Owen. I suppose one paper wanted to steal a march on the other. Frankly, the *Daily Mail* article, which came out the day after the start of the *Express* serialisation, was a very good one apart from a few bitchy remarks attributed to Owen's brother and mother. I'm quite sure they were taken out of context, as I had a good relationship with all of them and they knew Owen and I were still very close friends.

I don't greatly enjoy large, noisy gatherings, so, instead of a leaving party, the Beeb offered me a dinner for twelve at Browns Hotel in Mayfair and I chose the people I wanted – the Assistant News Editor Robin Walsh, a few of the weekend editors, an autocue operator, a newsroom secretary, a floor manager, Moira

Stuart, Bill Hamilton, and Eric. I was given some champagne glasses and other gifts and we all had a super evening. I also received an extremely complimentary letter from Ron Neil:

> This Saturday must be a very sad day for you indeed. You have been a very loyal and long standing servant of Television News for many years now and I just wanted to put on record this Department's appreciation for all that you have done in the past.
>
> You have always brought complete professionalism to the task of newsreading coping admirably with the many crises that have beset the weekends. Outside the building, you have at all times been a fine ambassador for Television News. In writing this letter I simply wish to express my thanks for the considerable contribution you have made and extend the good wishes of everyone in the department for your future.

He didn't have to write a letter like that, and yet they were getting rid of me. Strange! It further reinforced my view that there had been some 'behind the scenes' activity to effect my dismissal.

A few months later I was staggered to find myself accused of breaking the news of Sue Lawley's romance. It was front page of the *Sun* and in the Fiona Macdonald Hull Gossip column two days later, again in the *Sun*. That paper has always given me an inaccurate and bad time. I cannot think what I've ever done to offend them, except never buy the rag. Apart from the fact that Sue and I never socialised, I had no knowledge of her life whatsoever, and wasn't the least bit interested in her love life, so how the story became attributed to me was a complete mystery. James Kelly of IMG tried to get an apology from the paper but apart from protracted and long legal wrangling, there was nothing we could do. An appeal to the Press Council is well nigh useless.

I've often wondered whether my opinion of the BBC and the way in which I was treated was a fair conclusion but in the intervening years it has been interesting to read declamatory articles by people to whom the BBC gave a much better deal than I had and from whom the Beeb received tremendously good service and highly popular programmes. A couple of pieces stood out and these were by Selina Scott and Barry Norman. Barry must have given a quarter of a century of good ratings to the BBC. I would have expected him to be revered and treated well but he wasn't when his days were finally numbered. The other piece, written by Selina Scott – who always managed to keep her private life exceptionally private and rarely said anything to newspaper reporters – was incredibly hard hitting. On this occasion she was totally incensed by a BBC programme, *Fame, Set and Match*, which savaged her and other leading characters from the heyday of breakfast television. I didn't see it, and certainly wouldn't have watched a programme of that nature, but from what she wrote, it was a totally shoddy and unnecessary programme calling into question her sexuality and accusing her of only being interested in money and status. I've read other articles by BBC 'stars', who found themselves out in the cold with no advance notice after giving good years of service to the Corporation. And the dear old BBC does seem to be particularly good at not 'telling' folk when their services are no longer required. One tends to read it in a newspaper first – leaked by a friendly mole. It's interesting that a service built on communication has operatives who simply don't communicate.

I was worried about finance when leaving the News. I hadn't been paid a fortune but it was a good regular salary. My worries were unfounded. Leaving the BBC freed me up for all sorts of corporate work. I had what is referred to as 'credibility' and I don't think I ever took a job that would have been at odds with the trust that credibility brought. For a few years I was able to earn the kind of money I'd never dreamed of. I actually almost made the amount Anne Robinson had assumed I earned in the BBC. The agent took 25% and the tax man took 40% but I was delighted with what was left and put as much as I could into a pension fund – with Equitable Life. Not having been in pensionable employment, the future was beginning to worry me. Little did I know how worrying an investment in Equitable would become.

While I had been with the BBC, I felt it incumbent not to show any political leanings and had avoided association with any groups or attendance at any functions with political overtones. Now that I was free of that responsibility, I thought I could afford to 'nail my colours to the mast'. When I was invited by the Conservative Party to take part in their Wembley Rally, I readily agreed. I was even more thrilled when, on the day, I was asked to read a message from Sir Yehudi Menuhin, who was unable to attend. Years previously I had interviewed Sir Yehudi and was a great admirer.

Apart from demonstrating that I had the courage of my convictions, attending that rally was a very bad move professionally. For reasons unknown to me, one is allowed by the press to be a paid-up member of the Labour Party but having allegiance to the Conservatives is tantamount to being a fascist. I probably give as much support to charities and good causes as any Labour supporter and would have been prepared to pay more in tax had I been certain that the money was going to the genuinely deserving, the old, the sick, and those who could not support themselves, plus the health service and education. But when I see our hard-earned money being frittered away, given to fraudsters, minority causes, almost encouraging young girls to have babies, paying for more and more red tape and quangos, and a nanny state that takes away most of our personal responsibility and accountability, then I simply could not give my support to Labour. Mind you, I feel that most MPs of any party are out of touch with reality. They live and work in the cosmopolitan atmosphere of London, and woo minorities who are not representative of the country at large. I'm totally disillusioned with the lot of them.

I think my appearance at Wembley must have added ten stars to the black mark already in the BBC book. Still, I got two lovely letters of thanks from Norman Tebbit (later to become Lord Tebbit) and from Mrs Thatcher.

I had an interesting project to work on. HTV had invited me to present a ten-part series entitled *The West in Trust*. We were to interview and film the people behind the National Trust and look at how they oil the wheels to make it work. It was great to be with some of the members of the old firm – lighting, sound and cameramen with whom I'd worked a decade and a half previously. I love the West Country and am very interested in the workings of the National Trust, so filming the series was a delight. One of the most memorable programmes was covering the Fête Champêtre (rustic picnic) in the beautiful grounds of Stourhead in Wiltshire. A few of the Trust's larger properties hold these picnics in the summer. There is a theme and people dress accordingly, pay an entrance fee and come with picnics, which they consume while being entertained by music, drama and dance. The theme for Stourhead in 1987 was 'And All That Jazz', with Humphrey Lyttleton. Many bring not only picnics, but tables, linen and candelabra and really do the evening in style. As is often the way with our British summer, the weather was awful but we put up our umbrellas and made the most of the event. The series was very successful and I was invited to repeat the idea with the National Trust properties in the Lake District, but the money was never raised so the idea came to nought.

Eric and I were planning to take the children to Provence in the summer and to take a holiday on our own in Bali for the late summer. With the Bali holiday, there was one big problem, and that was the court case against my muggers. The culprits had been caught a couple of weeks after the event. According to the Sun, they were boasting about the incident in the back of a mini-cab. Only one was old enough to be charged, the others were minors. The eldest was being held on around fifty counts of theft (including possession of a police truncheon!) and one for the assault on me.

I had assumed that the case would be an open-and-shut affair. Little did I realise the machinations of the law. I was told that if the offenders pleaded guilty, I wouldn't have to go to court. If they pleaded not guilty, I would be put in the dock and cross-examined. They kept changing their plea, so we didn't know whether we could take our holiday or not. Eventually, a couple of weeks before our proposed holiday, I was given permission to leave the country. Off we went, only to hear on our return that they'd changed their plea yet again and a case, which to me appeared open and shut, took two and a half days. The two minors had already served time on remand so they were let off without further punishment. The eldest was sent down for five years, two for the burglary and three for the assault.

All that was far from our minds in Bali. We arrived in the evening and it was already dark as we drove into our hotel. The floodlit gardens were beautiful and we had a good feeling about the place in general. We had booked a standard room for ten days and were a trifle alarmed when the porter led us along a long passage and unlocked a door to the Agung Suite. It was palatial. 'They've made a mistake, we can't stay here. It will cost an arm and a leg,' I whispered to Eric. I refused to unpack until he went to reception to investigate.

I had twice presented the Awards for the Hairdressing Industry – prestigious affairs at the Hilton in London. We had become friendly with Derek Pace, who was on the management team. He knew we were having a holiday in Bali and, as he often stayed at the Nusa Dua on incentive travel holidays, he'd put in a word for us. As the hotel wasn't busy, and the suite was empty, it was ours for the same price as the room we'd booked. It was a lovely start to an idyllic holiday. We walked most nights under starry skies and I fully expected Eric to propose. We didn't need to get married, but when I love a man, I want to commit and to belong.

The remainder of the year was busy. There was corporate work, guest appearances on television and an exciting project to make a documentary for the actress Susan George and her husband Simon MacCorkindale, who currently stars in the soap *Casualty*. Eric and I had met them both at a dinner the previous year and we got on well. They lived not far from us and we socialised from time to time. They had set up their own production company, Amy International, and were to make a film about a couple of history's most renowned lovers, Héloïse and the twelfth-century philosopher Abélard. Abélard had been a celibate but fell in love with Héloïse. They had an affair resulting in a child. Héloïse's uncle, Fulbert, who saw her as a highly marketable property, was so incensed he arranged for Abélard to be castrated. Héloïse nursed her lover back to health but he decided to devote his life to God taking Holy Orders, and inviting Héloïse to follow suit. It is the correspondence between them through the years that provided the material with which to make a film.

It was called *Stealing Heaven* and was to be shot in Yugoslavia. The documentary was to be about the making of a film, from raising the money through choosing the actors to the actual on-set camera work. I flew to Yugoslavia with Susan and after we'd checked in at the hotel we drove out to Jadran films. It was fascinating to witness a film being made and a privilege and great fun to interview stars such as Rachel Kempson and Angela Pleasence, Bernard Hepton and the late Denholm Elliott. Abélard was played by Derek de Lint, well known on the Continent though not in England. I don't think I've ever encountered anyone who emanated such raw sensuality – it just came off him in waves. Kim Thomson, a virtual unknown at the time, was a very beautiful and credible Héloïse. The film launched her career as, after that, I often saw her name on cast lists.

Although the hotel wasn't much more than three stars by English standards, it was the best one could get in Yugoslavia and several well-known people were staying there whilst making their own films. One of the hotel guests was Telly Savalas (Kojak). He and Susan knew each other well, so I got an introduction to him. He was an absolute charmer.

The documentary was never transmitted on TV, but I thoroughly enjoyed working on it and my glimpses behind the scenes of *Stealing Heaven*. I am totally entranced by the story of Héloïse and Abélard. I was so taken with their story that the next time Eric and I visited Owen and Mireille in Paris we made a point of visiting the Père La Chaise cemetery to see their tomb. Père La Chaise is a necropolis on the north-east side of Paris. Now it is a closed cemetery, but it houses the mortal remains of dozens of famous people: Chopin, Bizet, Sarah Bernhardt, Edith Piaf, Oscar Wilde just to mention a few. So many lovers visit the tomb of Héloïse and Abélard and so many have tried to take pieces of stone as mementoes, that the whole edifice is now surrounded by huge iron railings. Invariably you'll see single red roses scattered all around the shrine.

Eric was 40 that December and I arranged a surprise dinner at the English Garden Restaurant in Chelsea. It was owned and run by Michael Smith. He used to appear on *Pebble Mill* talking about 'posh nosh' and the cuisine for the TV series *Duchess of Duke Street*. I'd interviewed him many times and he helped me choose the menu. I'd never arranged anything like it before and think I got as much fun out of planning it as I hoped the guests would out of being there. Eric very much liked Radio One's Dave Lee Travis, so he and his wife were on the list, as were John Blackwell and his wife. After all, had it not been for John, Eric and I would never have met. Henry and Anne Ploszek came. Not only were they very old friends of Eric's and new friends of mine, but it was Anne who had counselled Eric in Cyprus. When he was going through his torment of what to do and what not to do, he had confided in Anne. It was she who suggested that if he couldn't sustain his marriage and really loved me, there really wasn't much option. Somehow or other I managed to convince Eric that it was just the two of us having a special dinner on the town. He didn't suspect anything and was totally taken aback when he opened the door to the private dining room and saw his friends there.

At Christmas I was to be the Good Fairy in a panto at Wimbledon. How a Good Fairy figures in *Robinson Crusoe* is beyond me, but then pantomime suspends belief at any time. The stars of the show were Dennis Waterman and Rula Lenska, whom I knew because they were near neighbours of ours. Colin Baker, an ex Dr Who, and Sam Kelly from *'Allo, 'Allo* were also in the cast and rehearsals were great fun. I was most worried about singing on stage, so took myself off for singing lessons. I had a very lovely but quite difficult song to sing, and it was performed with me suspended from the prow of a boat. As if that weren't bad enough, I had a load of little darlings as waves beneath my feet. Never work with children and animals as they will always upstage you, and they invariably did. We performed nine shows a week, including one on Sunday afternoons. That brought its own bonus. Eric did the cooking and welcomed me home with a roast dinner each Sunday of the run. Although we had Christmas Day off, it was just like old times at the Beeb – working over the holiday.

We tried to get to Provence as often as possible and whenever we did, we always made a point of going to Salon and having coffee and a brandy by the mossy fountain. It had become a romantic tradition. On 4 April 1988, as I was trailing my hand in the water of the fountain, Eric put his arms around me and asked me to marry him.

CHAPTER TWELVE

THE LUCKIEST WOMAN ON EARTH?

I very much wanted to be Eric's wife. I suppose I'm old fashioned and despite my failures, was still willing to commit to the man I loved. Mind you, life was not a bed of roses emotionally. We were having a great deal of difficulty, both with the relationship between Jonathan and Eric and also the general interaction between Eric's children and Jonathan and myself. It is only natural to experience difficulties with step-relationships. I've spoken with so many folk who've had to deal with the 'step' situation and taking on offspring of any age, from babies, through toddlers, teens, middle-aged and even retired sons and daughters, is never easy. Relationships within families are not always plain sailing, so why should total strangers, brought together by an accident of love, fare any better? There are the natural jealousies and possessiveness. Looking back, I should have coped a great deal better. My only excuse is that I was extremely busy, saw too little of Eric, and very often had to share him with the children. I'm sure, quite understandably, they would far rather have had their father to themselves, but I was around. And Jonathan was possessive. So we were all performing a juggling act. However, our love for one another was not in doubt and I left it to Eric to plan when, where and how we would marry.

Then, as far as my future broadcasting career was concerned, I made an even bigger mistake than I'd made when I attended the Conservative Rally in 1987. In April, I recorded a Party Political Broadcast for the Tories. The *Sunday Mirror* headline read 'Labour Fury at "Tory" Jan'. The story was written by the paper's political editor, Alastair Campbell. It stated that, 'Senior Labour figures wanted to ban her as a presenter of factual programmes if she ever returned to her former career. Labour's communications director Peter Mandelson wrote to deputy director general John Birt and said "People are amazed that a personality with such strong BBC links should be promoting the Tories."!!!!!! He asked Mr Birt what contractual restrictions are placed on BBC stars "to prevent this sort of *abuse*." Mr Mandelson said later that it didn't matter that Miss Leeming no longer works for the BBC ... while the BBC said she was free to do whatever work she wanted.' Call me naive but I'd absolutely no idea I was considered to have such *importance* or *powers of persuasion*. Apart from guesting on the odd programme, I have never done any substantial work for the BBC since that date.

I don't know what corporate work I may have lost due to my political affiliation but I know of one definite cancellation. I'd been booked to make a presentation in the North of England. The date was cancelled and the people were quite upfront with my agent about the reasons why. They didn't like my politics!

Later that month, I was invited to a reception at No 10 Downing Street. I also received a letter of condolence from Cecil Parkinson over my treatment in the *Sunday Mirror*. Although I was flattered, it really didn't compensate for the bad odour caused within the BBC. Still, it was my own silly fault. I should have thought it through more fully, but then, you can't sit on a fence all your life, can you, and surely you should have the courage of your convictions? Except mine appeared to be out of step with the Establishment at the BBC.

Meanwhile, plans were progressing for our wedding. We wanted to marry abroad. It wasn't quite as easy to make arrangements as it is today. Now, there are companies devoted to organising overseas weddings – from the flowers, cake and dress through to the ceremony and reception. We originally fancied the Seychelles, but the political situation there was unstable. Because we wanted the children to be part of the celebration, we eventually decided to wed in France. The French have even more red tape than we do, added to which I had to provide proof of my change of name by deed poll. My standard poodle Fleur had chewed it up years ago. Fortuitously, I had kept the bits in an envelope and had to stick the whole thing together – all twenty pieces. Add to that the need for birth and divorce papers to be translated and notarised and it proved a legal nightmare for Eric.

We told absolutely no one in England of our plans, not even my parents. Owen and Mireille were in on the secret, as they were to be 'best man' and 'matron of honour' and were to look after the children on our wedding night. They had tried to synchronise their own wedding to be on the same day, but somehow didn't manage to bring it off; that really would have set the villagers gossiping.

We were to marry on a special Monday, totally forgetting that much of Provence is *fermé* on that day. The French don't have rich fruit cake for their celebrations, they go for a pyramid of profiteroles covered in spun sugar. We wanted to do everything the French way, but no – the Croquembouche has to be freshly made and they couldn't oblige for a Monday. We settled for a superb concoction of sponge and my favourite fruit, raspberries. Because it was closing day, I couldn't have a bouquet of fresh flowers either. So a lovely mixture of silk flowers was arranged in a posy to match my outfit. The dress was by a French design house called Chacok. I liked their clothes and often purchased them from a lovely dress shop in Beaconsfield. I'd bought the outfit months earlier, with no intention of using it for our wedding. It was just a simple summer dress in light cotton muslin in delicate shades of blue and green, but it seemed ideal for the occasion.

We set off for our usual Provençal holiday with no one suspecting what we were going to do. Eric had chosen the date of 8 August. Apparently, the eighth day of the eighth month of 1988 was an auspicious date in the Chinese calendar. It also reads the same backwards as forwards. We have no leanings towards China – despite my name, 'Lee-ming'! – but it seemed like a good luck omen.

We indulged in our usual holiday pastime of going to the local pool with the children, our lunch of baguettes, cheese and ham and a bottle of wine in the cool box, and good thick books to read. Despite our ages, and previous marriages, we had decided to be traditional and not spend the night before our wedding together so that Eric would see the bride for the first time at the village *mairie* – town hall. So Eric trotted off up the road to Owen and Mireille's house, leaving me with the children. The morning turned into a French farce. I was getting ready when there was a knock at the door. Owen said, 'You're going to have to go the *notaire*'s office. Neither of you has signed a marriage contract.' The form is a bit like a prenuptial agreement and in France it is obligatory. We'd got very little to leave each other, but the legal requirements had to be fulfilled.

I had my hair in rollers when Owen arrived, so I threw a scarf over my head, pulled on some clothes and off we went. Our village was too small to sustain a notary, so we had to drive to the neighbouring town of Lambesc. The staff must have thought we were really weird. Owen marshalled us around the offices in order to keep us apart. We signed the documents and, panic over, I returned home to get ready.

At the *mairie*, Monsieur Van Loo, the village mayor, greeted us wearing a tricolour sash over his suit and led us upstairs to a function room. Behind his desk was the bust of a female who symbolises the French Republic. She was also sporting the French tricolour. Owen explained that the facial features of the bust are changed from time to time and are always modelled on the face of someone famous. When we married the bust had been modelled on Brigitte Bardot. The ceremony was conducted in French and we said 'Oui' in the right places. At the end, Eric put a wedding ring on my finger and kissed my hand. Then the mayor's assistant handed me a booklet covered in brown plastic. I gave it to Mireille, who burst out laughing. What was the cause of her mirth? She explained that as we'd

married under French law, under that same law I had been
issued with the equivalent of a maternity allowance book
allocating funds for up to eight children! I was 46 years old.

By now we knew some people in our village. We'd invited a
couple with whom we'd socialised a few times. Henri had been
a member of the Patrouille Aérobatique de France (PAF), the
French equivalent of the Red Arrows, so he and Eric had a lot
in common. His wife Arlette was a teacher and a very pleasant
lady. There were several English couples who, like us, had
fallen in love with Provence, and had holiday homes in the
village. The mayor and his wife made up the little party. We had
champagne and the cake, off-loaded the children on to Owen
and Mireille, and set off to celebrate our wedding. Eric is a
fantastic organiser of surprises and always comes up trumps.
He had decided on one night of unadulterated luxury rather
than a week elsewhere. He'd chosen to book us in for dinner
and a night at the renowned five-star Ousteau de Beaumaniere
at Les Baux, which has hosted most of the crowned heads of
Europe, including our own Queen. When we arrived mid-
afternoon, we were initially very disappointed to find that we'd
been allocated a room in their annexe. The annexe was not
even next door to the hotel and restaurant but half a mile down
the road. The porter set off on his little moped and we followed
in the car. We were miffed. Then, when we got to the annexe
and saw the suite with its four-poster bed and the beautiful
swimming pool surrounded by exotic plants, we decided we'd
got the better end of the deal.

Eric is a romantic and he'd ordered my favourite roses –
peach – and a bottle of champagne. We'd already had
champagne at home in the village but we opened the bottle and
were decidedly squiffy and very happy by the time we went out
for a swim in the late afternoon. Beaumaniere is sited in the
valley below Les Baux and as we lay by the pool, looking up at
the mediaeval fortification etched against a Mediterranean blue
sky, we felt as if we were in heaven.

Dinner that evening was a fantastic gastronomic experience.
Wonderful though it was, I'd go pop if I ate like that too often.

There was a wine on the list from 1888 and Eric asked the price. The *sommelier* didn't come back. I think he worked on the principle that if you needed to ask the price you couldn't afford it. We couldn't have – and we wouldn't have – spent stupid money on a bottle of wine, but we were curious. Anyway, we did have some superb wine ordered through the 'ordinary' wine waiter. The weather was balmy, the photos were out of focus because the waiter took them, and I thought I was the luckiest woman on earth.

After dinner we walked up the hill and on into the Roman village of Les Baux, quiet, romantic and empty of tourists. We looked over the battlements, down into the valley at our hotel. To the south we could look across the Camargue to the Mediterranean. The sky was crystal clear and full of stars, so when we got back to our suite, we stripped and went for a midnight swim. I don't know why, but on the few occasions I've been swimming at night I can only describe the feeling of the water as being like velvet. It is a very sensual experience. Could you ask for anything more? Well yes, a few more days of the same! But, next day, we had to return to reality and reclaim the children. Apart from the joy of being married, we'd managed it without any intrusion from the press. It was almost two weeks before the story leaked. James Kelly arranged for the *Daily Express* to come out and take a photo and, as they had the exclusive, the other papers left us alone.

There were many exciting projects during the year, but the one that I most enjoyed was working on a documentary about Jack the Ripper. Representatives of Cosgrove Meurer, an American company, came to England and held auditions for the role of reporter and I got the job. The year 1988 marked the centenary of the appalling crimes carried out by the Ripper in the East End of London. The programme format was to look at various individuals who at one time or another have been seen to fit the profile of the Ripper. These ranged from the Duke of Clarence, to Queen Victoria's surgeon and a Polish man called Kominski. My role was to visit the various parts of Whitechapel where the bodies had been found, and scene-set. I remember the area of the first murder. It was in a road parallel to the Whitechapel market. Although it was a warm and sunny day, as I recorded my piece to camera, the hairs on my arms stood on end. I had to interview various experts in their different fields, people such as Colin Wilson, a well-known crime writer, and also Donald Rumbelow, the then curator of the Black Museum at London's Scotland Yard. On American television, there would be a panel of expert psychiatrists and psychologists to whom the profiles would be shown. Peter Ustinov was to chair the proceedings on the other side of the Atlantic. At the end, the panel and the television audience would be asked to vote for who they thought was the Ripper.

As we were working on different sides of the ocean, Mr Ustinov and I were not due to meet. Andy, the programme director discovered that Peter was going to be in London briefly for some filming and asked if it would be possible for us to get together. Peter agreed to meet Andy and myself for dinner at the Berkeley Hotel. We met at reception and he let slip that he was suffering badly from toothache. Immediately, we suggested the dinner be called off. Peter is a consummate professional and insisted we kept our date. What a magical evening that was. Another to be stored in my 'Special Memory Box'. Peter is a marvellous raconteur and he entertained us all evening with stories, lapsing into accents whenever required. Once again, I wished I'd had a recording machine with me. I remember the evening, but I can't remember the stories. Andy and I both felt privileged at having our very own 'Evening with Peter Ustinov' – the title of a show he brought into the West End not long afterwards. Perhaps we were by way of a try-out!

The programme was due to have a showing in England, but scheduling ruled it out. Granada television were making a film of their own, starring Michael Caine and Susan George. Although our programme was a documentary and very different, there was a conflict of interests and it didn't get a transmission here. But friends of mine in Australia and America saw it, and it went onto video, which you could purchase if you belonged to a Video Crime Club. Unfortunately, I didn't get royalties!

My friend from *Tom Tom* days, Richard Wade, had left the BBC and was working for Business in the Community and asked me to do some work for him. I attended one of their functions in Sheffield and as Prince Charles was their president and in attendance, we were introduced again. In the local papers, photos of the two of us look as though we were sharing an enormous joke. Maybe he remembered what he said to me at Beating the Retreat at the Tercentenary of the Royal Hospital!

It was going to be another working Christmas for me. I was to play Robin Hood in *Babes in the Wood,* with the comedians Little and Large, at the Reading Hexagon. This time I took singing lessons, as well as lessons in how to use a stave and how to shoot an arrow. Reading could hardly have been more convenient for me, as it was only a half-hour drive from home. The cast were great fun, especially Mia Carla, who played the fairy; she opened the show appearing out of the darkness in a frothy white tutu. Mia was a large lady with a voice to match and definitely not the archetypal slim and pretty pantomime fairy, but she was always ready with a rejoinder if anyone commented on her size. She was a very funny lady and my son Jonathan really fell for her. He played the tape of her show songs endlessly. Little and Large were very good to work with. They not only 'corpsed' the rest of the cast but they were always dissolving into giggles themselves. My Maid Marian was Eddie's wife Patsy Ann Scott. We like each other and worked well together although, I have to admit, it's very difficult romancing someone of your own sex. Eddie and Patsy live in Bristol and were great friends with my friend and hairdresser Jean. When she came to the show, in one of our love scenes, I deliberately planted a kiss firmly on Patsy's lips. Patsy went beetroot and we could hear Jean's laugh reverberate around the theatre. Jean's laugh would not only wake the dead but bring them back to life.

My friend Kit came over from Australia with two of her children. Having been born in England, she understood the tradition of pantomime but her very Oz offspring hadn't a clue.

Come to think of it, the whole thing is crazy. Men dressed as women and women playing lead men romancing lead women who are women. No wonder they'd no idea what was going on. I'm not sure the English children did either, but it was their letters which I treasure. They all carried drawings and paintings of the main characters and lines such as, 'What I liked best was when you kicked the sheriff of Nottingham'; 'My best part was when you got married'.

The year 1989 brought a fair amount of corporate work, but it was beginning to tail off. This was only to be expected. Companies want the latest 'hot' property to attend their launch, present their conference, grace their award ceremony. My professionalism was still the same but I'd been off mainstream television for nearly three years.

Eric's move to Caribiner was proving to be a mixed blessing. Despite more responsibility and a higher salary, the three to four hours of commuting each day into London was taking its toll. Also, after eighteen years of service integrity, he found it hard to tolerate the wheelings and dealings and the hypocrisy of the business world.

He took advantage of an opportunity to develop his training skills as a consultant, but work was spasmodic and there was a recession looming. 'One of us has got to earn a regular salary,' he said, 'your business is too fickle.' So he took out a large loan and retrained for a commercial pilot's licence. After a spell combining management training with freelance training, he was offered a position flying with British Midland and he took the job.

I had a few interesting media jobs during the year. Among others, I stood in for Steve Race on the *Steve Race Show* on BBC Radio 2. I enjoy writing scripts and found the programme quite challenging. I was also asked to be part of the team on a new magazine programme, *The Garden Party*. In 1989 Glasgow had been designated European City of Culture and this accolade signalled a revitalisation of the city. *The Garden Party* was a magazine programme, similar to the old *Pebble Mill at One,* and was to be transmitted from the Botanical Gardens, close to the BBC studios. *Pebble Mill* hadn't been the easiest programme from the technical point of view. as it came from the lobby of the studios in Birmingham but *Garden Party* was even more difficult. So long as it wasn't pouring with rain, we did most of the interviews outside in the gardens and our fall-back in case of inclement weather was a massive greenhouse called the Kibble Palace. So, as in the old *Pebble Mill* days, we froze or fried.

My colleagues were Paul Coia, Caron Keating and the soon-to-be-immensely-successful Eamonn Holmes. It was an interesting programme, but we didn't have as many of the big-name stars as we'd had at the *Mill*. Birmingham had been a difficult enough venue for attracting the stars who were in London promoting a film, book, or something else; Glasgow was just a tad too far. My fondest memory was my interview with Joss Ackland. He is such a lovely person, as well as being a fine actor. We exchanged Christmas cards for a few years and when I read recently of the death of his wife Rosemary I felt so sorry for him, because they were devoted. Long-lived marriages in the entertainment world are the exception rather than the rule.

When *Garden Party* came to an end, I went straight into making a series of ten inserts on crafts for *This Morning*. The series was funded by HTV who sold it on to Granada. I loved making them, as I've always been fascinated by the Arts and Crafts world, and we covered so many interesting subjects: the making of love spoons; creating lifelike pictures of animals from the dyed, dried grass Hare's tails; glass blowing; the making of automata. The series must have been popular, because we went on to make twenty more inserts. But, I know it wasn't financially viable for HTV. When the director rang to say Granada wanted another series – which he and I would have to fund, although the budget was so small that we'd be lucky to see a return on our outlay – I reluctantly declined. I really couldn't see why we should subsidise a production for a huge company like Granada, however much I enjoyed the work.

I had been having some run-ins with James Kelly at IMG and felt they weren't serving my best interests. I thought that basically, I was much too 'small fry' for them. They were used to dealing with clients who earned millions and I felt like a tadpole in an enormous lake. So I changed agents and joined Arlington Enterprises, run by Annie Sweetbaum. Corporate work was still coming in on a fairly regular basis, I was earning reasonable money and she was happy to have me as a client.

My hairdresser, Jean, knew I was unhappy with IMG and suggested that I phone John Miles, a neighbour of hers, who was a successful agent in the West country. Among the big mistakes in my life was in deciding to stay with a London agent and not making that phone call to have a chat. John is a hugely successful agent, a kind and caring man, and with hindsight, I feel he would have guided me at a particularly vulnerable time in my career. He is the agent who represents Carol Vorderman – need I say more!

Press coverage had died down to almost nil, which suited me admirably. There were the odd nasties but, in my eyes, they were totally expunged by a really kind piece written by Esther Rantzen. Although we knew each other and had socialised occasionally, we were by no means close friends, so nepotism didn't enter into it. I didn't even know she'd written about me until someone told me. Over the years hundreds of viewers have either written to me or spoken to me about the fact that they didn't know why, but they preferred the news when it was read by the likes of Richard Baker, Kenneth Kendall and myself. I maintain this is because we had theatrical backgrounds, in my case professional and in Richard's amateur, but we weren't 'journalists', which is what became the required prerequisite. In a three-column article Esther declared that '... she had the actress's skill in reading aloud, presenting the mix of the day's most important events, intricate facts and figures, unfamiliar foreign place names, so that we, half asleep on our sofas, could hear – and most important – could understand. Fashion killed Jan Leeming's career as a newsreader – the same fashion that swept away Richard Baker and Kenneth Kendall. Their mistake? To make it all look far too easy. So the decree went out that the news should be read with gritty authority by experienced journalists who could put their own stamp on the stories. But not all journalists are built like Sir Alastair Burnett. There have been some disasters – fine reporters reduced to stammering misfits in a claustrophobic studio, spotlit and sweating ... Fashions come and go in television ... and some bosses will return to the policy of the best writers writing the news and the best readers reading it.'

Well, the fashion didn't revert but I agree with what she said. Some fine reporters and correspondents made an excellent transition to newsreading, others ... well, they didn't. Sometimes, I wonder if they've been put through a course where they are told to stress every fourth or fifth word regardless of meaning. Wrong words are stressed, stories are badly and ambiguously written and it is sometimes difficult to understand their gist. The correct way to emphasise is by a change of pace or a slight alteration in intonation and the merest hint of a pause before a story of gravity. The art of presentation is totally different from that of journalism. Also, what is written to be read aloud is different from that simply to be read. Anyway, that's my private hobby horse, so I'd better get off it.

We were still on the guest list for some highly enjoyable social functions: Wimbledon, Ascot and charity balls. I have been fortunate to meet most members of the Royal Family but the closest I got to Princess Diana was at the British Paraplegic Sports Society Ball, held at Osterley Park House. We weren't introduced but we were only feet apart on the dance floor and I have to say, she was a stunner. Simon MacCorkindale and Susan George had a first night for *Stealing Heaven*. It was a World Charity Première in aid of SOS – The Stars Organisation for Spastics – now renamed SCOPE. I was a member of SOS and, as friends of Susie and Simon, we received an invite to the screening and to dinner afterwards at Les Ambassadeurs in London. It was a memorable evening and so good to see the actors again.

Although Eric and I weren't racing fans, the social side is enjoyable and one can do some interesting people-watching. At the Ascot end-of-season race meeting, I sat next to David Sieff from Marks & Spencer. When asked whether I shopped at their stores I replied that although I loved their food products, I didn't buy their clothes because, locally in Windsor and High Wycombe, they rarely had my size and I found the clothes dowdy. I didn't mean it as a challenge, but that's what it became and Mr Sieff invited me to their HQ in London to talk about my opinion. After lunch, we were invited to place a bet. I hardly know one end of a horse from another but I placed a bet on an outsider and won almost £200. With my winnings I took Eric and myself out for dinner and an overnight stay in an hotel. It was the first and last time I've ever won on a race.

Christmas 1989 saw me in panto again. This time I played Prince Charming in *Cinderella*. It was a short run of five weeks in Torquay. The production was made on a shoestring, but I have happy memories of aftershow dinners with the highly talented Leslie Randall and other cast members. The critiques weren't bad. I was praised for my acting ability: '... her background on the stage showed through, not just a former personality appearing in another guise. Unfortunately her singing voice failed to match her looks and acting skills.' Very fair comment, I felt.

Christina Foyle invited me to her luncheon for Peter O'Toole and asked me to be the Guest of Honour. Not only was I pleased to be asked but it meant sitting next to Peter, whom I'd worshipped from afar ever since the film of *Lawrence of Arabia*. I can usually find something to talk about with anyone, but not Mr O'Toole. (The only other person with whom I felt so awkward and inept was Mary Archer, Jeffrey Archer's wife.) After I'd got over the pleasantries of saying how much I'd enjoyed his performances in various films and plays, conversation stopped. I was very grateful to have Ned Sherrin on the other side of me. He hardly stopped talking.

The proposed lunch with David Sieff took place in February. He had asked me if I would commit to paper what I felt was wrong with my local M & S stores. I spent a couple of days looking around and putting my thoughts on paper and then went to London for the lunch. I was highly embarrassed when I realised it wasn't just a lunch between the two of us. He had also invited some senior members of his staff. I stated that, although their quality was as good as it always had been, other stores were catching up on the quality front and charging far less. The lack of changing rooms was off-putting, outside London the stores didn't have enough smaller sizes, and overall I felt many of the clothes were dowdy. The failure to accept anything other than a cheque or an M & S card was, in my opinion, a negative feature. I'd written all this and more down and was amazed when asked if I would let his staff have my typewritten pages.

We then had lunch and afterwards I was shown around their flagship store at Marble Arch. I remember commenting that if half the clothes at that store made their way to the provinces, I felt they would be far more successful. I only mention this incident because of the decline of M & S almost a decade later and for many of the reasons I'd highlighted. It's a bit like politics in that the people in charge are very often out of touch with the grass roots feelings of the populace. In 2002 they introduced their Per Una range and I have some smashing bejewelled jeans hanging in my wardrobe.

Eric and I went to the theatre to see *An Evening with Peter Ustinov*. We found it hysterically funny and, as I'd met Peter before, we ventured backstage after the performance. The commissionaire handed in our names and we were asked to wait, which we did. Eventually Peter's dressing room door opened and out swept Joan Collins. I'd met her over a decade previously, when she was a guest on *Pebble Mill*. She was stunning then and the years hadn't dimmed her beauty. Peter was charming to both of us.

Around this time, I was invited to be a judge on the NCR Book Awards. The final book list of ten contained esoteric works, from *Citizens* by Simon Schama and *The Shelleys and The Godwins* by William St Clair, through books like *Diana's Story* about the life and death of a woman suffering from ME, to light reading such as *A Year in Provence* by Peter Mayle. As

'The aim of the Award is to stimulate interest in non-fiction writing, publishing and reading in the UK', I took this to mean the kind of book that would be readily purchased from a shop such as WH Smith, so I opted for Peter Mayle's oeuvre. I was totally voted down because the book was seen as too popularist! Of course, it went on to be a major best-seller and made a fortune for Peter, whom Eric and I met later in the year in Provence. The original book had a front cover sketch of Peter's house. It was only a few miles from our village. Through his job, Eric is an excellent observer and we went out one day to see if we could find the house. No one was at home and I left a note saying how much I'd enjoyed the book and was sorry that it had not won the NCR Award. A few hours later we received a phone call inviting us to lunch with Peter and his wife Jenny. The house was charming and exactly as described in the book. Unfortunately, too many people found out where they lived and eventually they decamped to America.

In June I undertook a road show for Proctor and Gamble. They were one of the first companies to make a large investment of around £10 million towards becoming more 'green' with their products. It was action of which I approved and I was happy to endorse it. The tour comprised talking on radio shows and making one or two television appearances. I had to go to Belfast for one engagement, an interview on BBC Radio. Robin Walsh, who had been the Assistant News Editor in my days of newsreading, had moved up the ladder and was the Controller of BBC Belfast. As I was in the building, and he was available, we arranged to meet for coffee.

I am a Capricorn. I don't like loose ends and have to put everything in its right place. I had never got to the bottom of my dismissal from BBC News and it rankled with me. While we were having our coffee, I said, 'Robin, it's now well in the past and I'd like to draw a line under the matter, so please tell me why my contract wasn't renewed.' He hummed and hawed a bit and replied in his deliciously light Irish accent, 'Well, you know what was the reason.' 'No, I don't know the real reason or I wouldn't be asking.' Eventually he told me '… it was because you weren't a journalist'. 'Fair enough,' said I, 'but neither was Moira Stuart.' His coffee cup rattled in its saucer and he changed the subject rapidly by asking, 'Is Eric still flying?' So I never will get to the bottom of that mystery. Employers do not usually get rid of presenters whilst they are still popular with the public.

Life for me was slowing down. In many ways, I was happy to have more time to myself, but Eric was away a great deal of the time. Flying for a commercial airline is not good for anyone's social life. The hours are antisocial and not being given one's roster until a couple of weeks in advance doesn't allow you to plan much ahead.

Although we were still invited to many interesting functions and charity events, I was beginning to feel a lack of self-esteem and was worried about not earning an income. I'd worked all my life and having too much time on my hands was alien to me. I reached a stage where I was not at all happy with myself and felt worthless because of the lack of work. My doctor suggested some professional help wouldn't go amiss and sent me to see a psychiatrist called Professor Rees, the father of Angharad Rees the actress. I remember that first meeting quite vividly. He was such a lovely man and greeted me in his lilting Welsh accent, not as a patient, but as a fan, and initially couldn't understand why I was in his office at all. After I'd sat and poured my heart out to him for over an hour, he understood where I was coming from. It's very hard to have been, what seems to the outside world, at the top of one's profession and then to find oneself more or less on the professional 'scrap heap'. Even harder when members of the public so often asked why they didn't see you any more. I was finding it more and more difficult to look at the positives in my life, of which there were many. I had several meetings with Professor Rees and then he handed me over to one of his assistants, Mary Stones, who was a great help in restoring at least some of my belief in me.

At least Eric was a happier man now that he was back flying aircraft, albeit commercial ones. We had a worrying time in early '91 when British Midland started laying off staff, but Eric kept his job. I was very relieved that he was no longer on the

RAF Reserve List. Although I know he was itching to be in the Gulf, I didn't share the sentiment.

Some of Eric's colleagues from the Red Arrows had also gone into commercial flying. John Blackwell had joined Cathay, so we had a most enjoyable holiday in Hong Kong with him and his wife Annette. Henry and Anne Ploszek had gone to Dubai where Henry was the operations manager for the Dubai Air Wing looking after Sheik Mahktoum's fleet of aircraft. We had two glorious holidays with them and my favourite memory was of a barbecue evening. You think of the Gulf as endless sunshine but they do have rain and flash floods. On the evening of Henry's barbecue there was one such flood and the road outside their house was like a small river. Henry ended up doing the cooking in the garage wearing a wet suit.

In 1995 we planned our usual holiday to Provence. This time, Eric had decided that, rather than our normal dash down the motorway, we would take a more leisurely meander down through the Loire Valley. Mark couldn't join us at the start of the holiday as he was away with the school's RAF Cadet Force. So it was planned for Jonathan and Caron, Eric and myself to drive to Provence and later in the week Eric would pick Mark up from Nice Airport to join the rest of us.

The relationship between myself and Eric had always been passionate and fiery. We rowed, we made up and, as far as I was concerned, we went on loving despite the ups and downs. On that holiday, there was something very much amiss. Eric was incredibly short-tempered with all of us. He adored Caron, who was one of the easiest-going, sweetest children you could wish to meet, and even she managed to get on the wrong end of his tongue many times on the two-day journey to Alleins. He snapped at all of us and I couldn't do anything right. Tempers were so frayed by the time we got to our house, the two of us were hardly speaking. I couldn't make out whether it was work problems or money problems. I couldn't get Eric to open up to me.

It wasn't a happy holiday and yet he had booked the usual night at Beaumaniere to celebrate our seventh wedding anniversary. The atmosphere between us was so uncomfortable, I suggested that he cancel the booking, save the money, and just take us out for an ordinary dinner in Salon. He wouldn't hear of it and insisted we went ahead with our plans. We had a lovely evening and I thought whatever was wrong was sorting itself out. Then, on our journey home to England, we stopped at a Relais for the night and had the most almighty row, which started because of Jonathan. Eric had put a question to the children and as usual Jonathan was the one who spoke up. He was put in his place and I blew my top. I was fed up with Jonathan always being got at. The trouble was, and I knew it, Jonathan was a much more difficult child than Mark and Caron. But Jonathan was my son and I had to stand up for him. We seemed to get over that hiccup but Eric became more and more distant.

Jonathan was not only being difficult at home with us but also with his father when he went to visit. The atmosphere between him and Eric could have been cut with a knife and I was the piggy in the middle. Jonathan could wind me up very easily, resented any imposed discipline from Eric and I was getting regular stress headaches. After consultation between Patrick, Eric and myself, we thought it might be a good thing if he became a weekly boarder at his school, the Royal Grammar School at High Wycombe. I was finding my son too difficult to handle, as many parents will understand. Trying to instil discipline into a stroppy teenager is a difficult job for two parents. And when the discipline is meted out by a step-parent, it is even harder to accept. Although life at home was no bed of roses for him, and I genuinely believed he would enjoy the company of other boys, I was unprepared for Jonathan's reaction to the news of our decision. He begged and pleaded not to be made a boarder but we went ahead, thinking we were doing the best for everyone. After all, he would only be away from home four nights and back every weekend.

Earlier in the year, Eric had booked a week's holiday on the Nile to be taken in early September. He knew my interest in things Egyptian and there were some extremely good offers.

I thought the holiday was enjoyable for both of us but the distance was there and I couldn't get through to him. As the boat meandered down the Nile, I would often sit on deck painting and Eric would disappear for hours on end. I felt very lonely.

I had been attending watercolour classes for several years and an opportunity had arisen to go on a Painting and Conservation holiday to Zambia with David Shepherd, the celebrated wildlife artist. With Eric's blessing, I was booked to go in late September. It was an amazing experience. The Luangwa Valley in Zambia is teeming with wildlife and the sights I saw will remain with me forever. The only thing that spoilt the holiday was not having Eric to share it with. I sent him several postcards and took endless video film so that I could share the experience when I got home. He met me at the airport and, even after a fortnight apart, the distance was still there. I couldn't fathom it and whenever I enquired as to what was wrong, I was told, 'Nothing'.

Eric had become very active in the Parents' Association at the Royal Grammar School, because his son Mark was also a pupil there, in the year ahead of Jonathan. Eric was instrumental in organising an Auction of Pledges which I went to, accompanied by Patrick and Robin, who were now married to one another. Of the pledges on offer, there was a weekend on a canal boat. Patrick and Robin wanted it and so did we. We decided to share the weekend and made a joint bid.

We secured the trip and the plan was that Eric, the children and I would have the boat for the first night and then take it along the river and hand it and the children over to Patrick and Robin. It was Friday, 27 September and a miserable, wet day it turned out to be. I didn't want to have to cope with an unfamiliar cooking appliance on a canal boat, so made a spaghetti bolognaise, which I knew was one of the children's favourites, and packaged it up with all the attendant side dishes. We drove to the boat in monsoonal rain and then had to decant children, dogs – we now had another standard poodle, Tara, as a companion for Kiri – and luggage onto the vessel.

I heated up the dinner and was very aware of an atmosphere. I knew Eric treasured time with his children and got the distinct impression that I wasn't required, so I took myself off to the sleeping end of the boat and started to read. I was overwhelmed with loneliness and sadness. It must have been a presage of what was to come.

When Eric joined me in the double bunk we made love, but I knew he was miles away. Once again I begged him to tell me what was wrong. Was there someone else? The answer was a definite 'No'. Then it all came pouring out. He felt he needed time on his own. He was going through a black period and didn't want to treat me badly but said, 'I still love you, but I'm no longer in love with you.' Apparently I was stopping him doing things he wanted to do, such as flying and being with his children. I don't think I was doing any of this, but one person's perception of a situation is quite different from another's. I can't describe how I felt. You could have asked me to jump into a bottomless pit and I would have done it. My world was falling apart. We talked in the dark for four hours. He fell asleep but I didn't and by morning I was exhausted. I thought I had talked him around – that we had talked things through and could work out our problems together – but that wasn't to be. He definitely wanted a trial separation. Where had I heard that before? Jeremy in 1973.

I was so wrecked by the lack of sleep, I stayed on the boat while Eric took the children off for walks and lunch. I was like a zombie. The man I adored was going to go away. I vaguely remember the afternoon. Under other circumstances, it would have been beautiful. Late summer sunshine, fields with sheep grazing and quiet peace as we drifted along, but I was in turmoil.

We handed over the boat and the children to Patrick and Robin and declined a drink in the local hostelry. I can't remember the arrangements about cars, but somehow we were in our car and heading home. We were due to go out to dinner with friends that evening, but I simply couldn't cope. I was dying inside and the thought of making congenial conversation was anathema to me. When we arrived home, Eric gave me a large port and brandy to settle my stomach, and then another, and then another. I forgot I hadn't eaten all day and that, coupled with a totally sleepless night, made me intoxicated very quickly. I'd had too much to drink on occasions in the past but this was like nothing I'd ever experienced. It was as if my head was clear and functional and I was above myself looking down on a body that wouldn't obey me. I woke next day with the mother and father of a hangover. That night was the Annual Red Arrows Dinner and off Eric went to the celebration.

The next week was a time of lies and deception. I was convinced there had to be another woman and Eric kept denying it. I phoned my clairvoyant friend Kwesi and she said, 'Yes, there is another woman and has been for some time.'

Eric and I shared a study and on 7 November there was one item in the bin. I looked at it. A mobile phone bill with the same number coming up again and again and at all times of the day and night and five times on the day we left England for the family holiday in Provence. So that was why he was in such a mood with all of us during that holiday! He probably wanted to be with her. There was also another number registering very long calls late at night. Did he want me to see that bill? A man who was so meticulous about everything would surely not have let himself be found out by a misplaced telephone bill. I hasten to add that I'm not the sort of woman who goes through her husband's pockets, but the one bill in the bin was just too much of a coincidence.

I phoned the mobile but kept getting an answering service, so I tried the land line and to my surprise got an old woman at the end of the phone. I thought I'd mis-dialled, apologised and then rang again. Again I got the same person and asked if there were any young people in the house. 'Oh no,' she said, 'my daughter is down south at High Wycombe. She is a gliding instructor at Booker.' Then it all fell horribly into place. Mark, Eric's son, had been taking gliding lessons and had often been taken home by the gliding instructor. I stupidly assumed the instructor was male! I intimated that I couldn't reach her on her mobile and asked if she had another number. She did and her mother gave it to me.

I rang the number repeatedly and left messages asking that she phone Eric on his home phone number, knowing Eric was away and that I would answer the phone. I was beside myself.

I had to confide in someone and spoke to my friend Chloe. On 8 November, she descended on me early in the morning. 'Come on,' she said, 'You need to take your mind off things.' She was going to a Christmas cracker-making course and I was bundled along as well. The course was being held in Gaydon, just off the M40. During the journey, I continually phoned both the mobile phone number and the land line and eventually left a message saying we should meet.

At the cracker-making day arranged by a lovely lady who'd made crackers for Harrods, I worked like a dervish and made twelve to everybody else's six. They were good too! When Chloe dropped me off at home, there was a note on the mat from 'the other woman' agreeing we should meet. How did she know where I lived? I immediately phoned and suggested a rendezvous halfway between us at the Post House Hotel at High Wycombe. She declared she was a 'a very private person' and would rather come to my home. I started to give her directions and she said she knew where to come – she'd been at our home whilst I was away in Zambia!

When I opened the door at 7.30 p.m., I was shocked. I had expected to see a young glamorous woman. Younger she was but decidedly not glamorous. She stood on the doorstep in a puffa jacket and trousers with blonde unkempt hair. As she came into the hall, she bent down to unlace her boots and then asked where she should go. I was so angry I said, 'You obviously know the layout of the house, there's the sitting room.'

She stayed until 10.20 and consumed a very large amount of whisky. I remember little of what was said except her crying and saying, 'You're so beautiful.' I know I don't look like the back of a bus, but I do not think I am beautiful. Maybe her thought processes were, along the lines of, 'If she can't keep him, how will I?' She told me she never meant to get involved, that it was wrong, she felt he still loved me and should come back to me. At one stage, she was crying so much, I stood up and was about to put my arms around her. What the hell was I doing? This woman was taking my husband away from me and I was about to offer her comfort. I sat down again rapidly. It was the stuff 'B' films are made of, except that it was all for real and incredibly, horribly hurtful.

The next day Eric came home and we talked and talked and talked. He not only admitted this infidelity, but others. If you love someone enough, you will forgive them anything. Don't ask me why I loved him so much, but I did. I said – and meant it – that it didn't matter, that I forgave him and that we would get through it if he wished.

But he didn't wish to and was determined to go. He had married relatively young, had come straight from that relationship to one with me, and he wanted his 'freedom'. I think I could have taken a separation and waited, hoping that he would come back to me in time. But the element I couldn't come to terms with was that he was going to move out and into a house owned by her. He told me they wouldn't be living together as she spent most of her time at Booker Airfield in a mobile home, BUT it was still her house he was going to.

On Sunday, 12 November, Remembrance Sunday, Eric had been chosen to be the representative of British Midland and lay a wreath at Westminster Abbey. He wanted me to accompany him. My mood was the colour of my outfit – BLACK. He even told me how great I looked. There was a drinks party, which he insisted on attending, but I was so choked, I just stood like a dummy with a glass in my hand. As we were in London, Eric took us to lunch at the RAF Club. I could have been eating sawdust. He was going to leave the next day and I had to believe it. When we got home, he went upstairs to pack. I was in agony and still couldn't believe what was happening around us. In one respect, nothing had altered in our relationship. Our love life was just as good as it always had been, or as I had always believed it to be. I kept hoping he'd change his mind, especially when he hugged me and told me how wonderfully under-standing I'd been. However, despite this, he was adamant that he needed space and freedom and was definitely not going to change his mind.

On 13 November, I had to work on a corporate job that required an overnight stay. When I got back home on the 14th, I prayed that he'd be there saying it was a great big mistake, that he was sorry and could we make a new beginning.

Because of his early working starts to the day, and so as not to disturb me, Eric used to keep his clothes in a separate bedroom. His room was empty of furniture, his clothes had gone from the wardrobe and most of his belongings had been taken from the loft. It was the beginning of a living nightmare for me. One from which I hoped I'd wake up.

CHAPTER THIRTEEN

THE DARKEST DAYS

As the week wore on, I kept breaking down in tears and sleep totally eluded me. I had already been through weeks of anguish waiting for the day of departure and hoping it wouldn't happen. My doctor was already acquainted with my situation so he prescribed Prozac but it takes about ten days before the effect kicks in. He had also arranged for me to have sessions with a stress counsellor who worked within the practice and it happened to be the same Mary Stones I had seen a few years previously. Weight was dropping off me and within three weeks I had lost a stone taking me down to under seven and a half stones.

I had been invited to unveil a plaque in Lytham St Anne's, officially opening a Royal Air Force Association home. This had been in my diary for a long time. I didn't want to let them down and felt that getting out of the house and meeting people would be good for me. The invitation was for two to be flown to Lytham in a Chinook helicopter. When I originally accepted, Eric would have partnered me. This was now out of the question and I invited John Dobson's wife, Fenella, to come. You aren't offered a ride in a Chinook every day of the week and she was delighted to accompany me. It was an experience. You can't hear yourself think, let alone speak, over the noise of the engine and the rotor blades. Just as work is always good therapy for me, it was a tonic to be with people and we both enjoyed our afternoon. Driving from Strike Command, where we landed, back to my home meant going near High Wycombe and I needed to collect a registered package. I walked into the sorting office and there he was. He should have been miles away and the unexpected meeting completely unnerved me. Tears welled up and I turned away from him. He went outside, saw Fenella sitting in the car and asked her to find out whether I wanted to speak with him. I couldn't.

I had an engagement to present the Charter Mark Awards in the Queen Elizabeth Conference Centre. This necessitated a very early start so I took advantage of my associate membership of the RAF Club and booked a room for the night of 3 December. Somehow the confirmation note went to Eric and not me, so he knew where I was that evening. The 3rd was Eric's birthday and in my stupidly romantic way, I half expected a knock at the door, him standing there saying it had all been a silly mistake and could he come home. It didn't happen.

Because I had no regular work there was too much time to dwell on the whole horrible situation. We had some long phone calls, sometimes they were OK and at other times we said ghastly things to each other. I was accused of so much over the years, losing him his friends because I don't like drinking sessions, stopping him going off doing his aerobatic flying, dragging him round to all the things that I wanted to do. He said he had to clock-watch when visiting his children because I had a meal waiting. All this sounds so petty, but if you don't discuss your grievances within a relationship the tiny cracks become massive chasms. I'd no idea so much was eating him up.

To be fair to Eric, once or twice after he left he had asked if we could meet for lunch, so that we might discuss our problems, but I didn't feel strong enough to cope. I didn't want to be with him and then have him walk away from me to go home to another address. However, on one of the agreed periods when he was to use the office, I suggested we at least had a coffee. I had meant coffee but we ended up in each other's arms and inevitably in bed. He begged me to give him time and asked me to wait for him. Time I could give him, but it was his domestic arrangement that was totally unacceptable to me. After he left, I felt desolate.

I was in trouble on all fronts. I'd lost the man I adored, there was no work on the horizon and the future looked totally bleak. Mary Stones and many of my friends did their utmost to help me but I knew I was going into a decline. I have, from time to time in my life, suffered from depression, not manic, but bad enough to make me ill. Mary began to be worried and suggested that I need hospitalisation. I didn't want that. I felt it was too drastic a move and I was desperately worried about the press finding out. I've always taken refuge in flight so I phoned my friend Kwesi, who had moved back to South Africa, and lived in a beach front house at Umshloti just north of Durban. She readily agreed to my visit and I set about getting the fare together by selling some of my designer clothes and a few bits of jewellery.

During the early years of our relationship I had paid the mortgage and all the bills but the tide had turned. My earnings were dropping off alarmingly and Eric now had a good regular income. So apart from the mortgage, Eric paid for everything. He had given me a very generous allowance when he left but life wasn't easy.

Having a holiday in South Africa to look forward to made me feel a lot better and I had begun to feel angry. Most therapists will tell you to stop directing all the anger at yourself and start directing it towards the other party. After all, it takes two to make and break a relationship. I was angry but I still loved Eric and would have taken him back with no questions asked.

Although I couldn't understand his thinking, I knew that he too was in turmoil and, on several occasions, he begged me for time. And then the press found out and time ran out. We were put under phenomenal pressure.

On 11 December, I opened the front door to a man from the *Sun*. He started to ask leading questions and I slammed the door in his face and rang Eric immediately to forewarn him. There was nothing the next day and I wondered if we'd be left alone. Fat chance.

On the 13th the press were there en masse. They are like hyenas who smell blood and come to pick over the carcass. I rang Eric, who said he'd come back home and try to fend them off. We gave a statement to my agent saying that we were having a trial separation and would they respect our privacy. Of course, they wouldn't and didn't. At lunchtime, I had to go into London to the Albert Hall to rehearse the presentation and some readings for a charity concert to be held in aid of the Dyslexia Association. By the end of the afternoon eight newspapers had contacted my agent, most of them offering money for our story. The bidding went very high. But there was no way I was going to talk, nor was Eric. I wanted him back and wasn't going to let on about the other woman. Again I should have heeded the advice given by James Kelly back in 1987. Whether you give them a story or not, the papers will print. There were some unpleasant articles with headlines such as, 'Just why is Jan Leeming such a loser in love?' The simple answer is that I have a penchant for falling in love with womanisers. (I have a theory that most interesting and sexy men find it impossible to be monogamous. So you 'pays your money and takes your choice' – Dullsville or the risk of hurt.) As the press didn't know about the other woman I was blamed for everything and made out to be some kind of ogress. It was all so hurtful and I could feel myself near breaking point.

I've had some pretty nasty things said about me in the press and it never ceases to wound, but the one that took the prize for being the bitchiest I'd ever set eyes on was drawn to my attention by my friend Sandy Rowe Ham. She rang up to ask if I'd seen an article in the *Sunday Times* supplement entitled 'Relationship of the Week', by Chrissy Iley. Sure enough, it was devoted to myself and Eric. The trouble is that newspapers get it wrong so much of the time – it is then committed to micro-film and kept, along with all the other inaccuracies, and the 'what a friend or insider said' quote. The nastiness is ineradicable unless you can extract an apology. This is well nigh impossible.

Sandy and David were so incensed on my behalf that they contacted their solicitor in the late Lord Goodman's practice.

The gentleman read the article and spent twenty minutes on the phone to me. A summation of what he said was, 'Yes, we know of this young lady and her articles. What she has written is character assassination but unless you have the money to take on the paper and are prepared to spend a couple of years fighting your case, my advice to you is to let it drop.' And that, sadly, in my opinion, is why so much of this inaccurate journalism continues. Very few people can afford to fight so we just have to take it on the chin and yet more erroneous words, judgments, and valuations are committed to the microfilm for yet more journalists to use as the basis for their inaccurate outpourings, again and again. When I first joined the news in 1980, there was an article in a rag of a magazine and the headline was 'My trouble with men *by* Jan Leeming'. Down at the bottom, the article was credited to a journalist. What he'd done was to take various quotes I had made or was purported to have made, from different newspapers and magazines and cobbled them together. I had never even met the man, but there was nothing I could do about it.

Apart from the emotional hurt, the pressure on both of us was enormous. Eric had to take a few days' sick leave. When you fly an aeroplane, the safety of your passengers is your first priority. If you are being doorstepped and hassled your concentration cannot be at its best. British Midland gave him time off.

I was trying so desperately hard to understand Eric and eventually a mutual male friend suggested I went to a military psychiatrist who might be able to help me. Being military he might have a better understanding of the mind of someone who'd spent most of his adult life in a potentially dangerous and exciting profession. It was suggested that Eric should also see the man. He went a few times because he declared that he really did want to sort himself out so that we could live together again.

My son and I had several invitations to spend Christmas with friends. Poor Jonathan had put up with so much from me that I let him decide whom he would most like to be with over the festive period. He wanted to spend it with Lynne, the mother of Eric's and my godson Ronan. Jonathan is extremely good with very young and very old people. It was the ones in between, his peer group, with whom he had problems. He loved Ronan and it was a good decision for them to be together. Jonathan was very paternal with him. Lynnie is great fun to be with and is an extremely strong character. But, despite being supportive, she simply couldn't understand my continuing love for Eric. Nor could I, but then 'love is blind', and I was.

I didn't want to impose my misery on any one person for too long, so I had decided to split Christmas, and took Jonathan down to Cornwall to visit his godfather John Dobson, my 'long time ago boyfriend'. John is a very successful and sensible person but being a man, he, like Lynne, simply couldn't understand my continued love and faith in Eric. I must admit that I was beginning to feel like a rubber band stretched to breaking point. I put on a good face for Jonathan and my hosts and my salvation was the thought of a couple of weeks in the sun with Kwesi.

The New Year began with hope and within a week disintegrated into a meltdown situation. Eric and I had exchanged letters and phone calls and always the sticking point was the fact that he was living in her house, even if they weren't exactly living together. I had decided that I simply couldn't go on with the worry, the tears, the lack of sleep, the uncertainty. How on earth could Eric sort himself out and have space when he was continuing his affair with her. It wasn't fair on me, her or him.

On 31 December, I posted a letter to her asking for the truth about their relationship. The same day I phoned Eric to leave a message on his answer phone, thinking he would be at work, to make arrangements about his use of the study, which we still shared. He was just leaving to go to the airport. We had a furious row and he slammed the phone down on me. Half an hour later he rang to say he was prepared to give her up. I can't express the relief I felt – it was like a terrible weight being lifted off me. Although it was a foggy and miserable day, I took the dogs for a walk and felt happier than I had done for weeks. I had to go to bed early because of work the next day but, despite my new-found optimism, sleep eluded me until well past midnight.

I had been invited to read the news from 1–5 January on *The Big Breakfast* show. My instinct was to refuse but the agent persuaded me it would be good to be seen in a less sober light and the programme was watched by a large audience.

I was picked up by car at 5 a.m. and taken into the London studios. The news for *The Big Breakfast* came from a small studio at ITN, so I never met the presenters, Chris Evans and Zoe Ball, but, there were times during the programme when they interacted with the news presenter, and that was fun. The news journalists were welcoming and helpful and I very much enjoyed their company. Although it was only for a few hours, working kept my mind off my problems.

New Year's Day 1996 was nasty and foggy but, after catching up on a couple of hours' sleep because of the early start, I took the dogs for a walk in a spirit of optimism. Realising that I couldn't find my plane ticket to South Africa, I turned the house upside down looking for it and spring cleaned (in the middle of winter!) as I went along. I was just getting ready for bed when the phone rang. It was Eric to wish me a Happy New Year and to ask if he could come back to our house that night. I was longing to see him and be held in his arms but I couldn't bear the hurt of him going away again and refused his request.

On the 2nd, the gremlins were getting to me again and I decided to try one last time to make contact with Eric's girlfriend. She was in and, though I only wanted confirmation or otherwise as to whether they were cohabiting, she said she wanted to come and see me and we agreed a meeting for the next day, Wednesday.

I actually felt optimistic about my meeting with her, expecting her to be in turmoil because he had terminated their relationship. Was I in for a shock! When she arrived she talked non-stop and the story was quite different from what I'd expected. Apparently she had tried to end the relationship but Eric had persuaded her otherwise. They were planning a gliding holiday together and she told him the trip was off unless he had definitely finished with me. Guess where they were going and when? South Africa – a few days after my departure. I showed her some of the affectionate letters he'd sent me since leaving and played her some of the loving messages he'd left on the answer phone. Both of us were confused. And, now looking back, I can see what turmoil Eric was in too. But, we were all hurting so much, none of us could see further than our own raw emotions.

That night, phone calls were flying back and forth between the three of us. Eric was angry with me for putting a 'spanner in the works' and I was angry with both of them. The calls went on until 2.30 a.m., when it was agreed that Eric and I would meet in the study next morning and try to clear the air between us. I had to be up and on the road by 5 a.m. for my newsreading stint on *The Big Breakfast*. It was pure adrenalin that kept me going, as I'd had very little sleep for days.

I was so wrung out that I'd booked a massage to try and unwind. When I returned home and went to the study, I found not Eric, but a letter from him and on top of it was his wedding ring. The letter told me I'd not given him the space and time he needed, that he would be taking what few possessions of his which were left in the house, and that I could divorce him for unreasonable behaviour. By this time I think I was punch drunk and simply couldn't take it all in. I was due to take part in a 'Kit and the Widow' quiz programme that evening and wanted desperately to get out of the engagement but my agent insisted I did the job. I don't remember anything about the show and couldn't wait to fall into bed. The next day, the 5th, was my birthday.

They celebrated on the show with a cake and greetings and, as always in a working situation, I managed to keep myself together. The rest of the day passed in a blur of people phoning with birthday wishes, going to see Mary the stress counsellor and concentrating on the fact that I was just about to jet away to the sun for a fortnight. In the evening my mother and stepfather joined me to see Jonathan performing in an amateur dramatic production of *Alice in Wonderland*. He was one of the Tweedledum–Tweedledee partnership and was very good.

I returned home to a message on the answering machine from Eric wishing me a happy birthday. I should have left well alone, but, in my inimitable fashion didn't, and phoned him. We talked for three hours and so much came out. If only he'd been able to open up beforehand and talk about what bothered him and what was wrong with me and our relationship. I thought we were making some headway and asked if he would take his wedding ring back. He declined. Friends took me to the airport the next day and plied me with alcohol before I boarded the plane for Durban. I was also armed with a sleeping pill. I stuck the 'Do not disturb' sign on the headrest and only surfaced when we were about to land.

As I walked through the gate Kwesi swept me into her arms and just let me sob. Her home was separated from the beach by a small road and, as you looked out of the windows of her living room, there was the Indian Ocean. The weather wasn't very good, with only four days of sunshine in the fortnight I was with her, but Kwesi fed me, let me talk and took me for long walks on the beach with her dogs. It was very therapeutic.

We were walking the animals one day when I was almost knocked over by a big Alsatian. Dog people talk to other dog lovers and soon Kwesi and I were invited to coffee by the Alsatian's owner. His house was directly on the beach. He had a law practice in Johannesburg. Apparently, his wife had been gang-raped and murdered there and he'd decided to move to what he regarded as the relative security of Durban. We had coffee, then lunch and Kwesi left me to spend the rest of the day with our new-found friend. By the end of the day, Philip told me he loved me! He was a nice enough person, but really – who was he kidding? I'm inclined to believe the adage that 'Men give love to gain sex, and women give sex to gain love.' I wasn't about to give anything, but it was good for my ego to have some male attention and we had a few pleasant meals together.

I often crossed the road to the beach and looked northwards, knowing that Eric and his girlfriend were enjoying a gliding holiday somewhere north of Johannesburg. I fantasised that he would come to his senses and drive down to Durban. We'd be reconciled, sort out our differences and fly home together. That's the stuff of fairy stories!

I'd only been home a few days when I realised I still couldn't cope. I loved Eric so much, was so confused, felt so impotent and was so angry with myself for my part in the break-up of our relationship. Yes, he had been unfaithful, but I knew many women threw themselves at him. On several occasions they'd even said to me, 'If you ever get tired of him, send him in my direction!' He told me about the forwardness of some of the stewardesses. It would make your hair curl to hear how some of them behave. If you were a red-blooded male with a healthy libido, how would you react to a knock on your hotel bedroom door to be confronted by a girl in her uniform mac and nothing underneath? Eric was no saint.

I was totally faithful to him, but I'd been at fault in other ways. I had underestimated male pride in always being there with my hand in my pocket willing to pay for everything. He would have preferred we went without than that he was constantly beholden to me. I didn't see it that way at all. If I have, I share, and I share particularly if I'm in love. People were thoughtless without meaning to be in addressing invitations to 'Mr & Mrs Leeming' or to 'Miss Leeming and Guest', even though we'd been married for seven years. It all sounds so petty but as someone remarked to me recently, 'When you're first in love, you give and give without counting the cost. Then when the going gets tougher you expect a kind of "pay-back" time – you find fault – you count your sacrifices instead of giving willingly.'

Maybe I didn't fulfil all of Eric's needs, but he did mine. Not only did I love him greatly, I found him very easy to live with. Apart from my paperwork, which is always in piles on the floor (but I know where everything is within the piles!) we were both tidy people, both good timekeepers, both had a great deal of common sense; we were both sociable and enjoyed company and we both loved holidays. And he was a very practical man.

Probably the only thing he was short on was a sense of humour. I say all this because it is the little things in relationships that start to affect the overall situation, rather like rainwater creeping into rock fissures and expanding to the extent that the rock finally breaks apart. Even the way you squeeze a toothpaste tube can annoy to the point that it eventually becomes a major issue.

Not only did I miss my husband desperately, but there was no regular work to take my mind off the situation, and I was concerned about the future financially. I knew the house would have to go. It had always been seen as the largest part of my pension plan, to be sold when we retired and to capitalise on the asset. On my own, I couldn't afford to retain it.

I ran away again. This time I fled to my friend Kit in Australia and stayed away for five weeks. Kit lived north of Sydney at Pittwater, which is on the other side of a finger of land embracing Palm Beach where they film the Australian soap *Home and Away*. She had to work, so I was left to my own devices most of the time. Pittwater is situated on an estuary running into the sea. The view from Kit's flat, across the water to the National Park, was breathtaking – the sunsets divine. Most days I went to the beach and, when I wasn't reading or swimming, I became a beachcomber walking endlessly up and down looking for shells or anything else the sea brought in. On one particular day, the tide was in and as I took my usual walk, it was necessary to wade through the sea at some of the inlets. I walked on for an hour or so and when I returned the tide had receded, leaving the little coves swept and virginal, with no footprints or dogs' paw marks. I saw something glinting in the sunlight and when I bent to pick it up found that it was a Maltese cross. It wasn't rusted at all because it was made of lead. My belief in God had taken a severe battering over the years, but I saw this find as a sign and when I returned home I had it silver plated and wear it often.

I fitted in a brief visit to my friend Michael Laurence, who by now had decamped from the city and lived in a beautiful house in the Blue Mountains, a hundred miles west of Sydney. I'd last seen him in 1979 and though he's the worst correspondent on the planet he did keep in touch with a biannual letter. I knew he was happier and had found a certain peace by embracing the Catholic religion.

The Blue Mountains are incredibly beautiful but the climate is decidedly chillier than Sydney and whilst I was with Michael, it was sweater weather. We spent our evenings watching, at my request, many of the television programmes he'd scripted and which had been highly successful for him in America.

After my five weeks with Kit in the glorious sunshine and greatly enjoying the open-air life of Sydney, meeting her friends and going to barbecues and for midnight swims, I most definitely did not want to return to England, but I had to. I couldn't run away forever and I had a few corporate bookings in the diary.

I was still seeing Mary Stones, the stress counsellor, and though she was helping, there were many black days when I didn't feel I could go on. My friend from BBC days, Tim Marshall's wife Sarah, was wonderful. Despite having two small children, she was totally unstinting with the time she gave me. She was always willing to listen to my outpourings over the phone and regularly invited me to kitchen suppers, where I was accepted as one of the family and made to feel less lonely. My other close girlfriend, Chloe, organised many outings and involved me in her life in order to take my mind off my problems. Other friends were marvellously supportive, but Sarah and Chloe lived almost on my doorstep and their shoulders were there for me to cry on.

At half-term Jonathan and I went to Paris for a few days with Owen and Mireille and the two of us did the usual touristy things together. I enjoy Jonathan's company a great deal. In some ways he is very mature and we both share a pleasure in the artistic and cultural side of life, so our little holiday was great fun.

And then I don't know what happened. In June, my depression was getting very bad indeed. There were days when I found it hard to get out of bed. I was fine if there was something on which to focus, like a job or an art class or a social gathering. I was living a double life. On the surface it looked to everyone as though I was healing, but underneath I was being pulled into an ever-deepening pit. People who have not experienced depression cannot possible comprehend how helpless you are. Those who have will know exactly how it feels. There is a total sense of hopelessness. You are unable to think positively about anything. It is an effort to do even the most mundane everyday tasks. You feel as though all the blood has been drained from your body and sleep is what you continually crave. It's like being in a black hole and there's no way you can gain a foothold to climb out of it. You are unable to see any positive sides to life – everything is bleak and hopeless.

My only bright spot was looking forward to having Jonathan home from his weekly boarding. However, by the middle of June, not even his presence could shake me out of my deepening depression. I put on a brave face for him but I could think of nothing further than just not being any more. I wanted to die. It was impossible to weigh up the good and positive things in my life, such as my lovely son, my parents, friends.

June is often one of our most enjoyable months. The days are long and the weather warm. It was a lovely sunny Sunday when I took Jonathan back to school. I couldn't allow myself to consider the hurt I was going to cause, I simply couldn't go on. I had lost the will to live. Returning home in the early evening I wrote letters to my loved ones. With that task finished I went upstairs to bed, put on the outfit I'd worn the day we married and placed a photo of Jonathan on one side of me and one of Eric on the other. I had a glass of water and a tub containing a hundred paracetamol. I swallowed them like sweets until I simply couldn't swallow any more. And then I lay down in the hope that I would never wake up again.

I prayed to God. In my cock-eyed logic, I felt the pain I'd gone through over losing Eric had evened up the score – that I had expiated my sins and the pain I'd caused people like Robin. I believe in a God of love and felt sure he would understand and forgive me. It was an age before I fell asleep.

I didn't realise it at the time, but I had taken too many pills and instead of the desired effect, they made me ill. I came to at some time in the early hours of the morning. I had to crawl to the bathroom and was violently sick. I was sick several more times and finally fell asleep exhausted.

On waking, I felt totally spaced out and very, very wobbly. I managed to go downstairs, let the dogs out, feed them and crawled back to bed. I just kept drifting in and out of sleep. As there were 48 tablets left in the tub, I had taken 52.

That day, Monday 17 June, I'd been invited to the Garter Ceremony at Windsor Castle but was totally incapable of doing anything or going anywhere. I'd been intending to drop the dogs off at my mother's house and then drive to Bristol to stay with Jean and have my hair done the next day. I knew I couldn't drive, so I phoned her to apologise. I didn't realise how slurred my voice was and she immediately knew something was wrong, so I confessed to her. She wasn't surprised. Jean knows me very well and she knew the extent to which I was suffering over the loss of Eric. I think she'd realised for a while that I was close to cracking up. She didn't lecture me or tell me to pull myself together, which is the least helpful thing anyone can do under the circumstances. She seemed to understand and just said she'd be there for me if I needed her.

I can't remember much of that week except that I slept a great deal and by Friday everything had returned to normal and I went up to the Royal Grammar School to collect Jonathan for the weekend. I'd reached the crunch point, the absolute lowest point you can go, and after that there's no way but up. Life very slowly began to look as though it was worth living. I still ached for Eric but the kind of correspondence I was now receiving, on purely practical matters, made me realise that any hope I might have sustained about his return was a false one.

There was a date in the diary to look forward to. I'd been asked to go on a cruise up the Norwegian fjords in exchange for a few talks and mingling with the passengers. The invitation was for myself and partner, so I took Jonathan. It was of particular interest for him being a quarter Norwegian and he quickly became an unpaid member of the backstage crew who looked after the nightly entertainment. I still wasn't completely myself and, though I managed to socialise during the day, took to my cabin after dinner to read and have early nights.

Again it was great to be with Jonathan. We visited glaciers, fjords and the Land of the Midnight Sun. I began to thank God that he hadn't seen fit to take me and also to feel thoroughly ashamed of myself.

Despite everything, I still loved Eric, but realised he was not coming back. I am unable to let things drift and, knowing we had no future, I needed closure and initiated steps to divorce him. I needed that finality so that I wouldn't still be living in hope. I had to face the future on my own, to get stronger and thank God for all the good things in my life. One thing I couldn't face was losing my home, on top of losing my husband. Because of its location, I knew the house was eminently saleable so I made the decision to live on an overdraft pro tem until I had the emotional strength to let the house go and move on.

As I began to feel better I started entertaining. One of my favourite pastimes is having friends to dinner and it began to matter less that there was no man to play co-host.

The Femail Section of the *Daily Mail* was doing a series of articles entitled 'Dressed to Kill' in which set questions were asked of the subject, including their favourite item of clothing, the latter being the article in which the subject would be photographed. I'd been extremely fortunate in knowing the director who worked for Zandra Rhodes. I can understand Zandra's attitude, because if I designed gorgeous clothes, I'd be loathe to part with the prototypes. However, Zandra had thousands of gowns and she was persuaded that she really had to off-load some of them. So 'sales' were held, through invitation only, and I was a lucky recipient. To have owned a Zandra beaded creation, let alone several, would have been beyond my wildest dreams, but the 'sale' made it possible. As I reckoned this kind of opportunity probably wouldn't come again, I added the cost to my overdraft.

So, for the *Mail* article, I wore my exotic beaded green Zandra Rhodes creation and, not long afterwards received a letter, passed on by the newspaper. A state secondary school headteacher had a pupil who was doing a dissertation on Zandra and he asked if I would consider contributing an interview for inclusion in her work. This was August 1996 and, though I was mending, I was putting an enormous amount of correspondence and invitations on the ever-growing 'pending' pile. I often leave the 'pending' until it has 'pended' so far it is out of date and I don't have to answer. That's what I did with the letter, until May 1997. Going through a pile of 'pendings' I felt guilty at not helping the young girl and wrote an apologetic letter to the Head. In the post a few days later was a very artistic card that said, 'Dear Jan, Thank you very much for the trouble you took in writing. Very best wishes, Chris Russell'. The address at the top of the card was his private one. And that might have been that, but I chose to reply, stating that the card was lovely and an unusually artistic choice for a man!

CHAPTER FOURTEEN

KENT AND CHRIS

We corresponded for six weeks, by increasingly attractive cards, and then we met. Chris shared a close relationship with one of his deputies and had obviously taken her into his confidence. It was his female deputy, Carol Donovan, who suggested that he might take me to the theatre. The offer was proffered and accepted and we arranged a date for Saturday, 21 June.

Over the period during which we'd corresponded I'd gleaned that he was a divorcé and had been single for seventeen years. He had three daughters in their twenties and still had a good relationship with their mother. After my experience of step-relationships, I sighed with relief that they were adults and independent. Chris told me he worked hard and was always setting his sights on improving and obtaining better facilities for Astor School in Dover. He also told me that, though he had been on his own for a long time, he was no monk! I wouldn't have expected him to be.

We were to meet at Brown's in St Martin's Lane, have a light meal and then go to see *The Herbal Bed* – a play about Shakespeare's daughter and her wrongful persecution for dealing in natural healing; today we call it homeopathy. I knew what Chris looked like because when he originally wrote to me, he'd sent the school prospectus, probably to prove his credentials.

My words have been well documented in newsprint so I can't deny that my first thought on seeing him at the restaurant table was, 'Nice, but not my sort.' And where had 'my sort' ever got me but failed marriages and a regularly bruised and battered heart?

We enjoyed each other's company, the play was good, and he made me laugh. It was flattering to be in the company of someone who found me attractive. I had been invited to a silver exhibition at Aspreys for the Thursday following our meeting and decided that, if I liked him, I would invite Chris to come along. I did like him so I proffered the invitation. He readily accepted and told me afterwards that, to do so, he'd had to completely reorganise a governors' meeting.

The exhibition was interesting and even more so for me because someone I'd interviewed years ago was another of the guests. I remembered Professor David Watkins well because he came onto *Pebble Mill* with a range of the most incredibly modern and expensive jewellery made out of acrylic fibre. His wife was also at the exhibition, someone whose work I'd admired for years, the jeweller Wendy Ramshaw. Her rings are almost unwearable with all their excrescences of jewel-topped gold and silver, but they are fabulous pieces of sculpture. I possess two of her early, more modest, and more wearable designs.

After the show, Chris took me back to my car and acted with total propriety – not even a peck on the cheek. I was going on holiday with two friends to Malta the next day so we agreed to meet again on my return.

When I got back from holiday I was greeted by an excited message on the answer phone. Lili, who looked after me at Arlington, had been approached by a highly respected literary agent who wanted to meet me. The three of us arranged to get together for lunch at Cliveden in Berkshire. The agent wanted me to write an autobiography, which he wished to call 'Betrayal'. It would only have addressed my relationship with Eric – how we met, 'what the early days were like, the passion and desire … first realisation of when it all started to go wrong … sense of betrayal, hurt and anger'. 'Betrayal' would be the anatomy of a passionate marriage that went wrong. I found it sad that he wasn't interested in my story when I suggested that

there was much more to my life than that one love affair. I've
had a great deal of success and happiness as well as the
downside and I wished to write, if ever I did, a more balanced
story. As I was also too close to the pain and hurt, I didn't feel
I could be objective. I declined his offer.

Chris was a highly successful Head, completely dedicated to
his job. When we met again the summer holidays were starting,
so he had time to court me. We went to the ballet, theatre, met
for dinner and I had the same feeling I'd had years ago with
Patrick, that this was a relationship building on a solid basis.
This was the right way to establish a permanence. We shared
interests and were gradually getting to know each other. I was
almost divorced, he'd been single for ages, and we weren't
hurting anybody. There aren't too many attractive single men
around in their fifties. However, I was very worried about a
rebound love and expressed my concern. I had been quite open
and honest about my feelings for Eric and the devastation his
leaving had wreaked in my life. Perhaps I am 'Addicted to
Love', but my life seems the poorer when I don't have a partner
with whom to share it.

Chris's parents were a super couple, absolutely devoted to
each other and very welcoming to me. I felt so at home with
them from the first moment we met. I've been incredibly
fortunate with my various in-laws – it's a pity I didn't fare better
with their sons!

'If only ...' are two of the most oft-repeated words in the
English dictionary. *If ifs and buts were candy and nuts, what a
wonderful world it would be.* If only we had taken longer to
become acquainted and spent more weekends together at his
house rather than mine. I'd lived at *Pela* for fifteen years and
had made it into a lovely home. It wasn't richly furnished, but
was comfortable and homely – a testament to the style and
value one gets at a John Lewis department store. I was still
being invited to a few exciting functions in London, so maybe
Chris got a false impression of my life and lifestyle. Although he
told me he was a 'very private person' he appeared to like the
profile and publicity. We saw each other for high days and

holidays, but we didn't live together. Our relationship had all the hallmarks of a 'holiday romance' and before we knew it, we were planning to get married!

I respected and trusted Chris more than any of the other men to whom I'd made a commitment. I knew John and Jeremy had an eye for the women, so did Patrick, and Eric was quite open about his past and yet I was drawn to these men like a moth to a flame. Chris was different, I thought. Our relationship had been built on a solid foundation, not on some rampant sexuality. I truly believed this time I really had made the right decision and we would grow old together. I even worked out that if we lived long enough, we'd be able to celebrate a silver wedding!

I believed this was 'It' and that as I would have money from my house sale and because my other weddings, apart from the one for which Daddy paid, had been done on a relative shoestring, I would go for broke with this lasting commitment. We were going to have a quiet civil wedding and then a few weeks later there would be a church blessing in my home village of Penn, followed by a reception at Cliveden – a beautiful National Trust property, previously home of the Astor Family and now run as a five-star hotel.

On 1 October, we married quietly at Canterbury Register Office and went back to Carol and Nigel Donovan's house in Deal for a celebration. In a short time I'd come to like Carol very much indeed. She is an extremely kind, caring and loving individual and she'd not stinted in her affection and acceptance of me. We hadn't told anyone of our impending nuptials, once again because we didn't want the press snooping around. By 1997, I believed they wouldn't be too bothered about me, but locally, Chris was a highly visible and colourful personality. So our civil wedding was a very small affair. The only people in attendance were our witnesses, Chris's deputies, Carol and John and the other guest was John's wife Unity. We didn't even tell our respective offspring!

Carol had arranged a magnificent buffet and decorated her dining room with highly scented white lilies and other white blooms, knowing they are my favourites. Carol's husband, Nigel, joined us and presented us with the smallest three-tier wedding cake you've ever seen. He is also a teacher and had arranged for his Domestic Science Department to make it. My favourite music is that played on the harp and the guitar and Carol had managed to find a harpist to entertain us for the evening. Mike Parker brought several harps with him, ranging from a copy of the original harp, on which all the others have been based through the ages, up to a beautiful concert instrument. He played everything from the classics to Gershwin and even let us have a go. It was great fun. At the end of the evening we walked down the road by the Deal seafront to spend our wedding night in the Royal Hotel, which is where Lord Nelson romanced Lady Hamilton!

We were about to go to bed when I mentioned breakfast arrangements and was astounded when Chris said words to the effect, 'Well, it will have to be early as I've got to get to school.' I then jokingly expressed my surprise that, as school was so important, he hadn't gone for a later wedding service. 'I tried, but that was the latest they had'! So I really had been wedged in between lessons!

Three weeks later we had our blessing in Penn. It was the last service the retiring vicar was to take, after which he hung up his cassock, so the occasion was special for him too. I arranged for baskets of white flowers with trailing ivy to decorate the lych gate and the porch of the ninth-century church. Inside, the flowers were in my favourite colours of blue, yellow and white. I'd always wanted to hear bells ring at my wedding and this was part of our present from very dear friends, Tim and Sarah Marshall. Carol Myers, director of the Stars Organisation for Spastics Charity, sang a selection of Rodgers and Hammerstein love songs. Carol had trained as an opera singer and her voice ringing out in that little old church sent shivers of pleasure down one's spine. The pews were full of family and friends and Jonathan read from Corinthians, Chapter 13, about love bestowed and given being the greatest gift. We walked into and out of the church to the sound of Widor's *Toccata* and then repaired to Cliveden. We'd booked lunch for forty in the Mirrored Dining Room. It is a beautiful room that was dismantled and brought over from a French château and its position is such that you look out over the terrace, down along the manicured gardens and view the Thames in the far distance. We asked Mike Parker to play the harp for us again and all the guests expressed their pleasure both at the lovely instrument and Mike's choice of music.

I'd never had a official wedding album throughout my marriages, so the boat was pushed out yet further and we booked Tina Hadley, an award-winning wedding photographer. She was so professional I think she could have made Quasimodo look good. We also used her son to make a video of the wedding and reception. It was only his second assignment and, apart from a few technical faults which only a professional would notice, it was a sensitive and beautiful memento of a lovely day. The photos were gorgeous.

I added the cost of everything to my ever-growing overdraft, knowing that I could pay it off when the house was sold. I loathe being in debt, but as this was to be the final marriage commitment, I wanted everything to be right.

I didn't mind that Chris had nothing materially and was living in a small house. I've never been a gold-digger and if I love someone, I don't really care where I live, provided it has a flush toilet and hot and cold running water! I had a saleable house and would make a very good profit on it. I'd lived in Buckinghamshire for over twenty years and in the same house for fifteen of them. My mother and sister had homes fifteen miles from me and I had an established social life and circle of friends. I was prepared to give all this up and move to Kent to be absorbed into Chris's world. What I didn't realise was that Chris had very little world apart from school. I had assumed that such a pleasant, witty and debonair man would have a large circle of friends into which I would be welcomed. Assumption is a grievous fault. He spent so much time at work he had little time for a social circle and had very few friends. At the weekends he was totally wrung out and just wanted to recharge the batteries, predominantly by watching sport on television. Because I respected his fatigue, I didn't like to suggest visiting and staying with my friends on a regular basis. We did go away for the occasional weekend but it was always a ghastly journey to Buckinghamshire round the M25 on a Friday evening and an equally rotten one back on Sunday.

Before our marriage, I spent a couple of weekends with him in Kent and on one of these met his daughters. He had non-identical twin girls and a younger daughter. One twin and the youngest still lived at home with their mother. The other twin was married with children and lived close to the family home. On meeting the girls the eldest twin greeted me with the words, 'We are very protective of our mother and we've never liked any of Dad's girlfriends'! It makes me shudder to think that I didn't see the obvious.

I'm sure they didn't deliberately set out to dislike me, but we were as different in our outlook and behaviour as chalk and cheese. Chris had a very good phrase when things weren't right for him: he used to say, 'I'm out of my comfort zone' and I'm afraid I was with his daughters. They didn't come to see us that often but when they did it was always as a pack and usually with the child and I felt like an outsider, who was only there to do the cooking. I asked them many times to visit singly so that I could get to know them. It takes two to make or break a relationship and I will fairly and squarely accept a share of the blame for the situation which developed between Chris's girls and myself. I felt very uncomfortable when they came to the house and this put me on edge to the point that I was not very welcoming. I asked Chris repeatedly to pour oil on troubled waters, perhaps to have a round-table discussion and bang our heads together, but matters were never sorted out. This, plus my incredible loneliness, strained our relationship from the word go.

On the other hand, Chris was good with my son. Jonathan was very unhappy at the Royal Grammar School in High Wycombe, a fact of which I was ignorant. He was bullied just as he was in preparatory school. I know my son isn't the easiest person in the world – he has a fiery temperament and is quick to get angry, but he forgives and forgets just as easily and is very loving. I have sometimes wondered if the threatened miscarriage, the medication at the time and his traumatic birth have contributed to his nature. Certainly coming from a broken home and having a difficult relationship with both his father and stepfather doesn't augur well for a placid personality. But, I'm not the sort of mother who thinks her offspring can do no wrong. In fact I've usually erred on the side of the teachers whenever there's been a problem at school and have assumed the faults were Jonathan's, but I was unaware of what a hard time he was having. He confided in my mother that he had even contemplated doing away with himself. So, when I married Chris, he chose to leave Buckinghamshire and attend Chris's state school. He wanted a change – and besides, Astor was co-educational!

Chris didn't want to live in a town like Deal, where he would have constantly bumped into teachers, parents and pupils. He gave enough of his life to the school that, away from it, he wanted privacy, which I could understand. I love the country anyway and was happy to live out of town. While searching for a house we'd encountered the usual disappointments accompanying the buying and selling of properties. We'd had a disappointing survey on one house, my sale fell through and we lost the place we wanted to other buyers with ready cash. It was an added difficulty that I was still living in Buckinghamshire and had to drive to Kent for viewings. I didn't know the area at all and Chris was too busy at school to come on all the appointments.

Buying and selling property is a thankless task at the best of times. We visited several barn and oasthouse conversions only to find that although on the outside they were delightful – they had to be because of being 'listed' – the interiors rarely lived up to expectation and had been done up hastily and cheaply. I was beginning to despair when we found 'Rose Cottage'. It was the right price and had character and a super garden. The fact that it also had a swimming pool almost put us off viewing the property. We saw it in the winter and immediately liked its cosy atmosphere. I didn't give a thought to the fact that there were very few neighbours, no shop in the village half a mile away, and that it was extremely isolated. It is very difficult to start up a life in a new neighbourhood when you aren't taking children to school and meeting other parents, where there is no village shop or where you don't have a regular job through which you make contacts and friends. There was a very good pub in the village but I just don't like the noise and the smoky atmosphere.

If only we'd known each other better or lived together, I'm absolutely sure we would not have married. On the surface we were both romantics and appeared to have similar likes and dislikes but, underneath, there were fundamental differences. I am the sort of person who speaks my mind, blows my top, gets over it and gets on with it. I don't harbour grudges and usually forgive and forget. Chris will not enter into a disagreement, argument or discussion and very often would put his hands up to end all talk, take the car keys and drive off for several hours. He is used to being a Head and what the Head says, wants and does is implemented. Although I am prepared to give my man respect, I'm too much of a free spirit not to voice my opinions, requirements and desires. What I didn't realise was that Chris could be quite hard, under his sensitive exterior. When I made remarks disagreeing with him or perhaps made a suggestion for improving productions at school, these were seen as criticisms and 'put-downs'.

The cottage was soaking up money like a sponge which worried me as I was paying all the bills. There were all sorts of areas that had to be rectified and improved. Chris kept saying that, as this was to be our home till he retired, everything had to be right for me.

Because of the nature of my freelance employment I was entitled to take my Equitable pension before the age of sixty and as I wanted independent income to run my car, buy clothes, pay any extra bills and meet any financial requirements my son might incur, I took it. After the Equitable collapse in 2001, I went to an independent financial advisor. He looked up from my file, took off his glasses (always a bad sign I think) and said, 'Do you realise that if you go on taking what you are drawing at the moment, you won't have any capital left in a few years?' Oops!

I'd got money in a bond to put Jonathan through university, but I felt that as Chris was 'keeping me' I should play my part by paying for our holidays and other luxuries. Before he met me, Chris said he hadn't had a holiday for eleven years. I found this absolutely amazing. I couldn't do without holidays to recharge the batteries. But I have met other men, like Chris, who get their buzz from their work and to whom holidays are almost an intrusion.

In our first year of married life, Chris tried hard to make up for my loss of family, friends and a life. By year two I was counting the cost, emotionally and financially, of our marriage, and was aggrieved that he spent so much time at school. I even joked that the only thing he needed in his sumptuous office was a pull-out-of-the-wall bed. He had everything else there, including a shower and loo.

I had hoped that I could integrate into school life – perhaps run drama workshops or help out in other ways with the expertise I'd gleaned over the years. Astor School mounts very good dramatic and musical productions, but there is always the amateur failing of no concept of breath control and voice projection. The youngsters put so much into the shows, but very often by first night they were losing their voices. I've never taught but I know the basics of what should be learned, from my experience in theatre. I asked Chris to help me plan some workshops. These never happened. Was it because the school was his domain and he didn't want me intruding?

At school functions, when governors and parents enquired whether I liked living in Kent, I replied quite truthfully that I didn't, with the caveat that it was because I knew no one, was lonely and my husband was so dedicated to his work I hardly saw him. I thought Chris would understand the praise I was indirectly giving him. But he saw it only as criticism and I was not forgiven for telling the truth. I should have maintained a stiff upper lip and lied through my teeth. That is not my way.

John Gray wrote a book, *Men are from Mars, Women are from Venus,* in which his basic concept is that men and women speak different languages. I believe this is absolutely correct. What one says and how it is interpreted by the other person may differ entirely from what was meant.

I began to wish that I'd let Chris leave me the first Christmas after our marriage. I still had my house in Penn at that stage. He and his family had enjoyed hospitality there over the festive period. We had a disagreement over something and in the middle of the night, he got out of bed and started packing. I pleaded with him to stay and suggested that we'd sort out our differences. Again, with hindsight, I should have owned up to the fact that we'd made a big mistake, faced the music (from the press of course) and let him go. Selling the house was inevitable for me as I hadn't the income to maintain it in the long term but, five years ago, on the profit I made, I could have bought a tiny place in the same area and still have had money to invest for income. Kent is a much cheaper county for property and a move down there took me irretrievably out of the Buckinghamshire house market.

I think neither of us would admit we had made a mistake. I'm sure we genuinely cared for one another but our lifestyles were so different. I honestly think teachers should stay within their profession. They are such an esoteric bunch that anyone outside the circle is like a square peg in a round hole. Chris was amazingly generous and understanding to his pupils and staff, often putting his hand in his own pocket to help, but did not appear to have the same tolerance for his immediate family – me! This is not an unusual phenomenon. At his memorial service, Jonathan's grandfather was eulogised by past pupils at King Edward's School, Birmingham, at which he had been Chief Master, but I know his family suffered because of his dedication to the school. Many a successful businessman is totally paternalistic with his staff but gives his family short shrift.

I genuinely cared for Chris and, for a while, I thought he loved me. But, after two years of marriage, I was very unhappy indeed and needed space to sort myself out. My friend Kit in

Australia had been through an horrific time with pancreatic cancer. She was having other problems too and mentioned that she'd love to take a holiday but hadn't any one to go with. Chris's school was facing an Ofsted inspection, which meant I would see him even less than I normally did. So I seized on the opportunity of visiting my friend, grabbing some sunshine and having time for reflection. I discussed the proposition with Chris and thought I had his approval.

While in Australia I gave our relationship a great deal of thought and came to the decision that I was fortunate. Chris was a good man whom I respected and cared for, our marriage was worth working at and I decided to do my utmost to create a life for myself in Kent and stop regretting all that I'd given up to marry him. I wrote and faxed home regularly. I didn't get much feedback but put it down to the pressure of Ofsted.

I returned on 14 February, St Valentine's Day. Chris didn't even meet me at the airport due to pressure of work but, when he arrived home late that evening, we had a happy reunion and I thought the past was buried and we were on to a new beginning. I really did try hard to make things work, but I'm far from perfect and Chris expected too much of me and didn't understand me at all. School was as demanding as ever but I organised some lovely holidays, which Chris seemed to enjoy. We went to France, visited friends in Spain and had three wonderful holidays in the Seychelles. Our first holiday there was a few days offered by *OK! Magazine,* as a sort of delayed honeymoon. We got complimentary flights and bed and breakfast, but had to pay for other meals. In exchange for the break, we agreed to give the magazine photographic coverage. So in our six days on Mahé, we spent three days 'working'. Fortunately we liked the photographer, and as he'd brought his wife along as well, we turned the 'work' into a pleasurable experience. When I went to Chris's office a few months later, I saw that he'd had the whole article mounted and framed and it hung on his office wall.

Chris enabled me to join him on some very interesting school exchanges and I was delighted to be given the opportunity of going to countries I'd never have thought to visit. Chris, Carol and John, the Head of Art at Astor, were taking an art and textile exhibition to a school in a 'closed town' in Siberia. A couple of dance students from Astor were also going on the exchange. These towns aren't on any maps and were erected in the days of the Cold War predominantly to manufacture armaments. In the early days, dissidents were sent there. We went to Zhelesznogorsk – a town halfway across Siberia. You will find a Zhelesznogorsk on the map, but it it not the place we visited. Our town required entrance by visa and you went through checkpoints and huge barbed-wire fences. Once inside, the wire fences, the ice and the temperature of -42° were forgotten and you were overwhelmed by the warmth and friendliness of the Siberian people. I was amazed to discover how incredibly romantic are the Russians. At a dinner, every guest will rise and make a toast and most of them quote a few lines from a love poem or a piece of romantic prose. It was a wonderful experience and I will remember Siberian hospitality to the end of my days.

I will also remember Muscovite bureaucracy and their almost illegal ways of making money. On leaving Siberia, our plane was delayed for eight hours. This meant we missed our connection in Moscow and our visas ran out. Getting a Russian visa is like getting blood out of a stone. The process is extremely difficult and enormously bureaucratic. You are given the visa with no extra time at either end of the days for which you require it. By missing our connection and arriving at Moscow airport at 11 p.m. on a Saturday evening, we discovered that we had to renew our visas to leave the country. There was no one at the British Embassy who could help us until Sunday morning. Chris and I took the youngsters to a nearby hotel and Carol and John slept at the airport guarding the cases and the exhibition material.

On the Sunday morning an employee at the Embassy told us what we needed to do – it sounded like something out of a James Bond movie. At the airport, Chris had to go to a grill in the wall, almost hidden by a Coca-Cola machine. He pressed a buzzer and then had to relay his request to the operative who was somewhere, we didn't know where, in the building. About half an hour later, a burly Russian approached us. He was carrying a canvas bag out of which he produced an ink pad and a rubber stamp. All our visas were 'extended' at the exorbitant cost of sixty American dollars each – cash, of course. I don't think we'd have minded so much except for the fact that when we went through the gate to board our plane and showed the precious visas, the attendant said, 'Oh, that's all right, you don't need to show them as you're going home'!

It was because of the missed connection that Chris and I didn't get to Jill Dando's engagement party. We had been at a charity function at the Natural History Museum in London when we bumped into Jill and her boyfriend Alan. We were engaged in a very interesting conversation when Chris suggested we took the two of them to dinner, as it was my birthday. I thought they'd have other things to do, but they seemed delighted to accept and we all trouped off to Langan's Brasserie. It was a lovely evening and I was incredibly flattered when Jill told me I'd been her role model in my days at HTV in Bristol. (Joan Bakewell had been mine.) We all got on well and, at the end of the evening, we were given an invitation to their party. At the time we didn't know it was to announce their engagement.

Alan proposed to Jill when they were on holiday in Australia and apparently she almost danced down the road carrying a huge bunch of sunflowers. At her memorial service the church was decorated throughout with those giant blooms. For me, sunflowers and Jill will always go together. When I see them, I see her smiling face. She was a lovely person and I'm sad we didn't have the opportunity to get to know each other better.

After my Australian trip, and our long discussions, I thought we were resolving our difficulties and that Chris was not expecting perfection from me any more than I did from him. To be honest, I'm not sure what he expected of me. He'd fallen for someone with a bit of get up and go and an interesting life and must have realised I could never be happy as a compliant stay-at-home housewife. I did try hard to alter the relationship with his daughters, but there was only ever a surface acceptance by them. We were both at fault. I wasn't relaxed enough with them and was too judgmental, but they didn't appear to see how awkward I felt in my own home with their tribal presence. I was made to feel an outsider to the point that even my father remarked on it. As he is my harshest critic, it was comforting to realise that the poor relationship between the girls and me wasn't all my fault.

Life went on and the relationship with Chris appeared to be all right. After my experiences, I've never expected perfection. Our life was relatively humdrum. We went out to theatre occasionally and I happily entertained staff from his school. I went away sometimes during the week to visit my friends but always ensured that I was back at weekends unless Chris was playing cricket.

Each year of our marriage appeared to bring yet more time consumed by school meetings, governors' meetings, parents' meetings, sixth-form meetings, meetings and yet more damned meetings. Chris appeared to be on a roundabout of never-ending meetings. By 2001, he was out late three to four evenings a week, often coming home between 11 p.m. and midnight. Often these meetings were sprung on me at the last moment. I'd ask him in the morning at what time he'd like dinner and was informed that he wouldn't – yet another meeting. For a brief moment I entertained the idea of hiring a private detective and dismissed the thought as unworthy. Chris was far too trustworthy. I was worried as even friends were questioning the amount of time he spent at school. 'No one stays at governors' meetings and staff meetings till that time of night' was said on more than one occasion when I complained about his working day.

In February 2001, we had been to a charity ball at which there was a Silent Auction of attractive lots. Many of them were exotic holidays but what did catch my eye was a week in a hunting lodge in the Lubéron region of Provence. As I had always wanted to retire to Provence and hoped to encourage

Chris to think the same way, I felt a week there presented a great opportunity for him to assess the situation. I put in a bid, little thinking I would be successful. The ball was patronised by some extremely well-heeled personages. A few days later I received a letter informing me that the hunting lodge was mine for a week of my choosing. After consultation with Chris, we decided to take the week immediately after the end of the summer term. The summer break itself is a difficult time for him to take leave as there is always some building project or other which requires his attention. In fact, he rarely took more than a total of ten days off in the break, and, although he'd go in later and come home earlier, for him it was business as usual. So our main holiday was taken at Easter.

We had both fallen in love with the Seychelles and, for the third year running, I planned our Easter vacation at the Plantation Club on Mahé. As a young man Chris was a red-head, so although he liked the sun, the feeling wasn't reciprocated. I would go off for hours 'shelling' on the fabulous beaches, leaving Chris in the shade with a good book. The previous year we had discovered the joys of snorkelling and had bought some decent masks and snorkels with us so that we could enjoy the incredibly colourful marine life on our coral reef. In the evenings, as neither of us was partial to buffets, lots of people and 'entertainment', we opted to eat in our room and watch a film or chose the more expensive option of dining in the hotel's superb air-conditioned French restaurant.

My friend and surrogate mother Cecily had not been enjoying the best of health and, several times in June 2001, Chris suggested that I should go down to Cornwall for a visit. I never needed an excuse to go and see her but was always mindful of leaving Chris on his own. I felt it my duty to be there to look after and cook for him. But he persisted and I made arrangements.

On Monday, 25 June, we kissed goodbye and I set off, first of all to have my hair done at Jean's in Bristol and then on to Cornwall. Chris was going to be playing cricket both days the following weekend so I was able to have the whole week with

Cecily and Jack and planned my return for Sunday. I sent Chris a card saying I wished he could have been enjoying the break with me and we spoke most evenings. I wanted to get back home so that we could have a meal together on Sunday evening but when I asked what time he'd return after cricket, he was slightly evasive and said, 'I'm not sure exactly what time. We're playing away.' I replied, 'Never mind, I'll aim to be home at seven and looking forward to seeing you.'

The drive home was a pleasure. The motorways were free-flowing, it was warm and sunny. I'd had a week with friends and was going home. As I always do on long journeys, I reflected on my life. I was settled at last with a husband and son I loved, two dogs and a cat. I lived in a cosy country cottage with a large garden to keep me busy. Perhaps I wasn't ecstatically happy but I was very content and maybe at the age of 59, with an emotionally stormy life behind me, contentment was definitely the preferred option.

There are several ways of reaching our cottage. If I'm in a hurry I'll come down the Canterbury bypass. As it was such a beautiful day and I enjoy the country drive from Canterbury through the villages, that was the route I took. Travelling that way brought me past Chris's cricket club at Worth. There were players on the field! That's odd I thought. I don't know much about the game or his club, but I didn't think they had a second eleven. And he distinctly said he was playing away.

Walking down the garden path, I noticed he hadn't cut the grass, but then he worked incredibly long hours and gardening was his least favourite pastime. As my key turned in the lock and I opened the door, I was surprised to find the alarm hadn't been set. I entered the hallway and my eyes were caught by an envelope propped in front of the telephone. Had Chris left a welcome home note for me? I went to pick up the envelope and suddenly had a sense of foreboding. A much-treasured Astor School poster had gone from the wall. Only one dog was barking.

It took a second or two for reality to dawn. I still remember the cold shiver that went through my body despite the warmth of the day. I felt dizzy and faint and heard an agonised cry from a long distance. I realised the cry was mine. 'No!' It could not, should not, would not happen again. Not again!

But it had. Just like all the others, my fifth marriage was ending in disaster, but this time totally without warning. The letter was a cold, clinical, unfeeling notification that my husband did not wish to continue living under the same roof with me and asked that I contact him only through his solicitor. It was the kind of letter you would write to someone to whom you were giving the sack. I suppose he was! I sank onto a chair with wave after wave of coldness washing over me. So many feelings were assailing me – the heartbreak, the aloneness, emotional worry, financial worry and the inevitable character assassination in the press.

Having been down the same path so often, shouldn't I have been stronger? But separation and the heartbreak that goes with it never gets easier, whatever your age. In fact, I think it gets harder. You lose your resilience and bounce as you get older. I couldn't face it again. I simply wanted the ground to open up and swallow me.

I don't remember whom I phoned first. I was in a complete state of shock. Also, being in Kent, I couldn't drive to my mother or to one of my supportive friends, such as Sarah or Chloe. I was very much on my own.

In his letter, Chris had indicated that he would be staying with Carol and Nigel Donovan for a few weeks until he sorted out some accommodation. He had asked me not to contact him there, but I couldn't stop myself. He was out, but Carol was very kind to me and listened patiently as I expressed my total incredulity that he'd walked out with no discussion, no warning, nothing. She was powerless to help but she knew Chris well enough to say, 'He's pulled the shutters down. He won't discuss it.'

He came back to the cottage three days later to talk about practicalities. I asked that Carol should come with him. I wanted her to be witness to the fact that we really did speak a different language. He was a cold as ice and gave no quarter. He had closed our joint bank account, which I only ever used for food. I paid for Jonathan, my needs plus any luxuries, holidays, car servicing etc. out of my own money. He indicated that he would continue to pay the mortgage and the bills until the house was sold. When I asked how I was supposed to survive, he replied, 'You have money.' It was an odd statement to make. Did he think I had sources of money that I'd kept from him? Apparently some women do keep sources of income hidden from their spouses.

I thought again about the circumstances in which we met. He had very little. I had a lovely home and he may have assumed, in line with most journalists and a huge proportion of the public, that I was very well off. My home was all I had.

He had obviously been planning his departure for some time and very methodically. How could he have kept up the pretence of a normal relationship and shared my bed, when he'd already made his decision? Leaving as he did, encouraging me to visit Cecily and then packing up and going without any discussion or warning was, in my opinion, a cowardly act.

It was not the action of a man I greatly respected. I began to wonder if he'd had a minor breakdown through pressure of work and whether, eventually, he would agree to speak to me. For weeks I wrote him affectionate letters, begging him to meet me for dinner to discuss the situation – to try and find a solution. He'd found *his* solution, my feelings did not enter the equation, and my letters went unanswered. I didn't find out till months later that, at the end of term, three weeks after he left me, he assembled the staff and announced that we'd separated 'by mutual consent'! Funny, I don't remember being in on the decision. As I was unaware of this announcement, and felt that with the summer holidays he would be under less pressure, I continued to write and ask for a meeting. I was totally ignored.

I spiralled into an unfortunately familiar pattern, losing three-quarters of a stone in two weeks, being unable to sleep and sinking into a depression. The Chair of Governors and his wife and a few of the teachers from the school bumped into me in Deal and expressed their shock at the way I looked. When I asked how they would feel under the circumstances, they were flabbergasted. They'd all swallowed the 'mutual consent' story.

Fortunately for me, I had one of the best doctors you could wish for. After a fortnight of hardly eating and not sleeping, I had to make an appointment. She couldn't have been more helpful or considerate. She prescribed Prozac and sleeping pills. This time round the Prozac made me feel peculiar and I had to stop taking it and the sleeping pills made me totally woozy. After trying several different brands of conventional medicaments, I opted for the homeopathic St John's Wort for depression and Valerian tablets to help me sleep.

I don't remember much of July, August and September. Sarah and Chloe took it in turns to phone me, check up on me and allow me to pour my heart out. They were a great help, but it wasn't the same as having one or other of them physically with me to put an arm around me or to offer a shoulder to cry on. At that time, I hadn't any friends in Kent so there was no one to whom I could turn. I went away on visits as often as possible, but I still couldn't accept the situation.

Three months after he left, I was still in a state of shock and wanted answers. As I couldn't get Chris to respond to my letters, sent care of Carol Donovan, and didn't even know where he was living, I decided that I would go to Astor School.

On the morning of 4 October, I phoned the school to ascertain whether he was there. I was told on his arrival at school, he would go to a management meeting after which he would be in his office. I drove to Dover and up the steep incline leading to Astor, parked my car and went in past the school office to Chris's domain. Carol was inside and looked startled when she saw me. Chris wasn't at school. His boxer dog Holly was ill and he'd taken her to the vet.

Carol ordered a coffee for me and closed the door. Not long after I sat down, the phone rang and I heard her say 'Is it negotiable?' When she put the receiver down she said, 'I'm sorry Jan, he won't come on to school premises while you are here.' Someone from the office had obviously told him of my presence. I was dumbstruck. Then his other deputy, John, arrived. John is a gentle chap and he'd been at our wedding. 'Have you come to evict me?' I asked. There was no response but I could tell he was highly embarrassed.

I finished my coffee and Carol escorted me to my car. I was sobbing with total incomprehension. I wouldn't treat a dog the way I was being handled. Carol, who had always been so loving and affectionate, didn't even shake my hand. I drove off down the hill and around the corner intending to drive home but something stopped me and I decided to wait. I phoned Chris's private number to leave a message begging for just ten minutes of his time. Almost immediately John rang me back and told me once again to go home, that Chris simply would not see me nor would he enter the premises until I'd gone. I was accused of harassing him. Is wanting a meeting with your husband regarded as harassment?

I sat for a few minutes and, realising the futility of the situation, started to drive home. I hadn't gone more than a quarter of a mile when I had to stop at a pedestrian crossing. Another car pulled up on the opposite side of the road. It was Chris in a brand new sports car. He once boasted that he'd never had a brand new car and that buying new was a waste of money. He stared straight ahead and totally ignored me.

After learning that he had made an open statement to his staff about our marriage breakdown, I am surprised that the story took so long finding its way to the press. There's usually an obliging mole or an unnamed 'friend' who spills the beans. I was doorstepped, or rather car-stopped, by some local reporters on Monday, 15 October. Would you believe that two adults could sit in a car from 8.50 a.m. until 5 p.m. with nothing better to do than try and get a picture or a quote? They got nothing, but I knew it wouldn't be long before the nationals started snooping. By Friday it was a reporter from the *Sunday Mirror* on the doorstep. I despatched him but phoned my one and only journalist friend for advice. He said the same as my ex-agent James Kelly had done years before – they'll print anyway, so give them the story and at least you'll have some control over it. I was offered a fee and accepted it. It helped to get me through the winter of 2001–2. I could have said a great deal more, but out of respect for his position and for the affection that had once existed between us, I tried to give a balanced interview. At the time, I was also blissfully unaware of what I later learnt, otherwise I might not have been so charitable! A very pleasant photographer came along to the house and took rolls of film but, as is only to be expected, the paper chose an horrendously uncomplimentary one. I suppose it helps sell their newspapers.

Another paper must have spent a great deal of money getting the low-down from my previous husbands. Owen phoned to tell me that journalists had tried to contact him in Paris but he was taking time out to write at his home in Provence. The reporters hired a car and drove six hours to his village in order to ask him about me. He relayed their questions to me and also the answers he gave. They didn't print the favourable comments! Jeremy was approached and made a comment or two. Patrick refused to talk to them and I don't know whether they approached Eric but I assume they did, although there was nothing printed. At least Chris had the decency to admit that he left me because of irreconcilable differences. His words were, 'My work might have been one of those differences. I did put in the hours. I appreciate she had it very difficult down here [in Kent]. I just wish her every success in the future.'

From that horrible day at Astor School, I knew our marriage was definitely over and although I strengthened physically, mentally I was a wreck. As anyone who has been through this scenario will know, you keep going over and over what went wrong, how did it go wrong, what could you have done to avoid it. It becomes a long trail of unanswered questions beginning with 'What if?' What if I hadn't done or said that? What if I had acted differently? On and on it goes until you are driven mental. One of chris's friends knows him very well indeed and she admitted to me that in her opinion he doesn't understand how to make a relationship or how they alter and change over time.

I had regular appointments with my doctor and she came up trumps again. She arranged for me to have acupuncture for my terrible headaches and to see a stress counsellor.

The acupuncture worked, but I had little belief in the counsellor's ability to help me. However, I went through the motions of making an appointment. Thank goodness I didn't wait to see the psychiatric specialist – it was seven months before that appointment was offered to me, by which time I could have been dead. I declined the visit.

Sandra, the stress counsellor, wore very short skirts and was also very with it, not at all the stereotype counsellor one would expect. As I entered the room, I expressed my negative attitude as to her being able to help me. 'Sit down and tell me all about it.' An hour and a half later I'd finished telling her the story of my life from broken home upwards. We hadn't got much time left but she said, 'Now stop feeling angry at yourself and aim that anger at Chris. It takes two to make a relationship and it takes two to break it. You've made errors but so has he.' I know these words sound simple and could be said, and have been said, by my friends but when the advice comes from a professional, you take more notice. Sandra was one of the best things that happened to me in a long time. She was very down to earth. There was no incomprehensible psycho-babble. We spoke woman to woman and called a spade a shovel. I saw her fortnightly and then monthly for a year and she has helped me turn my life around. She looked at the wedding photos and the video and commented on the body language. It was staring me in the face and I hadn't seen it. There was no interaction, his body was saying, 'Don't enter my space.'

I was beginning to have a social circle again and also signed up for some adult education classes. On returning from my silversmithing class one Friday evening, there was a message from a journalist I knew quite well. He sounded embarrassed and asked that I should phone him because rumours were flying around and that if they were true, there was a fee on offer. I couldn't imagine what the rumour was. There was no man in my life. It was late, so I left it till the morning to make the call. 'What was this rumour?' I asked. 'That you were seen in the Priory Clinic in the North of England and that your wrists were bandaged.' The Priory exists to treat patients for substance abuse, drug- and drink-related, and also for intended suicides. I had to laugh at this preposterous story. 'If you want to check where I was yesterday and the day before and the day before that, you can. My local friends will vouch for the fact that I've been here and not up north. And I can assure you that if I were to do anything stupid, I wouldn't slash my wrists.' 'No, I didn't think you would. I'd put you down as a pill person, myself!' Apparently, had the rumour been true, there would have been a fat fee to give an exclusive but the *Mail* weren't sure of their facts so they'd checked it out first, otherwise there would have been the mother and father of all damages claims.

It saddens me that, in my opinion, some nasty and inadequate person had seen a woman at the Priory, mistaken her for me and was prepared, for money, to spill the beans to a newspaper. Wouldn't it have crossed their minds to have compassion for anyone in such a state of trauma that they'd try to take their own life? People never cease to amaze me.

With regard to the ending of our marriage, I would have been happy to wait two years for an amicable divorce by separation. There was no one in my life and I'd no intention of getting involved again. However, my solicitor explained that I couldn't let things drift – finance had to be sorted out. I do think it is a crazy system, but until you lodge a petition for divorce, you can't sort out the financial side of things. My solicitor was worried that if the house sold quickly and no agreement had been reached, as she put it, 'You could be out on the streets sitting on your suitcase.'

As a two-year separation didn't appear to be an option, I lodged a petition on the only ground open to me, which was 'unreasonable behaviour'. Within days I had a letter from Chris contesting my decision, stating that it would be 'dreadful for him professionally to be spread all over the newspapers' and he would countersue. I knew it would be me, not him, who'd be hung, drawn and quartered by the press – yet another Leeming failure. The fact that Chris already had two failed marriages would not have been taken into account.

In the case of behaviour, the solicitors for both parties argue and discuss and usually come to some form of wording that doesn't desperately upset anyone. I understand one could even cite 'snoring' as unreasonable behaviour. I don't know who said it, but 'the law is an ass'. However, we live in a democracy and have to live by the law of the land. I had no desire to damage Chris in any way, despite his cold-blooded treatment of me, but I had to fight for financial survival. Tied up in the house was my capital, but I had virtually no income.

Chris continued to ignore me, so we couldn't circumvent solicitors and they are expensive. I won't go into the gory details but through all my failed marriages I've never experienced anything like it. John divorced me for adultery; my marriage to Patrick ended amicably with a two-year separation and I divorced both Jeremy and Eric for adultery. There was no money in any of my husbands' pots and as I always had a house and a job, I wasn't interested in taking anyone 'to the cleaners'. I still am not, but I had to fight every step of the way to try and recoup the capital I'd sunk into my marriage with Chris Russell. It was all I had other than my small pensions. To take the title of Jeffrey Archer's book, I wanted 'Not a Penny More, Not a Penny Less'. If I had won a million on the premium bonds, I would have walked away from the whole unpleasant scenario.

Jonathan left university in June 2002 and went straight out to Ibiza to do what young people do in Ibiza. I asked no questions. He gained his degree and reluctantly agreed to fly home for the degree ceremony. Patrick collected him from the airport and took him to his home in Haslemere, Buckinghamshire. I joined them and Patrick drove us up to Manchester, allowing four and a half hours for a three-hour journey. Unfortunately, there was a terrible accident on the motorway and our journey took six hours. We phoned the university and were assured that Jonathan could have his degree conferred in the following ceremony, although he wouldn't be with his peer group.

So there he was, in the back of the car, moaning about having to leave Ibiza for this wretched ceremony that he was only attending to please his parents. However, when we finally reached Manchester and the robing room, I saw a subtle change come over his face as the gown, hood, and mortarboard were fitted. I think he allowed himself a little satisfaction from his achievement and we parents were fairly bursting with pride. We did the usual posing-for-official-photographs bit and were duly emotional as he went on stage to collect his degree. It's always the case, isn't it – the photos you most want for the album are always out of focus. Mine were!

Patrick took us for a most enjoyable meal afterwards and then we dropped Jonathan at a friend's flat and started the long journey home. We talked about all sorts of things and then I made a comment about how different life might have been for me if Mark (Eric's son and Patrick's stepson) hadn't taken gliding lessons, which resulted in Eric meeting 'the other woman'. Patrick said in a very matter-of-fact way, 'Oh, they haven't lived together for two years. She's in the States.' Of course, Jonathan saw Eric from time to time when he visited his father and Robin. But I had given him strict instructions that he was never to mention Eric or tell me what was going on in his life. I dreaded hearing that she had had his child. I simply didn't want to know anything about him and had assumed he was still with her and happy. As we continued our journey down south, my mind was in turmoil. I knew what I wanted to do but realised I had to think on it. I had to think long and hard.

Patrick and Robin had been good enough to ask me to stay the night. I was overtired and emotionally overwrought, so I didn't get much sleep. I drove home and spent the whole of Saturday thinking about the situation and in the end decided that all I had to lose was my pride. I wrote a letter to Eric on the Saturday night in which I simply asked if he would like to meet me. By the Monday afternoon, he phoned. I was about to take off for a holiday in Spain returning at the end of July, at which time he would be holidaying in France with his son, Mark. So a meeting was arranged for mid-August. Initially he was going to come to my home but we both thought better of it. I reckoned anywhere with a bed would have been too strong a temptation! We decided to meet halfway, at the Copthorne Hotel, Gatwick.

As I drove to our rendezvous, I didn't really know what I felt – a mixture of excitement and numbness. We both like punctuality and I timed my arrival to perfection, drawing into the car park at two minutes to four o'clock. I walked into Reception – no Eric. I knew he wouldn't stand me up, but thought he'd been delayed on a flight. I'd left my mobile phone in the car and as I walked back to the car park, there he was in the distance. I couldn't see him clearly because I wasn't wearing my glasses, but his walk is unmistakable. As we approached each other, I began to shake. When I reached him, my legs gave way and I fell into his arms with silent tears streaming down my face. I felt such an idiot. That was not the cool, calm and collected 'I'm totally in charge of myself' woman he was supposed to encounter.

We had afternoon tea and talked and talked. He proposed a walk but it started to rain so we went for a drive instead and then returned to the Copthorne for dinner. We were able to talk as though none of the pain, the hurt and the intervening years mattered in the slightest. We were very at ease with each other. After dinner, he saw me to my car and I asked him what, if anything, he'd expected from our meeting. He replied, 'I thought it would close the book on our relationship but it appears to have opened another chapter. And you, what did you expect?' I replied truthfully that I'd absolutely no idea. There were no plans to meet again but we parted company with him saying, 'I'll be in touch.'

A week went by, then another and then another so that when the letter with the familiar handwriting dropped through the letter box, I guessed what it would say. I was correct. He'd thought about us, but too much water had flowed under the bridge. He concluded his letter with the words, 'Receiving this, you may well not wish to communicate with me again and if I don't hear anything from you I will understand. If your new philosophy is right then fate will decide our futures. I wish you well.' My philosophy, now, is that nothing happens by chance. In the great plan of things everything is meant to be.

I must admit I felt a bit sad, filled a large glass with brandy and dry ginger, picked up a book and went to bed. The one good thing that had come out of our meeting was a burying of the bitterness. People had often said to me, 'There must have been good times. Remember those.' But I was so eaten up with hurt, I could only see the negatives in our relationship. I now felt more at peace and no longer regarded our twelve years together as a waste of time.

The case for the Russell divorce was scheduled for 5 September 2002. I hadn't seen Chris Russell since he left me in early July 2000. Even in court, I only saw the back of his jacket. That night, I came home and wept. I cried for both of us. The cards and letters we exchanged in those early weeks of our relationship were loving and full of hope and now there was nothing – not even the possibility of a few civil words if we passed in the street. After our divorce, a few people told me that Chris was known as a womaniser. So I'd got it wrong again!

And then to cap it all, I received a letter from the woman with whom Chris had had a long standing eight year relationship before he met me. (The relationship was apparently over when Chris and I met). She enclosed a copy of a letter she had sent him in December 2002. It was obvious from the content that he had re-established a relationship with her before he left me and that he had 'relentlessly pursued' her and that now the relationship was over again. It was interesting that she made a comment about him 'having to have a new one [relationship] in place before you discard the old one!' She also referred to the fact that once the balloon of his ego was punctured there was no going back. I had definitely inadvertently punctured his balloon so was most definitely doomed. She also talked about his emphasis on 'public perception'.

It was a very harsh letter and I felt for her to the extent that I wrote offering my condolences as she had obviously been hurt by him yet again.

At his job, no one could find fault with Christopher Russell. He is an excellent Head Teacher and has pulled Astor School up by its boot straps to the point that it now enjoys College for the Arts status and in that respect I am delighted for him and for the school. But in the relationship stakes . . . enough said!

★　★　★

So here I am in my early sixties and everything I always feared has happened to me. I will have enough money for a tiny house or an apartment, but I've lost my beautiful home, I've lost my partner and have long-term financial insecurity. BUT, for some unaccountable reason, I am more optimistic than I've ever been in my life. I always feared the worst and it happened. Self-fulfilling prophesy? Maybe.

I've put my son through university and he has a degree. I am so sorry he didn't have a stable home background, but he knows he is very loved. We have a great relationship and talk to each other about virtually everything. If I could wave a wand and get him the right job, I'd do it, but I can't. I can only give him my everlasting love and undying support. He now has his own life to lead.

I have friends and our caring is mutual. I'm on my own. There isn't enough income for a comfortable life in England, so I shall probably go and live abroad. My first choice would be Australia, but unfortunately they require a very large sum of money in the bank plus enough to buy a house, unless you have a trade or skill they need. I don't, and I don't blame them for taking that attitude. Why should they be overloaded with the sun-seeking elderly putting a strain on their health system? My second choice would be France, because I love it. But not speaking French fluently and not having a nucleus of friends puts the lid on that idea. My experience in coming to Kent and having no friends has taught me a valuable lesson. I hasten to add that after Chris left me, it only took the friendship of one couple, Martin and Gill Garrod, and a whole network of potential friendships opened up.

So, I rather fancy I'm left with Spain. The weather and health service is better, the housing and living expenses are less than in France and decidedly less expensive than England and my state pension remains index-linked. And I have very good friends already living there.

So what more could I want? In the words of the sixties musical *Tommy* – 'I'm free'.

I would rather not have gone through the emotional pain that has dogged my life. But, as a friend of mine put it, 'I'm not a flatliner' – you know how the machine goes from rapid motion into a flat line when someone expires. I've had terrible downs but I've had fantastic ups in my life. I don't believe you can have one without the other.

1. If only I hadn't met John Staple.
2. If only Hayo hadn't died.
3. If only I'd returned to Australia.
4. If only I'd not met Eric.
5. If only I'd not married Chris.

1. I wouldn't have met Owen Leeming, who encouraged me and showed me wider horizons.
2. I wouldn't have had a television career and met so many fascinating people.
3. I wouldn't have had my beloved son Jonathan. Well, I might have had a child, but not him.
4. I wouldn't have had an enormously romantic and passionate experience.
5. I wouldn't have the exciting choices before me now.

I remember being highly embarrassed the first time I was questioned over my marriages. Surprisingly, the female interviewer turned the whole thing round and said, 'Count yourself lucky to have been asked. Some women never get the chance.'

I haven't stayed in touch with all my old loves, but it's not a bad record. Owen Leeming has been my friend for over forty years. John Dobson is Jonathan's godfather. Jeremy still phones from time to time. He rarely comes to England from Sweden, but has threatened to take me to dinner when he does. Patrick is the father of our child and our relationship has improved with time to the extent that we can share a laugh and joke together.

So, has Jan Leeming been so unlucky in love?

I may not have been wise in my choices, but I have been lucky enough to have received, and to have given, an enormous amount of love. I am sure I will love again in the future, but I will never ever give my total trust to a man.

In the words of Audrey Hepburn's character in the film, *Roman Holiday* – 'I was born with an enormous need for affection, and a terrible need to give it.' I am 'Addicted to Love'.

AND SO . . .

Because Chris walked out before we could take the holiday in Provence, and because I was in no fit state to go on my own, I phoned the owner of the hunting lodge and explained my predicament. He was extremely generous in suggesting that I could have the lodge for a week the following year but that it would have to be at a date suitable to him. I was very grateful. The date offered was a week from 6–13 September 2002.

I was very much looking forward to that break, but the date for the court case over the divorce was set for 5 September and was unalterable. That vacation in Provence really seemed jinxed. I offered the week to friends, but none was able to accept it. Again I phoned the owner and couldn't believe it when he said he'd got a free week at the end of September and the place was mine if I wanted. Too right I did.

Jonathan had finished at university and had immediately gone out to Ibiza. He was intending to return in September to look for a job and to give me support at the time of the court case. So, I tentatively suggested he might like a week in Provence, little thinking he'd want a holiday with his mother. He jumped at the chance.

Then another couple of generous friends offered me their property in the Dordogne for a week in the middle of September when it was empty between all their family commitments. I'd never been to that part of France and was delighted to accept.

Jonathan and I had a lovely week in the Dordogne, a mixture of sightseeing and sunbathing. There appears to be a château or a castle at every turn of the road and we explored many. We also visited several churches and cathedrals and in all of them I lit candles before the Virgin and prayed for help and guidance. I basically put myself into her hands and promised that I would try and cope with whatever was meted out to me.

At the end of the week we motored on down south to Provence and our hunting lodge. When we arrived the caretaker told us there had been a lightning strike that had put out the computerised workings on the pool. It was freezing cold and not usable. As we couldn't swim and sunbathe, we went sightseeing and visited many of the places we knew so well from our ten years of holidaying in Provence. Les Baux and Fontaine de Vaucluse were a must.

The owners of the lodge had very kindly allowed us to stay on for an extra night and were arriving themselves on our last evening. By way of thanks, I'd offered to cook for them. As I know my way around the supermarket in Salon as well as I know the local ones in England, and I love visiting the town anyway, I decided we'd go there to shop.

Tradition dictates that if we go to Salon, we must have coffee and a brandy by the mossy fountain. It was extremely windy and, despite the sun, quite cold, so we chose to go inside the café. Jonathan and I enjoy each other's company but we're very alike in some ways and, after two weeks together, relations were a trifle strained. We both needed space, so I left him in the café and arranged to come back between 4 and 4.30 p.m.

I walked around the streets with an overwhelming sense of sadness. Salon had meant so much to Eric and myself. Why should I be so upset now, seven years and one marriage later? I passed the pâtisserie where we'd ordered our wedding cake. The flower shop had gone and the building was under reconstruction.

I was in the old part of Salon, near the clock tower, when I stopped to admire some clothes. My gaze was drawn to an attractive ceramic crucifix on a lilac cord. Crucifixes were all the rage in 2002, but I felt one shouldn't wear it purely as a fashion statement. I had found my faith again, albeit weakly and tentatively, but I felt comfortable with a Christian commitment. The cross was most definitely a fashion item but I was drawn to it. I went into the shop and the lady in charge explained that the necklace was already sold and was waiting collection, but she could order one for me. If I cared to pay for it in advance, she would post it to me. All this chatting and negotiation took twenty minutes. The shop was a thirty-second walk from the fountain and the clock was just striking the half-hour.

I crossed the road to the café and was greeted with, 'Mother, guess who I've just met.' Although we'd been on holiday in Provence for years, we didn't know many people, so I was at a loss and admitted it. 'You've got just enough time to scarper – I bumped into Eric and he's gone to feed the meter.' If I hadn't stayed in the shop ordering the crucifix, Jonathan and I would have been on our way to the supermarket! The meeting would not have taken place.

I couldn't run away. Had I not met him in August I would have done so, but the worst was over and I knew I could cope with seeing him. He'd come into Salon to buy a particular type of garlic crusher, couldn't get what he wanted and was walking through the old town of Salon when he saw Jonathan. Words such as 'Bloody hell, what are you doing here' were uttered and when Jonathan said I'd gone off shopping, Eric suggested joining us for a coffee after putting money in the meter. We stayed chatting for an hour, very much at ease with one another. He was on another short break with his son Mark and they were due to leave the next day. Assuming that they'd be driving north up the motorway back to Calais, and the area in which we were staying was well worth a visit, I proffered an invitation for both of them to drop in for a coffee and maybe lunch at the hunting lodge. Eric said he'd consult Mark and we parted.

Jonathan and I did our shopping in the Géant Casino and set off back to Murs. By the time we parted I realised that Eric and

Mark were flying home from Marseille, so visiting us was way off their route. I expected him to phone and refuse my invitation, but Mark sent Jonathan a text and said they would call in the next day, though they probably wouldn't stay for lunch.

I felt amazingly calm and again experienced the feeling of numbness that I had had when driving to our meeting six weeks earlier. I expected nothing.

Mark and Jonathan saw each other regularly at Patrick's house, so their meeting wasn't at all strained. They went off to do some shooting. I don't approve, but as neither was an expert with a gun, I hoped the local fauna would be safe.

Eric and I sat by the pool and talked for hours. It was a cathartic and cleansing experience. There was a peace between us and so many romantic and wonderful memories we could share. I could finally look back on our twelve years together with happiness, remembering the good and forgetting the bad.

We'd had seven years of marriage and seven years apart. We'd had passion and much love; now there was forgiveness and understanding and ... maturity!

Where will it go? Maybe nowhere ... maybe another book!

384.54 Lerner, Mark   c.1
LER
    Careers with a
     radio station

DATE			

c. 1

© THE BAKER & TAYLOR CO

careers with a
RADIO STATION

Mark Lerner

photographs by
Milton J. Blumenfeld

Lerner Publications Company
Minneapolis, Minnesota

With thanks to my friend Jim duBois

LIBRARY OF CONGRESS CATALOGING IN PUBLICATION DATA

Lerner, Mark.
Careers at a radio station.

(An Early career book)
Summary: Describes fifteen careers, including announcer, sports director, sales manager, music director, researcher, traffic manager, promotions director, account executive, and chief engineer.

1. Radio broadcasting—Vocational guidance—Juvenile literature. 2. Radio—Vocational guidance—Juvenile literature. [1. Radio broadcasting—Vocational guidance. 2. Radio—Vocational guidance. 3. Occupations] I. Blumenfeld, Milton J., ill. II. Title. III. Series.

PN1991.55.L47   1983   384.54'023   82-20349
ISBN 0-8225-0312-3 (lib. bdg.)

International Standard Book Number: 0-8225-0312-3   Library of Congress Catalog Card Number: 82-20349

2 3 4 5 6 7 8 9 10 92 91 90 89 88 87 86 85 84

Would you like to work for a radio station?

The radio is a very important part of our daily lives. Radio entertains us with our favorite music and keeps us informed of the day's news. When we want to know what the weather will be like, we turn on the radio.

Everything we hear on the radio comes to us from a radio station. Some radio stations play rock music. Others play country songs. Still other stations report the news, weather, and sports throughout the day.

No matter what their radio station plays, the people who work there want as many people as possible to listen. In this book, you will read about some of the people who work for a radio station and what they do. Maybe you'll find a career that you'd someday like to try.

ANNOUNCER

Announcers play the music you hear on the radio. They choose which songs to play and when to play them. And when you hear weather reports, announcers are the people you're listening to. They give the important information that listeners need.

When announcers are not on the air, they often talk to listeners who have telephoned the station. Announcers like to play *requests,* or songs that these callers especially want to hear. Announcers also do *commercials.* Commercials are advertisements. Businesses pay to advertise on the radio to tell listeners about what they sell. It is very important for announcers to make commercials sound just like the businesses want them to sound.

Announcers must have very clear voices. They must also like to entertain people.

NEWS DIRECTOR

News directors write the station's news reports. Their reports cover national, state, and local news. At some stations, news directors then read the news over the air. At other stations, that job is done by announcers.

News directors often attend important speeches and meetings where they hear government officials speaking about issues that affect the community. News directors put the most important information they've heard into their news reports. During severe weather, news directors give listeners up-to-the-minute reports.

The news director in the picture is standing in front of a *teletype* machine, or "wire." News comes over the wire from reporters all over the world. This news director will use some of these news stories when he writes his own reports.

SPORTS DIRECTOR

Have you ever seen somebody at a ball game holding a microphone and tape recorder while talking with a player on the field? If you have, you might have been watching a radio station's sports director at work. Sports directors go to many sports events. There they talk to fans, players, and coaches. Sports directors *interview,* or question, players about past games, upcoming opponents, or about how they are recovering from an injury.

Sports directors tape record such interviews and then *edit* them, or decide which parts of interviews to include in the station's sports report. Sometimes sports directors do "live" interviews. A live interview is not taped. Instead, it goes on the air as it happens, so listeners can hear the interview as if they were right there.

Sports directors are big sports fans and know a lot about the games they cover. Many were once athletes themselves.

RESEARCHER

Radio stations want to play songs that their listeners like. So stations have researchers who telephone listeners and ask them which songs are their favorites. Researchers also play recordings of new songs for the people they call to see which ones people like. If they find that people like a new song, the station will play it often.

Many radio stations have contests and give away records, concert tickets, and other prizes. When researchers telephone listeners, they also ask them how they like the station's contests or how the contests might be improved. Stations often get the telephone numbers of contest winners. That's how they know who many of their listeners are.

MUSIC DIRECTOR

Music directors make up the station's *playlist*. The playlist is the list of songs that the station plays. Music directors decide how often to play the songs on the playlist. Announcers then choose songs from the playlist to play on the air.

Music directors always want to keep their listeners happy. They know it is important to play songs that their listeners like. To find out which songs are the most popular, music directors ask record companies which records are selling best. The station's researchers also tell music directors which songs are listeners' favorites.

New songs come out every day, so listeners' favorites change often. That's why it's very important for music directors to keep close track of what people like to hear.

PROGRAM DIRECTOR

Program directors decide what goes on the air. They make up the station's *program,* or how many songs, commercials, and news and weather reports to play each day. Program directors make sure that the station plays just the right balance of songs and commercials. Too many commercials might make listeners change radio stations. But too few commercials would mean less business for the station.

Program directors work closely with the station's announcers. They *schedule* announcers, or tell them which times to be on the air. Program directors also *critique* (crih-TEEK) announcers, or listen to how they're doing and tell them how they might improve.

This program director is pulling out a tape of an announcer's voice. He will listen to it and perhaps offer helpful suggestions to the announcer. Many program directors were once announcers.

ACCOUNT EXECUTIVE

Account executives sell radio time to businesses for commercials. Business people buy 30-second or 1-minute "spots," or radio commercials, that will tell listeners about what they sell.

Account executives explain to business people how radio advertising will help their business. When talking to business people, account executives discuss their station's *demographics* (dem-oh-GRAF-iks). Demographics tell how many listeners the station has at different times of the day, how old most listeners are, and where they live. This information is very important to business people. They want to buy radio time on the stations that most of their customers listen to.

Besides selling radio spots, account executives help business people decide how much radio time to buy and how often the commercials should be played. Account executives must like to talk to people and know how to get along with them.

SALES MANAGER

Sales managers are in charge of the station's account executives. They tell account executives which businesses to call on. And they decide how much radio time should cost. They know the station can ask higher prices for commercials during a time of day when the largest number of listeners are tuned in.

Sales managers keep track of the radio time that has been sold. Then they tell account executives which time slots are left to sell. Sales managers know that the station allows only a certain amount of time for commercials. Most of the time is reserved for music, news and weather, and special shows.

This sales manager is showing an account executive a rate chart. From the chart, she can tell business people how much their commercials cost at various times of the day.

PRODUCTION DIRECTOR

Except for the announcer's voice, everything you hear on the radio has been recorded. Music has been recorded on tapes or records. And most commercials have been taped. Production directors record the commercial tapes that radio stations play.

Production directors work in the station's production room, which is a small studio. There they decide what music or background sounds will best fit in with the words of a commercial. When they have chosen the music or sound effects, they record the commercial. For a commercial about a car race, for example, a production director might talk in a fast voice and play the sounds of a roaring engine in the background. Commercials like these can then be played on the radio again and again.

Production directors must have clear voices and be able to say all that's needed in exactly 30 or 60 seconds.

CHIEF ENGINEER

Chief engineers make sure that all of the station's equipment is working right. The most important piece of equipment is the *transmitter*. Transmitters are special machines that change sound into electrical currents that can be carried through the air. Transmitters send these currents into the air through the station's antennas. These currents are then picked up by *receivers* in radios and are changed into the music or voices being produced at the station.

Chief engineers tune the station's transmitter so that it sends out sounds of the highest quality. This chief engineer is taking a reading of the transmitter. He's checking to see how much electric power it's producing. If it's not producing enough, then the station's *signal,* or sound that listeners hear, is probably weak or full of static. The chief engineer will adjust the transmitter to just the right power level.

APRIL
CST
5:30 AM
7:00 PM
(Till April 25...

TRAFFIC MANAGER

Traffic managers make up the daily *log* that announcers work with. The log is a list of what the station will put on the air during the day, such as commercials and news, weather, and sports reports. The log also tells announcers when to take time for commercials. Traffic managers make sure all of the commercials that account executives have sold are put on the air when they are supposed to be.

Traffic managers schedule commercials so that one company's product is not being advertised right before or after a competitor's. For example, traffic managers would not schedule commercials for two ice cream companies in the same half hour. With all of the commercials that stations have to play, traffic managers must be very well organized.

CONTINUITY DIRECTOR

After account executives have received the orders for commercials, they give them to the station's continuity (kon-tih-NOO-ih-tee) director. The continuity director types the orders and then gives them to the traffic manager, who schedules when to put them on the air.

Some businesses tape their own commercials instead of having the station tape them. Businesses send their tapes to the continuity director, who keeps them in order at the station. When businesses supply only the *copy,* or words, for commercials, the continuity director tells the production director to add the music or background sounds.

Continuity directors send the businesses bills for the amount they owe for their commercials.

PROMOTIONS DIRECTOR

Promotions directors plan fun contests for the station to hold. The station might have contests with prizes of T-shirts, bumper stickers, or hats with the station's name on them. Or they might give away concert tickets. Promotions directors also design advertisements telling about these contests. Then they arrange to have the advertisements appear in newspapers or magazines. Promotions directors do all that they can to let people know what the station has to offer.

Sometimes promotions directors organize parties or dances. The station's listeners are invited to come to meet their favorite announcers.

Promotions directors also work with businesses that buy commercials on the station. They might, for example, hold a contest giving away a car made by a company that has advertised a lot on the station.

PROMOTIONS ASSISTANT

Promotions assistants keep track of the station's weekly playlist. Many stations call their playlist the "Top 40," because it includes the 40 songs played more than any others. Promotions assistants send the Top 40 lists to record stores. The store managers then know which songs people are listening to. This can help them decide which records to order for their customers.

When visitors come to the station, the promotions assistant shows them around. The promotions assistant in the picture is greeting a singer who just arrived in town for a concert. Now she will take him on a tour of the station, which often plays his songs.

GENERAL MANAGER

All stations have *markets,* or groups of people, that they try to have as listeners. Some stations try to attract young listeners by playing rock music. Other stations have many news and weather reports, which older listeners are often more interested in. General managers make sure that the station is always pleasing its market.

General managers do this by keeping close track of how many listeners the station has and by watching how popular the station's contests are. General managers also help to decide how much to charge for commercials. They want to earn as much money for the station as they can, without losing any customers by charging too much.

General managers hire and fire the people who work for the station, and they buy new equipment when it's needed. This general manager is checking to see if one of the station's antennas needs to be replaced.

Radio Station careers described in this book

Announcer

News Director

Sports Director

Researcher

Music Director

Program Director

Account Executive

Sales Manager

Production Director

Chief Engineer

Traffic Manager

Continuity Director

Promotions Director

Promotions Assistant

General Manager

A letter from a radio station executive

NORTH COUNTRY RADIO 1130

Dear Reader,

   For people who love people, radio is a great business to be in. Radio is simply a matter of communicating with listeners one on one, like a friend-to-friend relationship. The stations who do it best are the most successful in attracting people to listen and also make the most money.

   Air personalities are the most visible part of a radio station, along with the news people and other "on air" performers, but everyone in a radio station gets to share in the excitement of pleasing the listeners.

   Every job in radio can and should be very exciting and rewarding if you have the right attitude and are prepared properly. A college liberal arts education or a trade school course can help you prepare yourself academically. A love of people will make your radio career more fun.

Good Luck!

Dale G. Weber
General Manager

10332 BLOOMINGTON FREEWAY, MINNEAPOLIS, MINNESOTA 55420
• 50,000 watts • A Storz Station • NBC Radio Network News ℕ

The publisher would like to thank Storz Broadcasting Company of Omaha, Nebraska, and its station WDGY North Country Radio 1130, Minneapolis, Minnesota, for their cooperation in the preparation of this book.

Lerner Publications Company

241 First Avenue North, Minneapolis, Minnesota 55401